THE NEW CHARISMATICS

By the same author
THE YOUNG EVANGELICALS (1974)

RICHARD QUEBEDEAUX

The New Charismatics

THE ORIGINS, DEVELOPMENT, AND SIGNIFICANCE OF NEO-PENTECOSTALISM

DOUBLEDAY & COMPANY, INC., GARDEN CITY, NEW YORK 1976

This study is a revised version of the author's D.Phil. thesis, submitted to the Board of the Faculty of Modern History, Oxford University, during Trinity Term 1975.

Library of Congress Cataloging in Publication Data
Quebedeaux, Richard.
The new charismatics.
Bibliography: p. 233.
1. Pentecostalism—History. I. Title.
BX8762.Q4   270.8'2
ISBN 0-385-11007-3
Library of Congress Catalog Card Number 75–21242

Grateful acknowledgment is made to the following for permission to use copyrighted material:

ALUMNI ASSOCIATION OF FULLER THEOLOGICAL SEMINARY—Chapter VI is a revision of "The Old Pentecostalism and the New Pentecostalism" by Richard Quebedeaux, printed in Vol. XX, No. 1, March 1974 issue of *Theology, News and Notes*.

AUGSBURG PUBLISHING HOUSE—*The Pentecostals* by Walter J. Hollenweger. Copyright © 1972 by SCM Ltd. Used by permission.

AVE MARIA PRESS—*The Pentecostal Movement in the Catholic Church* by Edward O'Conner. Copyright 1971, Notre Dame, Indiana.

FOUNTAIN TRUST—Editorial from *Renewal* magazine, December 1970–January 1971. Reprinted by permission.

HUMANITIES PRESS AND OSLO UNIVERSITY PRESS—*The Pentecostal Movement: Its Origin, Development and Distinctive Character* by Nils Bloch-Hoell, 1964.

LOGOS INTERNATIONAL—*The Era of the Spirit* by J. Rodman Williams. Copyright © 1971 by Logos International; *These Are Not Drunken, As Ye Suppose* by Howard M. Ervin. Copyright © 1968 by Howard M. Ervin; *The Spirit Bade Me Go* by David J. du Plessis. Copyright © 1970 by Logos International; *Walk in the Spirit* by Michael Harper. Copyright © 1968 by Michael Harper; *None Can Guess* by Michael Harper. Copyright © 1971 by Michael Harper. Reprinted by permission.

Acknowledgments

For their special help and encouragement the author thanks
Roy M. Carlisle
Christian Aid, London
Michael Harper
Walter J. Hollenweger
Kilian McDonnell
J. Robert Welsh

and, particularly,
Bryan R. Wilson

*The Lord hath more truth
and light yet to break
forth from his holy Word.*

—John Robinson

CONTENTS

viii   *Contents*

Contents

x   *Contents*

Contents

INTRODUCTION: *The Nature of Charismatic Renewal*

Someone has said that the problem with the present is the future. If the future is merely the continuation of the present, will there be any future at all? It is almost a truism to say that we are living in very distressing times in which even our wildest fantasies cannot provide solutions to present dilemmas—the population explosion; the "energy crisis," and the general depletion of natural resources; uncontrolled inflation, and the widening economic gap between rich and poor nations; the rapid increase in pollution, corruption in government, and competition for employment; and the demise of the nuclear family. All of these enigmas vex rich and poor, educated and uneducated, white and black, male and female, alike. No one is exempt. At another level, the persistence of racism, sexism, militarism, and totalitarianism indicates that humankind is still riddled by grave uncertainty and fear—no less for the present than for the future. The once-powerful hope that science and technology would save us has turned out to be an illusion. In fact, the "civilization" produced by technology and science tends to dehumanize rather than save men and women. It deprives them of an identity, and reduces them to an economic entity at best, and exploited and tortured victims at worst.

The central message of the Christian gospel is "new life" now, and "new heavens and a new earth in which righteousness dwells" in the future. But somehow the institutional church has failed notably in getting this message across—in making it believable—to contemporary men and women. The church needs renewal. Many Christians, no less than others, find themselves dehumanized by our present society. They live frustrated and incomplete lives of faith, believing that they are forgiven and have been made new by

God, but not sensing in themselves the *certainty* that this has really happened. Likewise, many Christians are encouraged by the New Testament promise that Christ has come into their lives to give them a fulfilling and abundant expression of himself, and that, ultimately, the Kingdom of God will prevail; but they are burdened because they have little or no *experience* of the joy that would confirm this promise. Yet others believe that God has called them to a life of responsibility toward the oppressed for whom Christ also died; but they do not feel assured that he is actively affirming their decisions and actions to bring about reconciliation, healing, and liberation.

When Christ promised his disciples that he would bestow upon them his Holy Spirit after departing from them, he anticipated three practical needs the Spirit would satisfy in their lives: (1) confirm faith, (2) bring joy in the midst of suffering, and (3) assure, guide, and teach those who would choose to follow Christ. Yet to many, if not most, Christians, Christ's promise of his indwelling Spirit may be accepted intellectually, but it is not received experientially. Hence the promise is meaningless, and the question is raised again and again, "How do I *know* that the Holy Spirit dwells within me?" Charismatic Renewal offers an answer to this question—the baptism of the Holy Spirit, a powerful experience that *convinces* the recipient that God is real, that God is faithful to what he has promised, and that the same "signs and wonders" described in the Book of Acts can happen today—to *me!*

Charismatic Renewal rejects the liberal, nonsupernatural god who really isn't there anyhow, but it also rejects the rational evangelical god of the intellect—the great giver of propositional truth —in favor of the God you can feel, respond to, and love, the God who *cares* about our present and our future. It is the knowledge of this God, given through the experience of his Holy Spirit, that binds Charismatics together.

In a word, Charismatic Renewal is a celebration in our generation that God has not forgotten his promises, that he is, in fact and deed, a living God, totally committed to work in *evidential* ways through the lives of those committed to him. This is the theme of the present work and the topic to which we shall now give our attention.

CHAPTER ONE: *The Background*

Secularization may be understood to include two related transformations in the way people think. First, there is an increasing "worldliness" in the attitude toward persons and things. What is fundamentally involved here is the abandonment of emotional commitment found in the religious response, the response to the sacred and holy. Second, there is a rationalization of thought, the repression of emotional involvement in thinking about the world. Rationalization suggests a manner of thought that is comparatively free of emotion and in which logic replaces emotional symbolism in organizing reflection and speculation. The secularization of culture indicates that a religious world-view is no longer dominant as the frame of reference for thought.[1] By the mid-1960s, even theologians had come to accept, if not celebrate, the "secular" understanding of man and his world. But since that time, something has happened to indicate that "modern man" might not, in fact, be so free of religious needs and aspirations as was hitherto supposed. Already in 1948, Kingsley Davis suggested that the

> tendency toward secularization probably cannot continue to the point where religion entirely disappears. Secularization will likely be terminated by religious revivals of one sort or another.[2]

It is doubtful, however, that secularization can ever be *terminated*. But it is also apparent that secularization is not in all respects an irreversible process. The recent upsurge in the popularity of Eastern religious traditions, astrology, and the occult, the renaissance of evangelical and enthusiastic Christianity, affecting seemingly all strata of Western society, together point to the re-emergence of what Andrew Greeley calls "unsecular man."[3]

Religion is nothing less than a symbolic transformation of experience. If the design religion gives to life is looked upon by the skeptic as a set of rules and practices concealing chance events and cosmic indifference to human concerns, that same design is viewed by the believer as a revelation, often supernatural in nature, of the deeper meaning of experience—which is at the heart of religion.[4]

In the religious experience, men and women respond to the extraordinary, to power, to spontaneity and creativity. That experiential response, characterized by intense attraction and awe, leads to stable forms of thought, feeling, action, and relationship.[5] The religious experience is an attempt by man to respond to, and enter into, a relationship with what lies behind and beyond mere appearance.[6]

Yet basic to the very essence of religion is an unavoidable dilemma. Religious men and women must always live in relationship with two contrary realms of experience. They must relate both to the sacred and to the profane. And they must concern themselves both with the ultimate and the mundane, the spirit and the flesh. Out of this situation comes a multitude of problems for the church of all ages—not the least of which is the persistent effort to preserve the spirit of the New Testament and the primitive church in the changing conditions of each ensuing generation.[7] It is in this context that we shall examine closely one contemporary attempt to maintain and renew that spirit— "Charismatic Renewal," Pentecostalism in its newest expression.

PENTECOSTALISM OLD AND NEW

The beginnings of the modern Pentecostal movement can be traced back to 1901. "Classical Pentecostalism," to distinguish it from the more recent Charismatic Renewal or "Neo-Pentecostalism," arose at the turn of the century out of various Baptist bodies and "Holiness" groups that were reacting against the secularism and rationalism then seemingly dominant in the institutional churches. Pentecostal denominations that later developed from the early movement stressed an experience called "the baptism of (or in) the Holy Spirit" as a second or third stage (after "conversion," or conversion and sanctification) in the life of the believer. Evidence of this experience was most often assumed to be the *initial* speaking in tongues or glossolalia (Greek *glossa*, "tongue"; *lalia*, "a talk") "as the Spirit gives utterance." "Spiritual gifts" outlined in I Corinthians 12–14, for instance, including the *gift* of tongues (glossolalia as a *recurring* phenomenon), were understood as likely to follow in due course. Classical Pentecostalism has been characterized by its organization into many, often local, groups and distinct and separate national structures; its ardent fundamentalism; its ethical austerity; its separation (more or less) from the wider society ("the world") and the latter's institutions and values; its exclusiveness, both in attitude and in social structure; and its nature as a movement of the disadvantaged and deprived. Hence, sociologists often designate traditional Pentecostalism as "sectarian."

Neo-Pentecostalism, though grounded in the same religious experience (variously interpreted), differs markedly from its Classical forerunner and counterpart. In principle, Charismatic Renewal is a "transdenominational" movement of enthusiastic Christianity that emerged and became recognizable in the "historic" denominations only in 1960. It is theologically diverse but generally orthodox, and is unified by a common experience—the baptism of the Holy Spirit—with accompanying *charismata* (Greek "gifts") to be used personally and corporately in the life of the church. Evangelistic in nature, the movement is also genuinely reformist in character, and is represented largely by persons from the middle and upper-middle socio-economic levels of society. These dominant attributes (and other less pervasive tendencies), since they indicate a radical departure from the sectarianism usually associated with the Pentecostal movement as a whole, are highly significant.

Charismatic Renewal is, first of all, neither a church nor a denomination. It is, as Edward O'Connor, professor of theology at the University of Notre Dame, suggests, a "movement" (though not without qualification):

> The term *movement* . . . implies that numbers of people have joined forces in more or less concerted effort on a common project. This supposes a goal that is aimed at

and a deliberate pursuit of that goal; usually it connotes a considerable degree of organization and method. . . . [Neo-Pentecostalism] did not originate by the deliberate adoption of any goal, is not an organized enterprise, and it does not consist in a method. It is indeed a movement, inasmuch as it consists of a multitude of people moving in the same general direction, and influencing one another. But their unity does not derive, at least basically and originally, from any intention or plan of their conceiving. In fact, what is most remarkable about this movement in its early days is how unexpectedly it arose and how spontaneously it spread. Most of those who were involved in it at the beginning found themselves taken quite by surprise.

It is true [however] that in the course of its development it has become more aware of its aims, more deliberate in its efforts, and more methodical and organized.[8]

Michael Harper, Great Britain's foremost Neo-Pentecostal leader, emphasizes that

there are few signs yet of its being bureaucratised into impotence. Its main strength, and for many its attractiveness, lies in its spontaneity, and in the fact that it is so far comparatively unstructured.[9]

What organizations do exist within Charismatic Renewal are indeed loosely structured, and are concerned chiefly with communications (i.e., publishing) and with fellowship (meeting together for "expressive" rather than "formal," goal-oriented purposes).

PENETRATION OF "ESTABLISHED" CHURCHES

If Neo-Pentecostalism *is* a proper movement, its essential nature is transdenominational. Roman Catholics, Eastern Orthodox Christians, Anglicans, and Protestants of most historic denominations are included. Here the Pentecostal experience is understood to transcend denominational walls, while it clarifies and underscores what is authentically Christian in each tradition without demanding structural or even doctrinal changes in any given church body. Hence, Charismatic Renewal is also ecumenical, though not in the sense that it openly seeks institutional unity as a goal. Michael Harper stresses that the movement is more concerned with *spiritual* unity at the "grass roots" level than with organic union engineered by ecumenical planners:

> There is a sharing together at the deep levels of worship, prayer, spiritual gifts and ministries, and testimony, as well as biblical teaching. This is not to disguise the fact that there are still many differences between Christians and many difficulties in the pathway to unity. But those involved believe that this is where Christians should *begin* in their quest for unity, not at the conference table or the debating chamber. . . . The ecumenical movement seems to put the cart before the horse; whereas this new move of the Holy Spirit is indicating what we should be doing first.[10]

Nevertheless, Neo-Pentecostalism is generally friendly in its attitude toward the ecumenical structures such as the World Council of Churches and its regional counterparts. Furthermore, the Protestant-Catholic encounter within Charismatic Renewal is so intense and heartfelt that it is probably unparalleled in contemporary ecclesiastical experience. In view of this fact, Michael Harper again asserts "that this movement is the most unifying in Christendom today . . . *for only in this movement are all streams uniting, and all ministries being accepted and practised.*"[11] Already in 1952, David Du Plessis, then secretary of the Pentecostal World Conferences, called for a reconciliation of Pentecostals and other Christians:

> After nearly half a century of misunderstanding and ostracism, for which they recognize they have not been entirely without blame on their own part, the Pentecostal Churches offer their fellowship in Christ to the whole of His Church in this grave hour of her history. They believe they have something to gain by larger fellowship with all who truly belong to Christ. They are greatly en-

couraged by many world-wide tokens that old prejudices
are melting and a new era of mutual appreciation dawn-
ing. Brethren, let us receive one another, as Christ also
received us to the glory of God.[12]

The real beginnings of that reconciliation took eight years to ma-
terialize. And when the rapprochement finally did occur, it was
no mere "dialogue" between Pentecostal and non-Pentecostal
churches; rather it was a totally unanticipated *penetration* or
diffusion of the Pentecostal experience into the "established"
denominations.

Another characteristic of Neo-Pentecostalism is its theological
diversity. Protestants and Catholics, conservatives and liberals, do
not automatically discard their own theological and ecclesiastical
differences when they come together in this movement. Nor do
the movement's leaders themselves agree on a precise definition of
the baptism of the Holy Spirit or the exact nature of the *charismata* and their operation. Nevertheless, Charismatic Renewal is
indeed firmly rooted in "historic orthodoxy."[13] Furthermore, this
implicit orthodoxy is enhanced by the fact that whether one is
theologically liberal or conservative, it is felt that he, as a Neo-
Pentecostal, will invariably come to have a more vivid sense of
God as a *person*, since in the baptism of the Holy Spirit, God has
demonstrated his reality to him in a personal way. Likewise, it is
expected that the Pentecostal experience will initiate or restore a
person's interest in serious Bible study and will also give him a
new awareness of the efficacy of prayer. The Neo-Pentecostal, regardless of his theological and ecclesiastical outlook, must culti-
vate a fresh *openness* if he is to continue successfully within the
movement.[14] Charismatic Renewal manifests a kind of "unity in
diversity"—grounded in the baptism of the Holy Spirit, the Pentecostal experience. To Neo-Pentecostals, this experience is so dynamic that it produces an all-embracing religious enthusiasm and
renders denominational and theological barriers insignificant as
deterrents to Christian fellowship.[15]

A further aspect of Neo-Pentecostalism is its nature as an evangelistic movement. Activity often centers on an evangelism that
calls people to a personal (though variously understood) "acceptance of Jesus Christ as Savior and Lord," and that is expected to

result in a new relationship with God. This must always come prior to the baptism of the Holy Spirit, although it is felt that individuals are initially brought to that point in their lives through the activity of the Spirit. The Holy Spirit is understood to provide the *power* necessary to convince persons of their need for the experience, whether the latter is regarded as a "first-time decision" or a profound "renewal" of what has already happened in water baptism and confirmation. Charismatic Renewal is also evangelical in spirit. By "evangelical" we refer to those who actively seek to bring others what they see as a "God-man encounter." But the term describes a theological spirit as well, a kind of mediating position between the legalistic, literalist, and very exclusive tenets of religious (or politico-religious) "fundamentalism" and the humanistic naturalism of religious "liberalism."[16] This mediating evangelical spirit is demonstrated by the readiness of Neo-Pentecostals to participate in discussion with Christians of other persuasions, with the knowledge, of course, that such discussion itself can be a form of evangelism. The former believe that the person with an experience need never feel himself to be at the mercy of the person with an argument.[17]

Charismatic Renewal is, moreover, thoroughly reformist in character. There is very little if any interest in separating from old ecclesiastical structures and building new ones according to the Classical Pentecostal pattern. Rather, present institutions are to be "renewed" by the Charismatic activity of the Holy Spirit as it affects the membership of a church or other group through the continued presence *within* that structure of individuals who have been baptized in the Spirit. This stance as a norm of Neo-Pentecostalism was first articulated by Dennis Bennett, the pioneer of Charismatic Renewal, in his letter of resignation as rector of St. Mark's Episcopal Church, Van Nuys, California, in 1960—a resignation motivated by the strong disapproval of his Pentecostal experience voiced in powerful quarters of the parish:

> I am sorry for the furor, and for the pain that has been caused. I ask every person in St. Mark's whether they be for me or against me, *not to leave the Parish or cancel their pledge*. This is a spiritual issue, and will not be settled in this way. I myself am going to stay strictly out of

Parish work until the matter has been clarified one way or the other. Support whatever interim pastorate the Bishop and Vestry set up. . . .

Any rumors that reach your ears that in any way imply that I am leaving the Episcopal Church are false. . . . What I am standing for is to be found within the Episcopal Church; no one needs to leave the Episcopal Church in order to have the fullness of the Spirit. But it is important that the Spirit be allowed to work freely in the Episcopal Church, and it is to this that I bear witness, and will continue to bear witness.[18]

Initially, there were a few Neo-Pentecostals who discouraged others new to the experience from remaining in the more theologically inclusive denominations. In England, the typical argument used by "dissenters" from the established church (appropriately modified) was even raised.[19] But such vocal opinions were few and far between. The stage had clearly been set for the continued diffusion and "settling in" of Pentecostal phenomena in the historic ecclesiastical structures as "normative procedure" for the movement.[20]

Finally, we can say that Charismatic Renewal is characterized by a very large representation of individuals from the middle and upper-middle socio-economic levels of society. Among those in the movement, there are wealthy business people and other professionals, "mainline" clergy, even intellectuals—a fact manifestly apparent from the beginning. St. Mark's Episcopal Church serves an affluent community. And the Blessed Trinity Society, Van Nuys, California—one of the first fellowship and publishing organizations the movement produced—had several well-to-do patrons. An early sampling of the society found Republicans in a ratio of seven to one.[21] When Neo-Pentecostalism began to diffuse within the Roman Catholic Church in 1967, most of the first participants from that tradition were part of the academic community—undergraduates, graduate students, and university instructors (including theologians). With the growing involvement of Catholic bishops, priests, nuns, and lay people, the "WASP" (White Anglo-Saxon Protestant) stereotype of the movement no longer applies. And although *some* representatives of the poor and

minority groups are to be found in the ranks, no one can rightly
designate Charismatic Renewal as a movement of the economically deprived and disadvantaged—a description which still might,
to a large degree, fit Classical Pentecostalism.

Having looked at the essential nature of Neo-Pentecostalism
and, in broad terms, a few *dominant* attributes distinguishing it
from its Classical forerunner and counterpart (other differential
features will also be mentioned), we shall now examine the character of the Pentecostal phenomena themselves, their biblical (especially New Testament) justification, and their historical incidence.

THE SPIRITUAL GIFTS

At the heart of the Pentecostal experience is the baptism of the
Holy Spirit. It should be clarified from the start, however, that
the expression "baptism of the Holy Spirit" does not occur in the
New Testament. The noun "baptism" is never used in that way.
A few times the verb "baptize" is employed in this connection
with the Greek preposition *en*, which the Revised Standard Version (RSV) translates "with" (Matthew 3:11; Mark 1:8; Luke
3:16; Acts 1:5 and 11:16). All these refer to the same saying
ascribed to John the Baptist that the coming Messiah would
"baptize with the Holy Spirit." The one other appearance of the
phrase is in I Corinthians 12:13, where it is declared that "by
(Greek *en*) one spirit we were all baptized into one body" (i.e.,
the church).[22]

Pentecostals believe that certain sayings and incidents recorded
in Acts are a fulfillment of the prophecy that the Messiah (i.e.,
Jesus) would baptize with the Holy Spirit. Luke reports that at
Pentecost, Peter proclaimed that the gift of the Spirit was now
available to all who repent and are baptized in the name of Jesus
Christ (Acts 2:38)—a teaching very much in harmony with the
basic implications of the New Testament as a whole. But in the
case of Cornelius and his household, the Spirit "fell on" the converts immediately, before they were baptized (Acts 10:44–48).
We can also point out the case of the Samaritan converts who
were baptized by Philip, yet whose reception of the Spirit was
delayed until Peter and John had come from Jerusalem and had

laid their hands on those new believers (Acts 8:12–17). Somewhat similar to the last incident is the status of various disciples Paul met in Ephesus (Acts 19:2–6) who had been baptized with only "John's baptism." They had not received the Holy Spirit "when" they had believed (i.e., had been converted—the King James Version rendering, "since ye believed," is incorrect). These individuals were then baptized by Paul "in the name of the Lord Jesus," and "when Paul had laid his hands upon them, the Holy Spirit came upon them; and they spoke with tongues and prophesied" (Acts 19:6).[23] Thus it is difficult to ascertain any one consistent pattern in Acts of the sequence of conversion, reception of the Holy Spirit, and water baptism. In this respect, it is clear that (as an interpretive principle) Pentecostals give primary attention to the *historical* parts of Acts as normative over, perhaps, other *doctrinal* portions of the New Testament, which some critics believe are more important.[24]

For Pentecostals, the physical action of "laying-on-of-hands" by clergy or lay people (or both) who are already "filled" with the Holy Spirit in a manifest way, during prayer, is usually (but not always) the manner in which an individual receives his Spirit baptism (an action that is not regarded by Catholic theologians as sacramental or even quasi-sacramental in character[25]). While the candidate prays, it is generally (but again, not always) anticipated that he will experience at least an initial outburst of glossolalia in the course of his prayer—when he actually receives "the blessing." Such speaking in tongues is viewed as evidence of the manifest "fullness" of the Holy Spirit and may in due course, if not immediately, be followed by reception of the *gift* of tongues (recurring glossolalia) or other spiritual gifts. Edward O'Connor describes the laying-on-of-hands as follows:

> When a person is seeking the "baptism of the Holy Spirit," it is a common thing for others, especially those who have already been thus blessed, to lay their hands on his head and to pray for him. The same form of prayer is frequently used when other graces [or gifts] and needs are being sought for also.
>
> The adoption of this gesture has been inspired by biblical precedents, especially those in which the Holy Spirit

was given to someone through the laying-on-of-hands. However, its continued use is motivated above all by the power that it seems to have. De facto, God seems to use it in a remarkable way to bestow grace . . . the effects of this prayer are quite manifest, in the gift of tongues, or in a sudden powerful experience of the grace of God, or even in a miraculous healing. These occur often enough that people in the movement are deeply convinced of this form of prayer and strongly attached to its use.[26]

Glossolalia, though generally the most observable, is certainly not the *only* spiritual gift for which an individual baptized in the Holy Spirit may aspire. "Spiritual gifts" is a comprehensive term for all the extraordinary and sometimes "miraculous" powers possessed by many Christians in the Apostolic era. These *charismata* had their origin in the gracious (Greek *charis*, "grace") action of the Holy Spirit and were given in order "to equip God's people for work in his service" (Ephesians 4:12, New English Bible).

The most important section of the New Testament dealing with spiritual gifts is I Corinthians 12–14:

12

Now concerning spiritual gifts, brethren, I do not want you to be uninformed. You know that when you were heathen, you were led astray to dumb idols, however you may have been moved. Therefore I want you to understand that no one speaking by the Spirit of God ever says "Jesus be cursed!" and no one can say "Jesus is Lord" except by the Holy Spirit.

Now there are varieties of gifts but the same Spirit; and there are varieties of service, but the same Lord; and there are varieties of working, but it is the same God who inspires them all in every one. To each is given the manifestation of the Spirit for the common good. To one is given through the Spirit the utterance of wisdom, and to another the utterance of knowledge according to the same Spirit, to another faith by the same Spirit, to another gifts of healing by the one Spirit, to another the working of miracles, to another prophecy, to another the ability to distinguish between spirits, to another various kinds of tongues, to another the interpretation of tongues. All these are inspired by one and the same Spirit who apportions to each one individually as he wills.

For just as the body is one and has many members, and all the members of the body, though many, are one body, so it is with Christ. For by one Spirit we were all baptized into one body—Jews or Greeks, slaves or free—and all were made to drink of one Spirit.

For the body does not consist of one member but of many. If the foot should say, "Because I am not a hand, I do not belong to the body," that would not make it any less a part of the body. And if the ear should say, "Because I am not an eye, I do not belong to the body," that would not make it any less a part of the body. If the whole body were an eye, where would be the hearing? If the whole body were an ear, where would be the sense of smell? But as it is, God arranged the organs in the body, each one of them, as he chose. If all were a single organ, where would the body be? As it is, there are many parts, yet one body. The eye cannot say to the hand, "I have no need of you," nor again the head to the feet, "I have no need of you." On the contrary, the parts of the body which seem to be weaker are indispensable, and those parts of the body which we think less honorable we invest with the greater honor, and our unpresentable parts are treated with greater modesty, which our more presentable parts do not require. But God has so adjusted the body, giving the greater honor to the inferior part, that there may be no discord in the body, but that the members may have the same care for one another. If one member suffers, all suffer together; if one member is honored, all rejoice together.

Now you are the body of Christ and individually members of it. And God has appointed in the church first apostles, second prophets, third teachers, then workers of miracles, then healers, helpers, administrators, speakers in various kinds of tongues. Are all apostles? Are all prophets? Are all teachers? Do all work miracles? Do all possess gifts of healing? Do all speak with tongues? Do all interpret? But earnestly desire the higher gifts.

And I will show you a still more excellent way.

13

If I speak in the tongues of men and of angels, but have not love, I am a noisy gong or a clanging cymbal. And if I have prophetic powers, and understand all mysteries and all knowledge, and if I have all faith, so as to remove mountains, but have not love, I am nothing. If I give away all I have, and if I deliver my body to be burned, but have not love, I gain nothing.

Love is patient and kind; love is not jealous or boastful; it is not arrogant or rude. Love does not insist on its own way; it is not irritable or resentful; it does not rejoice at wrong, but rejoices in the right. Love bears all things, believes all things, hopes all things, endures all things.

Love never ends; as for prophecy, it will pass away; as for tongues, they will cease; as for knowledge, it will pass away. For our knowledge is imperfect and our prophecy is imperfect; but when the perfect comes, the imperfect will pass away. When I was a child, I spoke like a child, I thought like a child, I reasoned like a child, when I became a man, I gave up childish ways. For now we see in a mirror dimly, but then face to face. Now I know in part; then I shall understand fully, even as I have been fully understood. So faith, hope, love abide, these three; but the greatest of these is love.

14

Make love your aim, and earnestly desire the spiritual gifts, especially that you may prophesy. For one who speaks in a tongue speaks not to men but to God; for no one understands him, but he utters mysteries in the Spirit. On the other hand, he who prophesies speaks to men for their upbuilding and encouragement and consolation. He who speaks in a tongue edifies himself, but he who prophesies edifies the church. Now I want you all to speak in tongues, but even more to prophesy. He who prophesies is greater than he who speaks in tongues, unless some one interprets, so that the church may be edified.

Now, brethren, if I come to you speaking in tongues, how shall I benefit you unless I bring you some revelation or knowledge or prophecy or teaching? If even lifeless instruments, such as the flute or the harp do not give distinct notes, how will any one know what is played? And if the bugle gives an indistinct sound, who will get ready for battle? So with yourselves; if you in a tongue utter speech that is not intelligible, how will any one know what is said? For you will be speaking into the air. There are doubtless many different languages in the world, and none is without meaning; but if I do not know the meaning of the language, I shall be a foreigner to the speaker and the speaker a foreigner to me. So with yourselves; since you are eager for manifestations of the Spirit, strive to excel in building up the church.

Therefore, he who speaks in a tongue should pray for the power to interpret. For if I pray in a tongue, my spirit prays, but my mind is unfruitful. What am I to do? I will pray with the spirit and I will sing with the mind also. Otherwise, if you bless with the spirit, how can anyone in the position of an outsider say the "Amen" to your thanksgiving when he does not know what you are saying? For you may give thanks well enough, but the other man is not edified. I thank God that I speak in tongues more than you all; nevertheless, in church I would rather speak five words with my mind, in order to instruct others, than ten thousand words in a tongue.

Brethren, do not be children in your thinking; be babes in evil, but in thinking be mature. In the law it is written, "By men of strange tongues and by the lips of foreigners will I speak to this people, and even then they will not listen to me, says the Lord." Thus tongues are a sign not for believers but for unbelievers, while prophecy is not for unbelievers but for believers. If, therefore, the whole church assembles and all speak in tongues, and outsiders or unbelievers enter, will they not say that you are mad? But if all prophesy, and an unbeliever or outsider enters, he is convicted by all, he is called to account by all, the secrets of his heart are disclosed; and so, falling on his face, he will worship God and declare that God is really among you.

What then, brethren? When you come together, each one has a hymn, a lesson, a revelation, a tongue, or an interpretation. Let all things be done for edification. If any speak in a tongue, let there be only two or at most three, and each in turn; and let one interpret. But if there is no one to interpret, let each of them keep silence in church and speak to himself and to God. Let two or three prophets speak, and let the others weigh what is said. If a revelation is made to another sitting by, let the first be silent. For you can all prophesy one by one, so that all may learn and all be encouraged; and the spirits of prophets are subject to prophets. For God is not a God of confusion but of peace.

As in all the churches of the saints, the women should keep silence in the churches. For they are not permitted to speak, but should be subordinate, as even the law says. If there is anything they desire to know, let them ask their husbands at home. For it is shameful for a woman to speak in church. What! Did the word of God originate with you, or are you the only ones it has reached?

If any one thinks that he is a prophet, or spiritual, he should acknowledge that what I am writing to you is a command of the Lord. If any one does not recognize this, he is not recognized. So my brethren, earnestly desire to prophesy, and do not forbid speaking in tongues; but all things should be done decently and in order.

Here Paul presents three lists of such gifts (I Corinthians 12:8–10, 28, and 29–30). It is useful to compare the lists, starting with verse 28, in which the apostle enumerates the first three gifts in a definite sequence ("first . . . second . . . third"). I Corinthians 12:28: (1) apostles, (2) prophets, (3) teachers, (4) workers of miracles, (5) healers, (6) helpers, (7) administrators, and (8) speakers in various kinds of tongues. Somewhat analogous is the sequence found in I Corinthians 12:8–10 and 29–30 (numerals in parentheses refer to the list in I Corinthians 12:28, and to the same or similar gifts). I Corinthians 12:8–10: (1) utterance of wisdom, (3) utterance of knowledge, faith, (5) gifts of healing, (4) working of miracles, (2) prophecy, ability to distinguish between spirits, (8) various kinds of tongues and the interpretation of tongues. Then, I Corinthians 12:29–30: (1) apostles, (2) prophets, (3) teachers, (4) miracles, (5) gifts of healing, (8) speaking with tongues and interpreting (tongues).[27]

In I Corinthians 12:29–30, "a word of wisdom" and "a word of knowledge" seem to refer to discourses or briefer utterances that either express Christian truths and their relations to one another or that put forward ethical instruction and practical exhortation. "Faith" here can hardly mean mere "saving faith" but must indicate some exceptional degree of potent faith that can work miracles (cf. I Corinthians 13:2). "Prophecy" in the primitive church was not so much the predicting of future events; rather, it was primarily the gift of understanding and expressing by teaching or preaching the nature of the will of God for a particular situation, resulting in "upbuilding and encouragement and consolation" (I Corinthians 14:3). The "ability to distinguish between spirits" refers to an intuitive power enabling its possessor to discriminate between true and false prophets—to judge whether their teaching comes from God or is an illusion (cf. I John 4:1).

THE MIRACULOUS AND THE NONMIRACULOUS

What is clear is the fact that, in general, the gifts may be divided into the miraculous and nonmiraculous. Included among the former are workers of miracles and healers; among the latter are gifts of character and mental and spiritual endowments—exhortation, contributing, giving aid, and administering, for instance.[28] By way of summary, *charismata* can be defined as endowments and capacities needed for the edification and service of the church—given by the Holy Spirit—through which its members are enabled to use their natural faculties to serve the church or are endowed with new abilities and powers for that purpose.[29]

Pentecostals firmly believe that they have a biblical warrant for their exercise of the spiritual gifts. A special significance is attached to the prophecies of Joel, to which Peter referred on the Day of Pentecost.[30] Feeling compelled to account for the strange manifestations that puzzled onlookers, Peter declared that

> this is what was spoken by the prophet Joel: "And in the last days it shall be, God declares, that I will pour out my Spirit upon all flesh, and your sons and your daughters shall prophesy, and your young men shall see visions, and your old men shall dream dreams; yea, and on my menservants and my maidservants in those days I will pour out my Spirit; and they shall prophesy" [Acts 2:16–18; Peter is citing Joel 2:28–32].

It is because of their zealous use of the *charismata* that Pentecostals are often characterized as prone to ecstasy and enthusiastic demonstrations. If glossolalia appears to be "ecstatic utterance," however, it is probably only so in the sense that the speaker "may feel emotionally lifted, inspired by God's Spirit, not that one behaves in an irrational and trance-like manner."[31] Pentecostalism is indeed an enthusiastic form of Christianity; but the caricature of the "holy roller" (one who literally "rolls" in the aisles during services of worship) is applicable only to Classical Pentecostalism in its very extreme manifestations. Kilian McDonnell, a Benedictine monk and scholar, asserts that the typical activities associated with Pentecostal worship, including hand-clapping, shouting, screaming, running around the assembly (the "Jericho march"), "dancing in the Spirit," and, ultimately, rolling in the aisles, are merely examples of Classical Pentecostal "cultural baggage" and are not to be confused with what is essential to the nature and operation of the spiritual gifts.[32]

In Charismatic Renewal, the Pentecostal experience has been subdued. Not only has much of the cultural baggage been suppressed, but the protracted sequence of events in the spiritual life characteristic of Classical Pentecostalism has been shortened as well. Gone are the days when an individual might have to

"seek" or "tarry" perhaps months or even years in order to become experientially "sanctified," freed from sin, and then receive
the baptism of the Holy Spirit—often "praying through" the
night and waiting patiently for evidence of the blessing to appear.
For the Neo-Pentecostal, reception of the Spirit in a manifest way
is generally accomplished after only a brief session of prayer with
the laying-on-of-hands. Likewise, other Classical Pentecostal practices such as fasting and exorcism, though not discarded in Charismatic Renewal, have been modified or put under restraint. In the
matter of exorcism, some Neo-Pentecostals believe that Christians
can be obsessed or possessed by demons and, therefore, encourage
and provide a ministry of "deliverance." Others totally disagree.
But in all aspects of the Charismatic operation, strict emphasis is
placed on Paul's dictum that "all things should be done decently
and in order" (I Corinthians 14:40).[33]

THE CHARISMATICS IN HISTORY

If it seems that Pentecostal phenomena disappeared altogether
during the period between the Apostolic era and the twentieth
century, this is not really the case at all. But references to the
phenomena are often unclear, and it is probable that manifestations of the more spectacular charismata in (and outside)
Christian history were fewer and farther between than some Pentecostals have maintained.[34] Although reports of healings and other
miracles are not uncommon in the corpus of surviving Christian
literature, evidence for the appearance of glossolalia, at least from
the late second century to the eighteenth or nineteenth century, is
scarce and frequently obscure. Quite often, for example, speaking
in tongues is not clearly differentiated from the gift of prophecy.
After the first century until the modern period, there are only a
few references to glossolalia in Christian discourse. Hence, some
authorities believe that the gift of tongues was insignificant in the
development of the early church. Others feel that since glossolalia
was easily misunderstood by nonspeakers, the divulgence of such a
gift would arouse public hostility. It does seem certain, however,
that the Montanists of the second century, a schismatic group of
Christians in Phrygia—ardently apocalyptic—practiced speaking
in tongues and other charismata as well, although we have only a

few cryptic "sayings" of Montanus and his disciples to examine as primary sources (the writings of such movements in the church considered less than orthodox were often destroyed). In fact, most of our information about the Montanists comes from the comments of orthodox writers and historians (such as Eusebius) who were clearly antagonistic toward the movement and must be read with much caution.

There is some question concerning the espousal of glossolalia by Tertullian, a major formulator of Christian doctrine during the early third century. Some authorities feel that he was quite specific as to its existence and real values. Others find the references less specific or even ambiguous—also pointing out the passing influence of Montanism on his writings. Origen, in the third century, and Chrysostom, in the fourth, both disparaged the accounts of speaking in tongues, and rejected its continued validity. Augustine, early in the fifth century, asserted that glossolalia was a sign adapted only to biblical times—though some scholars believe that he did, in fact, uphold the legitimacy of speaking in tongues, and that it was still practiced in his lifetime.

Biographies of the great missionary saints such as Vincent Ferrer (1350–1419) and Francis Xavier (1506–52) have long perpetuated the notion that these persons possessed the gift of tongues—in the sense that they could speak existing foreign languages previously unknown to them (some people define glossolalia in this way). But careful study of the facts indicates that the biographies in question were subject to the power of myth.

Data exist suggesting that speaking in tongues was practiced infrequently in sixteenth-century Germany by the Anabaptists, and in seventeenth-century France by the Jansenists. In 1685, Louis XIV of France called upon the Protestant Huguenots to return to the Roman Catholic Church, and reinforced his urgings with severe persecution. During this time, some of the Huguenots (the Camisards) reported phenomena among them such as "strange sounds in the air; the sound of a trumpet and a harmony of voices." Those affected were known as "prophets of the Cévennes mountains," and the episodes continued until 1711.

The French prophets also toured England and probably influenced Mother Ann Lee and the Wardleys, originators of the

Shakers (evidence points to the possibility of glossolalia among the Shakers in mid-eighteenth-century America). According to clergymen who examined her, Ann Lee, although only semiliterate, spoke in several known languages. Various splinter groups of the early Quakers espoused speaking in tongues as a significant religious experience—among these, the so-called Ranters in England.

In the course of the nineteenth century, the Irvingites (founders of the Catholic Apostolic Church, which still exists in Germany and the United States) practiced glossolalia—as did others in Sweden, Norway, and America. Especially interesting here are the obvious similarities between the Irvingites and Classical Pentecostals. First, it is thought that the Irvingites believed that the occurrence of speaking in tongues among them was of the same nature as that which took place on the Day of Pentecost —an evidence of Spirit baptism. Second, they appear to have regarded such an experience as a prerequisite for obtaining one or more of the spiritual gifts mentioned in the New Testament. Third, the Irvingites insisted that the *charismata* manifested at Pentecost and in the primitive church were a permanent possession of the church—withheld only because of the unfaithfulness of Christian believers. And fourth, Edward Irving and his Charismatic followers were expelled from the Presbyterian Church and were forced to establish a new denomination.[35]

Belief in the gifts of the Spirit ("the gift of tongues, prophecy, revelation, visions, healing, interpretation of tongues, etc.") is indicated in the "Articles of Faith" of the Mormon Church, founded in 1830 by Joseph Smith. Finally, scattered references are found suggesting that glossolalia occurred in Orthodox Russia in the nineteenth century (e.g., among Presybterians in the Armenian village Kara Kala in 1880 and thereafter).[36]

Other possible occurrences of speaking in tongues in Christian history (and in non-Christian cultures as well) could be cited. But in so many cases—those mentioned, and others—we cannot be certain at all that the verbal behavior alluded to was anything like modern glossolalia.[37] Whatever importance may be attached to the historical incidence of speaking in tongues and Pentecostal phenomena in general since the end of the Apostolic era, it is only since this century began that the church as a whole has been confronted by a widespread manifestation of the Pentecostal experience within its ranks. Once more, that confrontation (especially since the advent of Charismatic Renewal in 1960) has increasingly attracted the interest of psychologists, historians, sociologists, anthropologists, and theologians, who have produced notable scholarship on Pentecostalism both from within the movement and from the outside. It is also worthy of comment, moreover, that most of the best and most influential works have appeared just since 1964. What is striking about the more recent investigations by non-Pentecostal scholars is the relatively large amount of favor shown toward the Pentecostal movement as a whole (even toward glossolalia), which was not evident in most earlier studies. (See Appendix, "Scholarly Investigations.")

CHAPTER TWO: *Beginnings in America*

Nils Bloch-Hoell, a Norwegian scholar, puts forward a number of cultural and religious facilitating circumstances that he considers underlie the rise of the Pentecostal movement in general, and its emergence in the United States at the turn of the century in particular.

The first underlying circumstance was the pervasive diversity characteristic of American church life. At the beginning of this century, the United States represented an immigrant conglomerate, and each national or ethnic group had its own heritage. There was no one dominant religious style; yet, unconventional appearance and antiritualism were common features of American Christianity as a whole. In this context, Pentecostalism was from the start opposed both to regularity and orderliness.

Second, religious tolerance and denominations—again, distinguishing features of American life—greatly facilitated the rise and prosperity of the Pentecostal movement, which itself then contributed to the ever-increasing number of American religious denominations.

A third underlying circumstance in the emergence of Pentecostalism was the principle of voluntary association distinctive of American life. Voluntary church membership has promoted intense religious activity in the United States—activity which, especially on the frontier, produced fervent evangelism in the form of revival campaigns. Traditional churches and clergy did not exist on the frontier, where preaching was undertaken largely by uneducated laymen or "circuit riders" who appealed more to the emotions than to the intellect. From 1800 onward, revivalism was closely connected with "camp meetings," which attracted thousands of people for days at a time. Mass conversions, both at rural camp meetings and, later, in urban revival campaigns, were the consequence. Pentecostalism re-emphasized the old camp meetings, and its advance was associated with the persistence of revivalism in general—predominantly in the southern and western states, where the Pentecostal movement reaped its richest harvest.

Fourth, the general climate of American individualism—a product of the frontier—indirectly contributed to the rise of Pentecostalism. Fundamentalism, of course, has often led to individualism. But the increasingly popular theological liberalism of the nineteenth century, with its principle of critical evaluation, was often also decidedly individualistic. Denying both biblical and creedal authority, it ended up as a form of religious subjectivism. The empiricism of natural science demanded that something had to be proved by observation, verified by the senses, or demonstrated by logical argument. Like individualism, subjectivism favored the emergence of the Pentecostal movement whose empiricism became emotional. Religious truth was confirmed by experience.

A fifth underlying circumstance was the pervasive optimism of the nineteenth century. This optimism—motivated by great discoveries and inventions, social awakenings, and long periods of peace—profoundly influenced religious and ethical thinking. No less than the Social Gospel, the Holiness movement (as the precursor of Pentecostalism) was an outcome of the optimistic belief that moral perfection—entire sanctification—was indeed a very real possibility.

Sixth, the rootlessness connected with the Industrial Revolution and the mass immigration to the United States in the late nineteenth and early twentieth centuries contributed to the emergence of the Pentecostal movement. The sudden change in milieu —from Europe to America, from country to city life—led almost inevitably to political and social rootlessness. Many immigrants may have had unsatisfied religious needs met more readily by an enthusiastic form of Christianity than that represented by a static church.

A seventh underlying circumstance in the rise of Pentecostalism was the thoroughly democratic character of American society, which affected religion deeply. This democratic attitude resulted in the predominance of low-church principles and practices, as well as an esteem for personal religious experience and "nonliturgical," informal worship. When university-trained clergymen replaced the circuit riders and brought with them formality and "culture" to many churches, several groups of believers no longer felt at home—socially and at worship—and reacted by forming their own associations, some of which became Pentecostal (emphasizing enthusiasm and informality).

Eighth, the new structure of industrial society itself may have facilitated the emergence of the Pentecostal movement. With an apparent increase in class prejudice, the poor naturally became more open to "radical" and oppositionist movements. Pentecostalism was, in a sense, a class movement of the poor and uneducated.

A ninth underlying circumstance in the rise of Pentecostalism (as well as the Holiness movement before it) was the stiffening institutionalism, secularism, and "modernism" of the greater American churches. As the masses of people became seemingly indifferent, there arose a strong desire on the part of numerous Christians to *demonstrate* by some palpable evidence the truth of Christianity to an unbelieving society. The Pentecostal movement found that phenomena such as glossolalia and divine healing (the latter of which was also stressed in the Holiness movement) strengthened revival work by offering "proofs" of God's presence and activity to antagonists, removing intellectual doubts about Christianity, and providing additional means to conversions.

Tenth and finally, the Pentecostal movement was facilitated by the interdenominationalism of American revivalism, which allowed it to cross ecclesiastical boundaries and to spread among Christians of various denominations—especially Methodists and Baptists, who were the prime supporters of the revivals. In so doing, Pentecostalism was generally influenced by Baptist congregationalism, antisacramentalism, and biblicism, while it adopted Methodist sanctification and empiricism.

Thus, whatever other circumstances may have helped usher in the Pentecostal movement, it is clear (if we accept Bloch-Hoell's assertions) that Pentecostalism has been characteristic of certain elements of American Christianity and culture as a whole, and it has absorbed and intensified many features of American religion particularly apparent at the turn of the century.[1]

THE FUNDAMENTALIST BIBLE SCHOOL TRADITION

The Pentecostal movement had its beginning among humble folk in the fundamentalist Bible school tradition. Charles Parham, a Holiness preacher, founded the short-lived Bethel Bible College, Topeka, Kansas, in October 1900. His students had been studying the Scriptures (especially Acts), hoping to determine if there were some sort of special *witness* to the fact that a person had been baptized with the Holy Spirit; and one Agnes Ozman asked Parham to lay hands on her and pray that she might "receive" the Holy Spirit after the pattern in Acts. (In the Holiness movement, Spirit baptism was a familiar concept, but it had been linked to the experience of sanctification alone—"baptism" as a cleansing from sin, as Donald Gee describes it.[2]) When Parham prayed for her at a traditional New Year's Eve "watch night" service on December 31, 1900, Ozman began to speak in tongues, and she continued to do so for days thereafter. John Nichol points out that the significance of this event was not the mere manifestation of glossolalia itself (which had been witnessed and practiced before), but that for the first time the idea of being baptized or filled with the Holy Spirit was connected to an outward sign— speaking in tongues. Prior to Agnes Ozman's experience, glossolalia had been regarded simply as one of the spiritual gifts referred to in I Corinthians.[3] During January 1901, the whole Bethel Bible College student body of forty—twelve of whom held ministerial credentials with Methodist, Friends, or Holiness churches— engaged in fervent prayer for the baptism of the Holy Spirit with the initial evidence of speaking in tongues. Soon, the majority of students and Parham himself testified that they had experienced a dynamic Spirit baptism and had indeed spoken in "other tongues." Feeling newly empowered by this experience, many went immediately into evangelistic work.

For the first two years of their evangelistic efforts in Kansas, Parham and his students were relatively unsuccessful. But the Pentecostal preacher's fortunes changed dramatically when, in October 1903, he was invited to conduct a revival campaign in

Galena, Kansas. Numerous healings were said to have occurred in the course of this three-month revival; hence, news of the happenings spread quickly, and many people were attracted. As a direct result of this effort and Parham's further endeavors, by 1905, "Pentecostal" or "Full Gospel" ("full," since it includes the Pentecostal experience) meeting places had sprung up in Kansas, Missouri, and Texas. It is estimated that by the winter of that year, Texas alone had twenty-five thousand Pentecostal believers and about sixty preachers. From Texas, small bands of Pentecostals fanned out through Alabama and western Florida during 1905 and 1906.

As an adjunct to his Houston campaign in 1905, Parham established a Bible school in that city, which was patterned after the one he had directed in Topeka. Among his students there was a black Holiness preacher, William Seymour, who later became pastor of the well-known Azusa Street Mission in Los Angeles. Seymour was called directly from Houston to a Nazarene mission on Santa Fe Avenue in Los Angeles; however, his first sermon to this Holiness congregation was offensive, for in it he maintained that the baptism of the Holy Spirit is not mere sanctification, but something more—to be verified by speaking in tongues. Thus, Seymour was ousted; but friends invited him to conduct worship in their home at 214 Bonnie Brae Street. There, on April 9, 1906, seven "seekers" received their Spirit baptism and spoke in tongues. People started to come to services from seemingly everywhere, forcing Seymour and his followers to secure an old frame building (once a Methodist church) in the industrial section of Los Angeles, at 312 Azusa Street. Meetings lasted typically from 10 A.M. to 10 P.M. or later (sometimes until 2 or 3 A.M.). In the beginning, sermon topics were unannounced, and the revivalistic singing was without accompaniment—no musical instruments, choir, or hymn books. Although a semblance of structure and additional staff were features of the growing mission later in its development, spontaneity was always the notable characteristic of services. Glossolalia, healings, testimonies, shouting, dancing, and other manifestations of religious enthusiasm were an integral part of worship at the Apostolic Faith Gospel Mission on Azusa Street.

It is hard to explain its magnetism, but the ramshackle Azusa

Street Mission became a topic for the international press and a veritable Pentecostal mecca to which pilgrims from all over the world came and from which the news of supernatural signs and wonders were broadcast. By 1912–14, the mission congregation had become entirely black; William Seymour died in 1923; and the work ended in 1928, when the building was demolished. But numerous evangelists whose ministries were "revolutionized" at Azusa Street in those early years carried the Pentecostal message from there to the world—and that is why it is remembered even today.[4]

DISTINCTIVE RELIGIOUS STYLE

From the beginning, the Pentecostal movement was marked by a distinctive religious style, which still characterizes large segments of contemporary Classical Pentecostalism.

Services of worship were basically unstructured, and were marked by informality and spontaneity. They lacked not only formal liturgy, but also any type of fixed order at all. Together with "after-services" at the altar, they might last for several hours or even an entire day or night; if set time limited for worship existed, it was easily disregarded. So as not to "quench the Spirit," Pentecostals felt free to exercise the *charismata* at just about any time during a service, which itself might be characterized by repeated outbursts of enthusiasm—spontaneous testimonies, shouting, screaming, and dancing—not untypical of the black worship experience as a whole.

Pentecostalism has vigorously promoted evangelism. And although the stress has clearly been on "soul-winning," sanctification, and, of course, Spirit baptism, Pentecostals have also emphasized the "reclaiming" of "backsliders" fallen from grace. Pentecostal theology has always been Arminian,* and thus the fall from grace has not been an uncommon occurrence. Every Pentecostal believer was expected to be an evangelist—evangelism itself being an integral part of every service of worship.

---

*Jacob Arminius was a sixteenth-century Dutch theologian who opposed the absolute predestination of strict Calvinism. Rejecting the notion that Christ died only for "the elect," he maintained that salvation is open to all by an act of "free will," which must be continually reaffirmed by a godly life. Arminians do not accept the Calvinist doctrine of "eternal security" applied to believers who fall back into sin.

Pentecostalism took on other theological and cultural features of revivalism as well. Revivalistic preaching, the use of "gospel songs" (e.g., "I'll Fly Away" and "The Meeting in the Air") in place of traditional hymnody, and a thoroughgoing biblicism prevailed. By and large, the culture of the wider society—particularly its amusements, mores, and education—was rejected. "Separation from the world" was the watchphrase.

The Pentecostal movement emerged with an inherent individualism and subjectivism. Despite the emphasis on biblical authority, it was really personal experience that validated religious belief and commitment. Experience and testimony preceded doctrine. Individual piety took the form of moral negativism (e.g., taboos against drinking, smoking, and social dancing) and unconcern about social issues, while adherence to the Protestant ethic ("hard work, little play") remained firm.

In one sense, Pentecostalism was a product of nineteenth-century optimism. It upheld the possibility of ethical perfection, but in a privatized way that did not reflect the "social holiness" of John Wesley nearly so much as it did the culture-rejecting, even gnostic elements of later revivalism. The Pentecostal movement's moral negativism and social unconcern were reinforced by the dispensational† pessimism which permeated fundamentalism in general, at least after the appearance of the Scofield Reference Bible in 1909, if not before then.

Pentecostalism was a highly democratic movement from the beginning. Rooted in antisacramentalism, there was never much distinction made between clergy and laity in the Pentecostal concept of ministry. "Brother" or "Sister" seemed like a more appropriate ministerial title than "the Reverend" or even "Pastor." Lack of formal education was no bar to ordination, although Pentecostalism established its own Bible schools in the fundamentalist fashion (e.g., Central Bible College, Springfield, Missouri; and LIFE College, Los Angeles). A sense of "calling" was often enough to warrant local or congregational ordination. And because of the informality and spontaneity of worship, the laity

† Dispensationalism originated in Great Britain in the early nineteenth century with the writings and ministry of J. N. Darby, founder of the Plymouth Brethren. This school of theology divides history into several "dispensations" each of which signifies a *different* way in which God relates to humanity, and in which humanity utterly *fails* to please God.

could easily assume an important role in services—almost as great as the minister himself. Women, like ordinary workingmen, also became pastors, missionaries, and evangelists (half of the staff of the Azusa Street Mission in 1906 were women).[5] To the average Pentecostal layman or -woman, a full-time ministerial vocation offered a measure of social status denied that person in the workaday world. Pentecostalism was clearly a working-class movement in which even oppressed minorities, no less than physically, economically, or socially disadvantaged and deprived whites, could find recognition.

If the religious style of the Pentecostal movement was indeed grounded in elements of the American cultural and religious experience dominant at the turn of the century, that style was also reflected in its organizational character. Like revivalism in general, Pentecostalism emerged largely among Baptists, Methodists, and Holiness people as an interdenominational movement; but, given the ease of legitimation for leadership through spiritual gifts, it soon became structured into a large number of denominations distinct and separate from each other. And although Pentecostalism was integrated at first, it was but a short time before racially segregated churches and denominations were established. Within denominational structures, low-church principles predominated. Some denominations, like the Assemblies of God, took on the congregationalism of their Baptist parents; while others, like the Church of God (Cleveland, Tennessee), retained a strong, centralized ecclesiastical polity characteristic of their Methodist parents. Like fundamentalism as a whole, but even more so because of Holiness influence, the Pentecostal movement created its own "society" and "culture" as a substitute for that offered by "the world"—a "haven of the masses."[6]

BASIC THEOLOGY AND ETHICS

A close kinship exists between Pentecostalism and the Holiness movement from which it emerged. Holiness as a movement was an outgrowth of "perfectionist" teaching and revivalism both before and after the Civil War. Its development was greatly facilitated by certain Methodists (and others) who revived a faded interest in John Wesley's doctrine of sanctification (Christian perfection) neglected in Methodism by that time; and although the movement grew largely under Methodist leadership, it actually operated on an interdenominational basis—to stimulate religious piety as an antidote for the "worldliness" thought to prevail in an "apostate" institutional church.[7] In this connection, Prudencio Damboriena, a Roman Catholic scholar, puts forward five basic reasons for the evolution of the Holiness-Pentecostal movement in the late nineteenth and early twentieth centuries. These include (1) an apparent departure from "the true faith" in the historic churches (signaled by their increasing acceptance of Darwin's evolutionism, Kant's rationalism, Schleiermacher's religion of experience, Bushnell's theories on Christian nurture, and Rauschenbusch's Social Gospel); (2) the dead formalism of the established denominations; (3) the pervasive worldliness in the churches, especially in Methodism, where separation from the world was by then a dead issue, and in which traditional prohibitions—from card playing to drinking—had been rescinded; (4) the substitution of personal religion by mere knowledge and external profession; and (5) the resistance of endorsement of urgently needed reforms by denominational hierarchies.[8]

William Boardman, an American Presbyterian, and Robert Pearsall Smith conducted Holiness meetings in England that resulted in the famous Keswick interdenominational conferences for the deepening of spiritual life. In America, the Holiness movement was greatly aided by the use of media fast disappearing in the established churches—revival campaigns, camp meetings, and inexpensive printed literature. Its theological thrust was the belief that when the Holy Spirit makes his abode in the heart, it will be evidenced by a definite emotional experience—a "second blessing," Spirit baptism.[9]

Because of mainline ecclesiastical opposition, recurrent outbursts of fanaticism among Holiness fellow travelers, increasing attacks on the Holiness doctrine of sanctification, and the growing activity of urban Holiness preachers in city missions and social work, it became expedient for these Holiness bands to withdraw from the already established churches and form their own denominations—such as the Church of the Nazarene, Church of God (Anderson, Indiana), and the Christian and Missionary Alliance.[10]

In terms of theology and ethics, the debt owned by Pentecostalism to the Holiness movement is sizable. In fact, a number of Holiness churches in the South finally came to believe that speaking in tongues is indeed the outward sign of Spirit baptism and thus joined the emerging Pentecostal movement. Among these were the Pentecostal Holiness Church, and the Church of God (Cleveland, Tennessee). But more generally, the doctrinal influence of Holiness on Pentecostalism can be summarized by the following points suggested by John Nichol: (1) There is a second blessing to be sought and received *after* conversion; (2) a believer must seek the Spirit's leading in all of life; (3) revivals and camp meetings are crucial not only for evangelism but also for the rejuvenation of the spiritual lives of believers; (4) believers ought always to expect the imminent return of Christ (a doctrine repopularized in the late nineteenth century); and (5) Christians should shun "the world" and all manifestations of worldliness (including "appearance of evil"—I Thessalonians 5:22, King James Version) such as luxuries, cosmetics, jewelry, amusements, alcohol, and tobacco.[11]

Pentecostal theology and ethics have reflected the basic tenets of American fundamentalism. Important here is the acceptance of what became known as "the five fundamentals of the faith"—biblical infallibility, the virgin birth of Christ, and his substitutionary atonement, physical resurrection, and imminent, visible, and personal second coming. In addition, a strict biblical literalism—reinforced by dispensationalism—and a moral negativism wedded to social unconcern have been equally important. Pentecostal distinctiveness, however, lay in the emphasis of Holiness sanctification and the present-day operation of *charismata* (particularly glossolalia and divine healing) in the life of the church as the result of Spirit baptism. In due course, to be sure, a number of Pentecostal denominations "officially" rejected the cultural and theological excesses of fundamentalism by aligning themselves with the emerging Neo-Evangelical movement and joining the National Association of Evangelicals (NAE) at its inception in 1943. But in practice, Classical Pentecostal theology and ethics have reflected the older American fundamentalism more than its moderated counterpart, evangelicalism.

RECRUITMENT

The initial (and continued) success of Pentecostalism can be tied directly to its ideology and method of recruitment—aggressive evangelism.

In the early years, the Pentecostal message was directed at the nominal Christian, the apathetic believer, rather than the unconverted. It was felt strongly that the baptism of the Holy Spirit would provide the means of more effective Christian service for those who were already followers of Christ. The initial nondenominational character of the Pentecostal movement allowed it to infiltrate various segments of the church. And Pentecostal belief in the imminent second coming of Christ brought a sense of urgency to evangelism; every Pentecostal believer was expected to be an evangelist in that he was obligated to "witness" boldly to his faith and experience.

Feeling uncomfortable in the increasingly middle-class Baptist and Methodist congregations, many people from the lower income groups severed their affiliation with these churches. It was primarily from the masses of such alienated working-class men and women that Pentecostalism recruited its membership in ways that attracted *their* interest particularly. Like the Methodist circuit riders of a bygone era, Pentecostals did not wait for individuals to come to them; they went out eagerly to meet the people where they were—singly or collectively.

Early in the movement's development, Pentecostal leaders discerned the potential good effect mass meetings of various sorts could have on their followers. Tent meetings and camp meetings, it was thought, would not only offer an opportunity to evangelize non-Pentecostals, but would also function as a means for Pentecostal believers themselves to experience a sense of belonging to a community—a fellowship often denied them in the wider society. Thus American Pentecostals employed evangelistic and healing revivals as a primary method of recruitment.

In addition to mass meetings, inexpensive tabloid newspapers became an effective means of Pentecostal evangelism. These early religious newspapers dealt chiefly with the nature of the Pentecostal experience, and presented moving testimonies by persons who had been baptized in the Spirit or who had experienced a dramatic healing. Distributed throughout the world, the newspapers also conveyed information and announcements concerning Pentecostal activities and institutions—from newly founded missions to revival campaigns.

In early Pentecostalism, there was little or no discrimination on the basis of sex, race, national origin, or social status—a fact that certainly aided recruitment.

More than anything else, perhaps, it was the certainty of their convictions, the vivid sense of reality emanating from them, that attracted people to the Pentecostals. They were convincing, because they themselves were convinced. And in other lands, Pentecostals often found a special welcome both for their missionaries and their message largely because of the Pentecostal movement's manner of establishing indigenous churches, allowing local people to conduct their work, ministry, and worship in a manner that conformed best to the latter's own interpretation of the Christian faith.[12]

MAINLINE ECCLESIASTICAL DISAPPROVAL AND RAPID SPREAD

Luther Gerlach and Virginia Hine, anthropologists at the University of Minnesota, have suggested that a key factor in the success of a modern religious movement is the perception of opposition among its adherents.[13] Without a doubt, the Pentecostal movement was aided by the tactics of its opponents.

From its early days, Pentecostalism became the object of abusive attacks from the pulpits of established churches and from the religious and secular press. Ministers and missionaries, both participants and sympathizers, were summarily removed from their pastorates and dismissed by their mission boards. Some Pentecostal leaders were even subjected to violence. These occurrences took place not only in the United States, but also in Canada, Sweden, Great Britain, Chile, and in other countries.

The pejorative label for Pentecostals, "holy rollers," was often not entirely inappropriate. Indeed, it was the seemingly extreme excesses of enthusiasm that commonly marked Pentecostal worship from the start that constituted one of the chief reasons for such severe opposition. Pentecostals, however, are quick to apologize for these extravagances by explaining that (1) hyperemotional outbursts were primarily a reaction against the dead formalism of the churches from which they came; (2) most early Pentecostal leaders had been afraid to "restrict" enthusiasm lest they "quench the Spirit" in the process; and (3) early Pentecostals tended to attribute *everything* (even inappropriate behavior) to the Spirit's leading. As spiritual gifts, glossolalia and healing were perhaps most often abused. But so was prophecy—in the sense that many Pentecostals used the gift to correct, rebuke, foretell, and otherwise direct at will. There were just too many prophets, it appeared to outsiders, prophesying out of their own spirit rather than *the* Spirit.

Many denominational leaders were also disturbed by the apparent "transient" character of Pentecostalism. They were unhappy about their own members' withdrawing to join a tent meeting or a store-front mission only to see the tent soon folded up, the mission abandoned, and the itinerant Pentecostal evangelist move on his way. This caused mainline pastors to refer to Pentecostalism as a "fly by night" religion. But they also condemned the movement as inherently anti-intellectual and spiritually elitist. The early Pentecostals did emphasize the fact that they themselves were the special recipients of both the baptism of the Holy Spirit and the *charismata*. Yet it has to be underscored here that this feeling was motivated by the attitude of other Christians toward *them*. Mainline clergy most often viewed Pentecostals as "the scum of society" and their religious posture as something suitable only for poor whites and minorities (especially blacks).

Of course, there were other reasons why the established churches quickly became hostile to Pentecostalism. These included its asceticism, its denunciation of doctors and medicine in favor of divine healing, its opposition to ornamentation—from neckties to jewelry—and its aggressive (and seemingly questionable) methods of evangelism.[14]

We have said that mainline ecclesiastical disapproval helped rather than hindered Pentecostal expansion, which advanced at a fast pace. Technically, Pentecostalism was the last great wave of "sectarian orthodoxy" and the first religious movement to have the *full* advantage of telegraph, telephone, and inexpensive mass

media. We have noted already, for instance, the publicity given
the movement by the secular and religious press which, although
uncomplimentary, served to draw attention to its progress and
aroused the interest of a curious public. Likewise, we have seen
that Pentecostalism made effective use of tabloid newspapers
(e.g., *Pentecostal Evangel* and *Church of God Evangel*) to carry
its message to the far reaches of the globe, while it employed mass
meetings centered on Charismatic activity as a successful means
of evangelism (in the United States, at least). Revival campaigns
and camp meetings could be set up easily, and itinerant evangelists often were content to live "by faith"—to subsist on a mar-
ginal income derived only from the "love offerings" of the people.

It can also be said that the Pentecostal movement spread rapidly because of its highly dramatic style. Although outbursts of enthusiasm did on occasion occur in services of the Holiness movement, its characteristic manner was far quieter than that of
Pentecostalism. The Holiness experience of sanctification appeared as little compared to Pentecostal Spirit baptism evidenced
by speaking in tongues and the consequent reception and exercise
of *charismata* in services of worship. Supernatural signs and wonders happening among the poor and otherwise disadvantaged not
only functioned to validate religious truth in their minds, they
also demonstrated to these people that God has indeed "put
down the mighty from their thrones, and exalted those of low degree" (Luke 1:52).

If the Pentecostal movement was from the beginning opposed
by the established denominations, it suffered from *internal* dissension and controversy as well. The baptism of the Holy Spirit was
not enough of a unifying experience to prevent fragmentation
from occurring almost immediately. Pentecostalism had not once
received organizational form. Its spirit was in itself anti-organiza-
tional. Thus there was no one beginning, no basis for agreement,
but rather diverse, simultaneous, local, varied, uncoordinated, and
perhaps finally unreconcilable positions taken by different
churches and congregations.

Pentecostal believers in America (and Europe) very early came
to associate their initiation into the movement with the particular
ministry of an outstanding personage in their own general locality
(e.g., Charles Parham in Kansas and Texas; William Seymour in

Los Angeles; and, as we shall see, Alexander Boddy in England). These leaders soon captured the allegiance of their followers to the point that adherents even copied the mannerisms of each respective leader. Partisanship arose already at Azusa Street, and not one single leader could ever speak for the Pentecostal movement as a whole. Furthermore, some Pentecostals insisted on following the Spirit's "direct" leading apart from *any* human authority; but waiting for a voice from within, or Charismatic announcements alone, only added to the confusion. These people tended to ignore human direction completely. Finally, much dissension was rooted merely in the fact that the early Pentecostal leaders themselves had come from a variety of ecclesiastical backgrounds (e.g., Methodist, Baptist, Lutheran, Anglican, and Holiness) and saw no reason to renounce (entirely, at least) their inherited views and preferences regarding baptism, liturgy, and church polity.

One important controversy had to do with church organization itself. Some leaders favored the continuance of a decentralized movement structure, while others discerned serious problems in independence—doctrinal instability, conflicting ethical standards, vulnerability of local congregations to unscrupulous pastors, and financial inefficiency. Thus, to this day, there exists side-by-side in Pentecostalism a multitude of denominations, some weak and others stronger, as well as numerous completely independent local assemblies.

Another divisive issue early in the movement's development was the doctrine of sanctification. Pentecostals who had emerged from the Holiness movement stressed sanctification as a distinct, experiential "second work of grace" subsequent to conversion—whereby one's inner nature was thought to become "dead to sin," totally free from sinful inclinations. But Pentecostals from a Baptist background, for instance, felt that a second work of grace was really superfluous; for them, conversion (salvation) changed a person's heart as well as his nature. Basically, the problem centered on chronology. Holiness people were used to thinking that Spirit baptism is imparted only after a period of cleansing (sanctification). Pentecostals of Baptist background, on the other hand, were quick to point out large numbers of non-Holiness people who had been baptized in the Spirit—*without* the experience of sanctification after conversion. They understood sanctification not as distinct from, but as somehow related to the conversion experience itself—or as an ongoing process in the Christian life. The present-day Church of God (Cleveland, Tennessee) and the Pentecostal Holiness Church reflect the former view; the Assemblies of God, the latter.

In Great Britain and Germany, there also occurred early dissension over the prominence of certain spiritual gifts—particularly glossolalia, the interpretation of tongues, and prophecy—in the life of the church. There was a tendency here for a minority of Pentecostals to say that the gift of prophecy was actually co-equal with the authority of Scriptural revelation—even as the basis for church government. But this tendency never became popular in the United States.

Another important controversy was designated in mainstream Pentecostalism the "Jesus only" heresy. Spokespersons for the "Jesus only" school of thought (best represented today by the United Pentecostal Church) denied the doctrine of the Trinity, and baptized with water in the name of Jesus alone. They felt that while God is indeed a threefold *being*—Father, Son, and Holy Spirit—there is only one *person*, Jesus. The emphasis of these people on the name of Jesus with the promise of additional power to all who would embrace their doctrine greatly facilitated the popularity of "Jesus only" groups in the source of Pentecostal development.

Yet another early area of dissension had to do with cultural attitudes—degree of strictness concerning characteristic prohibitions. Pentecostal believers from a Holiness background most often held very strict views regarding dress, entertainment, eating habits, medicine, and the like, which other Pentecostals did not always accept. Also to be mentioned here might be the use of wine (rather than unfermented grape juice) in communion, foot-washing as an ordinance (adopted by the Church of God [Cleveland, Tennessee]), baptism by immersion (optional in the Pentecostal Holiness Church), divorce and remarriage (the latter generally forbidden until the death of one spouse), the use of tobacco (a special problem in the tobacco-growing South), eating of pork, drinking of coffee and "soda pop," and participation in the military and labor unions (prohibited by some denominations).

Even the doctrine of the necessity of glossolalia as an accompaniment to Spirit baptism was not held *universally* among Pentecostal groups. The Elim Pentecostal Alliance (in England), for instance, endorsed the view that there *may* be signs of baptism of the Holy Spirit other than tongues alone.

It should be manifestly clear by now that the widespread diversity of opinion within early Pentecostalism and its fragmentation into groups favoring different degrees of spontaneity and ritual, ecclesiastical independence and hierarchical control, legalism and tolerance, would seemingly preclude the development of a unitative Pentecostal movement. The establishment of separate Pentecostal denominations—distinct not only from those already existing in Protestantism, but also from each other—was inevitable.[15]

We can say, therefore, that the Pentecostal movement arose as separate denominational organizations for the following reasons, at least: (1) the virulent and belittling opposition raised especially by the increasingly middle-class established denominations toward Pentecostal phenomena and adherents; (2) the internal diversity of the movement itself, marked by dissension; (3) the feeling among Pentecostals that their testimony would be hindered without the establishment of some kind of ecclesiastical regulation of polity and doctrinal-ethical norms; and (4) the character of fundamentalism itself (still dominant in Classical Pentecostalism), which has always discerned "apostasy" in unitative Protestantism and insisted on a basically separatist stance.

The oldest and most prominent Holiness-Pentecostal bodies in the United States include (1) the Church of God (Cleveland, Tennessee),[16] (2) the Church of God in Christ (a black denomination), and (3) the Pentecostal Holiness Church. All three have strong central hierarchies after the Methodist pattern. The Assemblies of God,[17] structured by a curious combination of (congregational) Baptist and Presbyterian elements—lacking a really powerful ruling hierarchy—constitutes the most important Pentecostal body holding to a "progressive" rather than instantaneous doctrine of sanctification. Another very significant American Pentecostal denomination is the International Church of the Foursquare Gospel, founded by an ex-Assemblies of God minister, Aimee Semple McPherson.[18] Although this denomination reflects characteristic Assemblies of God theology, it has a much stronger central bureaucracy, now led by Sister Aimee's son, Rolf McPherson. Finally, we should mention the most important "Jesus only" (unitarian) denomination in America, the United Pentecostal Church, which also has developed a powerful central administration.

In Great Britain, the oldest and most prominent denominational organizations include the strictly hierarchical Apostolic Church,[19] which relies largely on prophetic utterances in matters pertaining to church government; the Elim Pentecostal Alliance (or Elim Church),[20] founded as the result of George Jeffreys' revivals and later molded into the most centralized Pentecostal denomination in Great Britain; and the Assemblies of God.[21] The British Assemblies of God, interestingly enough, have not incorporated in their services of worship the American revivalistic altar call. At the same time, unlike their American counterparts, they emphasize the ordinance of communion, which is celebrated every Sunday morning with very little (if any) preaching. As a whole, British Pentecostal congregations are smaller than those in the United States, less enthusiastic in worship, and constitute a far smaller percentage of the total ecclesiastical constituency than do American Classical Pentecostal churches. There are, no doubt, cultural as well as purely theological reasons accounting for these differences.[22]

DIFFUSION OF THE MOVEMENT

The Pentecostal movement, as we have said, spread rapidly from Azusa Street (and later from New York City as well) to other parts of America, and soon crossed the Atlantic. Great Britain was fertile ground for the new Pentecostal thrust—having had its own Holiness movement, best represented by the Keswick conventions of the late nineteenth century, and the Great Welsh Revival of 1904, led by Evan Roberts. To these British conclaves came many continental clergymen, who returned to their own pastorates challenged by the message of Holiness. Reuben Archer Torrey, the Yale- and Leipzig-educated American fundamentalist evangelist and pastor, took the Holiness doctrine to Germany—stressing the baptism of the Holy Spirit (sanctification) as necessary for an effective Christian witness. News of the Pentecostal beginnings from Topeka and Los Angeles thus created a great deal of interest both in Germany and Great Britain.

Thomas Barratt, a native Englishman who had been resident since childhood in Norway, where he was a Methodist minister, visited the United States in 1905–6 to solicit funds for his work. Just prior to his returning to Norway, Barratt received the Pentecostal Spirit baptism in New York City (he may have also visited Azusa Street), and returned to Kristiania (now Oslo), where he introduced Pentecostalism to Norway and founded the Filadelfia Church in 1916. In January 1907, a young Baptist pastor in Sweden, Lewi Prethus, became intrigued by a newspaper account of Barratt's revival in Kristiania. Prethus later traveled to the Norwegian capital and experienced the baptism of the Holy Spirit, which led him to spread the Pentecostal message within his own country—assisted already in 1907–8 by Barratt himself, who held several revivals in Sweden during those years.

Partly because the happenings in Kristiania had often been featured in the secular press, Barratt's fame spread widely. Another visitor to Kristiania to observe the happenings there was an English Anglican vicar from Sunderland, Alexander Boddy, who had been influenced by the Welsh Revival. Boddy returned to his home parish in Sunderland to advance the Pentecostal experience in England. Subsequently he invited Barratt to preach at All Saints Church, Monkwearmouth, where people from all branches of Christendom flocked in 1907, as they had done a year earlier at Azusa Street. Word of the Sunderland revival was quickly broadcast throughout the British Isles in the newspapers and by word of mouth.

Yet another person drawn to the Norwegian capital was Pastor Jonathan Paul of Berlin, who took the Pentecostal message back to Germany and began to preach it throughout that country —supported by the efforts of Barratt and two Norwegian evangelists, Dagmar Gregersen and Agnes Thelle, who traversed Germany and Switzerland in 1907–8.[23] Pentecostalism was popularized in Finland no later than 1912 through the evangelistic work of Pastor Gerhard Smidt from St. Paul, Minnesota, and William Pylkkanen, a Lutheran missionary who had recently returned from China. Although it does appear that a small amount of Pentecostal activity developed in France and a larger incidence of Pentecostal phenomena occurred in the Netherlands in that time, no major Pentecostal revival took place in other European countries until 1923 in Austria, and 1925 in Poland and the Baltic States.[24]

The Far East, Africa, and Latin America, together, are another matter completely. By 1909, Pentecostalism had spread to India (and even beyond, as far as Korea) by the initial efforts of a well-educated Christian woman, Pandita Ramabai of Mukti, and through the labors of Pentecostal missionaries from Great Britain and the United States. The Pentecostal movement took root in China—Hong Kong, Canton, and Shanghai—in 1908–10, furthered initially by American "graduates" of Azusa Street and later by Pentecostal missionaries from Scandinavia, the Netherlands, and Canada.

Sometime before 1910, the Pentecostal message took hold in Johannesburg, South Africa, through the efforts of two American evangelists, John Lake and Thomas Hezmalhalch, and soon spread across that country both among whites and nonwhites.[25] Central Africa was evangelized by Pentecostals no later than 1914–15—by two Englishmen, William Burton and James Salter. In the western part of the African continent, Nigeria has been the most receptive to Pentecostalism. The majority of Pentecostals there affiliated either with the Apostolic Church (Great Britain) or the Assemblies of God of Nigeria (established initially in 1940 with the help of American missionaries).

In Latin America, Chile and Brazil were permeated with the Pentecostal ideology very early. Pentecostal phenomena first appeared in a Methodist church in Valparaiso, Chile, in 1907. Its pastor, an American named Willis Hoover, was finally ordered back to the United States by his distraught Methodist superiors in 1910; but he remained in Chile instead to help found the Methodist Pentecostal Church there. Later, the ranks of Chilean Pentecostalism began to swell dramatically.[26] In Brazil, the Pentecostal revival has continued unabated since 1910. The work in that country was begun by Louis Francescon, who left for São Paulo from the United States in 1910, and by two Swedish-American missionaries, Daniel Berg and Gunnar Vingren, who arrived in Pará from Chicago in the same year. The latter two were joined in a short time by Nels Nelson and Samuel Nystrom, Pentecostal missionaries from Scandinavia.[27]

With respect to North America, once more, Canada was evangelized for Pentecostalism in the early years of the movement's history. The Pentecostal Assemblies of Canada received a Dominion charter in 1919—and two years later affiliated with the Assemblies of God (U.S.A.). Unlike the Americans, Canadian Pentecostals did not emphasize their differences and thus did not proliferate nearly so much. The movement also spread through Mexico during the early years of its growth, attracting, for the most part, men and women of the masses—peons on haciendas, common people on ranchos, in pueblos, and the ciudades.

Returning to South America, we note that the Pentecostal message was first introduced to Argentina by a group of Italians from Chicago who brought the experience in 1909 mainly to their own people who had settled there. But the larger work in Argentina was undertaken only in 1921 with the arrival of Swedish and Canadian missionaries in Buenos Aires.

Pentecostalism was slow to develop in Australia. Although there had been isolated cases of Pentecostal phenomena in Victoria during the first decade of this century, no widespread Pentecostal revival occurred in Australia until American and British evangelists like Smith Wigglesworth (1921), Aimee Semple McPherson (1922), and A. C. Valdez (1925) arrived to conduct large campaigns in Melbourne, Sydney, and Brisbane. The Pentecostal movement was introduced in Indonesia by two American missionaries in 1921, and its growth over the decades since then has been especially significant.

During World War II, Pentecostalism entered a "settling down" period during which its rapid expansion subsided. After that time, the Pentecostal movement experienced a late growth in Latin (Roman Catholic) Europe—although it had been introduced in France already in 1909, and in Italy in 1908.[28] Until recently, its development in these lands (including Spain and Latin America) had been, more or less, hampered by the Catholic Church[29]; but with the diffusion of Pentecostalism within Roman Catholicism itself since 1967, opening channels of communication between Catholics and Pentecostals, Catholic opposition to Pentecostal Christians has abated.[30]

John Nichol stresses that the post-World War II period has not only been marked by substantial Pentecostal gains throughout the world, but also by what he feels are significant trends within Classical Pentecostalism suggesting a gradual modification of its characteristically sectarian traits. Among these, he includes (1) the decision of the Assemblies of God (U.S.A.) and the Church of God (Cleveland, Tennessee) to join the National Association of Evangelicals in 1943; (2) the organization of regular Pentecostal World Conferences since 1949; (3) the formation of the Pentecostal Fellowship of North America (PFNA) in 1948–49 and other national and international cooperative ventures; (4) the admission in 1961 of two Chilean Pentecostal denominations to the World Council of Churches (followed later by a Brazilian Pentecostal body); (5) the increasing pervasiveness of liturgical order in Pentecostal worship; (6) a growing interest among Pentecostals in higher education; (7) the emergence of a social awareness and concern in Pentecostalism—seen most dramatically in the efforts of Assemblies of God Pastor David Wilkerson to rehabilitate teen-agers of the drug and delinquent subculture (by organizing in the ghettos of New York City his now international Teen Challenge organization); and (8) the new willingness of Pentecostals to engage in a measure of self-criticism (though very little evidence for this trend is yet apparent).[31] Furthermore, the development of strong bureaucratic Pentecostal denominations in the non-Communist countries of the world, and the advent of Neo-Pentecostalism in 1960, together have made it impossible to neatly categorize Pentecostalism as a totally "sectarian" religious movement by whatever definition.

Our purpose here has been just to sketch briefly the diffusion of Classical Pentecostalism since its beginnings in 1901. In so doing, we have merely touched on the introduction of the Pentecostal message to various (but not nearly all) nations in North and South America, Europe, Africa, and Asia.[32]

Reliable statistics on world Pentecostal growth and present constituencies are most often lacking. Nevertheless, thanks to Prudencio Damboriena and Walter Hollenweger's work, we can offer a very approximate estimate of total Pentecostal adherents in nations where the movement has had a measurable impact as follows (for example): U.S.A., 1,400,000; Great Britain, 70,000;

Scandinavia, 200,000; Italy, 200,000; India, 190,000; Nigeria, 130,000; Zaïre (the former Belgian Congo), 200,000; South Africa, 470,000; Indonesia, 1,000,000; Mexico, 120,000; Chile, 460,000–1,000,000, where 80 per cent of the Protestant population is Pentecostal; and Brazil, 4,000,000.[33] These statistics are for Classical Pentecostalism alone, and they probably should already be adjusted upward.

What is particularly noteworthy is the phenomenal growth of Pentecostalism in Indonesia, Chile, and Brazil. Within Latin America as a whole, Classical Pentecostalism is clearly the fastest-growing religious movement of any kind, and it continues to make important advances elsewhere as well (especially in the Third World). There is no doubt that Pentecostalism in its denominational expression is indeed a significant Third Force (in addition to Catholicism and Protestantism) in contemporary Christendom.

IN GREAT BRITAIN: AN "EXPERIMENT" THAT FAILED

We have talked about the rapid change in Pentecostalism from a nondenominational movement to a distinct form of (now moderated) denominational sectarianism in the United States. But this same process took much longer to occur in Great Britain.

Alexander Boddy, an Anglican priest and one-time lawyer and author of travel books, became vicar of All Saints Church, Monkwearmouth, Sunderland, in 1886. In later years, he became a stanch supporter of both the Keswick movement and the Great Welsh Revival. During March 1907, Boddy visited Thomas Barratt in Norway and was deeply impressed by the Pentecostal happenings in Kristiania—with the result that when the Anglican vicar attended the convention at Keswick later in 1907, he distributed thousands of tracts he had written entitled *Pentecost for England*. This undertaking, however, met with a very cool reception there.

In August 1907, the vicar of Monkwearmouth welcomed Thomas Barratt, whom he had invited to conduct a preaching mission (or revival) at All Saints Church. Barratt preached the same evening that he arrived in Sunderland (August 31), and the first three members of All Saints were baptized in the Spirit that night (the service lasted until 4 A.M. the next day)—"speaking in other tongues as the Spirit gave them utterance." Without delay, the national press carried the sensational news.

Barratt's mission in Sunderland lasted seven weeks. Meetings, all comparatively quiet and orderly, were held in the church's large vestry. During this time, both Alexander Boddy and his wife actually received the baptism of the Holy Spirit, and Mrs. Boddy introduced the experience to a plumber from Bradford who was destined to become one of England's great Pentecostal evangelists —Smith Wigglesworth. Before long, All Saints Church had become a mecca for those seeking the Pentecostal experience, no less than Azusa Street had become the previous year.

Although Alexander Boddy encountered much opposition, he also did not lack support. Mail *poured* into his Sunderland vicarage, forcing him to hire two full-time secretaries. In 1908, Boddy decided to hold a Whitsun (Pentecost) convention at Sunderland—the first of many such gatherings. The vicar himself sent out invitations, and admission was by ticket only, restricted to persons in full sympathy with the Pentecostal message. Strict rules regarding order at the meetings were drawn up and kept—so uncharacteristic of the beginnings of Pentecostalism in the United States. At about the same time, the Anglican vicar first published *Confidence*, a magazine on the Pentecostal movement which, although originally intended just for England, was rapidly circulated throughout the world.

Associated with Alexander Boddy's leadership was another Anglican, Cecil Polhill, who inherited Howbury Hall (an eighteenth-century country house near Bedford with extensive grounds) in 1903. Educated at Eton and Cambridge, Polhill had experienced an evangelical conversion in 1884, and became a missionary to China the following year. On a visit to Los Angeles after Pentecostalism emerged there, the squire of Howbury Hall was baptized in the Spirit, returned to England, and immediately joined forces with Boddy. In 1909, he commenced the well-known non-denominational Pentecostal meetings at Zion College, London. This "college," on the Thames Embankment near Blackfriars, had been founded in the seventeenth century by a vicar of St. Dunstan's Church in Fleet Street as a place where clergy could "maintain love by conversing together." Smith Wigglesworth was one of the first speakers at Zion College in 1909, and the regular meetings there (like the Sunderland conventions) became recognized as a place where one might expect to hear Pentecostal speakers from all over the world. According to Donald Gee, the British Assemblies of God leader, writing shortly before his death in 1966, a hall of the college is still available for religious gatherings. He declares, "Pentecostal people have appreciated the gracious hospitality of this Church of England establishment for many years."[34] But nondenominational Pentecostalism in Great Britain did not last after World War I.

The Sunderland Pentecostal conventions ended in 1914 and moved to Kingsway Hall (Methodist), London, where Cecil Polhill took the chairmanship from Alexander Boddy. By 1918, Boddy's leadership in Pentecostal circles declined measurably. And although he remained vicar of Monkwearmouth until 1922, Boddy played no further active role in the Pentecostal movement. By the end of World War I, Pentecostalism in Great Britain followed its American counterpart into separate denominations. The Church of England and the Free Churches had barely been touched. Like Cecil Polhill, Alexander Boddy never left the Church of England; but as an Anglican Pentecostal, in the words of Michael Harper, he was a "prophet few listened to, and most forgot."[35]

Why did the Pentecostal movement in Great Britain take so much longer to become denominationally sectarian than its counterpart in the United States? We can argue that the pervasive respectability of a national ecclesiastical establishment in Great Britain (the Church of England) often has tended to discourage the formation and subsequent growth of new denominations side-by-side. In America, on the other hand, initial resistance to a non-sectarian Pentecostalism was no doubt facilitated by the absence of such a national church and by the general ease in starting new religious organizations—especially in the West, Midwest, and South. There is no evil connotation to the concept of religious sectarianism. With respect to the case of Alexander Boddy in particular, we have to remember that it was he, as a Church of England clergyman in good standing, who primarily influenced the early development of the Pentecostal movement in Great Britain; and Boddy never left the Anglican Church.

Modern Anglicanism has had a reputation for inclusiveness. For instance, the Church of England has been able to keep under one roof at least two very contrary ecclesiastical parties—Evangelicals and Anglo-Catholics—without a great deal of conflict. Furthermore, it was also the case that after the nineteenth century, Anglican bishops as a whole tended to display more tolerance of seemingly aberrant priests who themselves found it inherently difficult to leave the national church—because in so doing, the latter would not only lose their stipend and position, but their *respectability* as well. This fact, of course, may have constituted one reason why Alexander Boddy always remained faithful to the Church of England.

Donald Gee puts forward a few suggestions why the sectarian process in British Pentecostalism developed rather slowly. He emphasizes again that the dominant leaders in the earliest years of the Pentecostal movement in Britain never encouraged the formation of separate Pentecostal assemblies or denominations as such. The counsel usually was given, rather, to "receive the baptism in the Holy Spirit, but remain in your church, whatever the denomination may be."[36] Gee points out that Alexander Boddy was particularly fortunate in having an exceptionally lenient bishop in the person of Handley Moule, bishop of Durham, who allowed the Pentecostal meetings at All Saints Church to continue unabated. And Cecil Polhill, though not an ordained priest, found his denominational connection as an Anglican layman no hindrance to his roving Pentecostal activities. With such early Pentecostal leadership in Great Britain, denominationalism was simply not encouraged.

Yet other factors did lead ultimately to the organization of British Pentecostal denominations. Gee goes on to declare that in Britain "the Pentecostal Movement probably received the most determined, capable, and prejudiced opposition that it encountered anywhere in the whole world."[37] As in the United States, therefore, vehement opposition fostered the establishment of separate, exclusive Pentecostal denominations in Great Britain. Furthermore, Gee suggests that the Pentecostal message there had actually been hindered in the early years for lack of proper ecclesiastical control. He states that a "crude, and ungifted ministry" emerged in many areas of the British Isles:

> Consecration was deemed enough, not only for personal discipleship, but for leadership also. The baptism in the Spirit was construed as making its recipients not only "witnesses," but competent preachers in the assemblies. . . . A handful of kindred spirits [following a devoted but incompetent minister] could make a happy little company to enjoy fellowship among themselves; but it scarcely seemed to be realized that there was a complete lack of any ministry sufficiently powerful to attract and move the masses outside.[38]

Some kind of bureaucratic authority over the increasing number of independent Pentecostal assemblies, therefore, became necessary to regulate pockets of "fanaticism," set qualifications for the ministry, and foster overseas missionary work.[39]

Thus, nonsectarian Pentecostalism in Great Britain came to an end by the conclusion of World War I. It had been an "experiment" that failed. For the rebirth of nondenominational Pentecostalism, the world had to wait until 1960, when—in an Anglican parish in California—another Alexander Boddy emerged to lead a New Pentecostalism, with very different consequences for the church.

CHAPTER THREE: *The Path to Renewal*

BEGINNINGS IN THE 1950S

Although Charismatic Renewal, as a recognizable movement within Christendom, became recognizable only in 1960, the beginnings of Neo-Pentecostalism can really be traced to isolated incidents of Pentecostal phenomena among clergy and laity of the historic denominations by the mid-1950s[1]—but very little documentation for these incidents exists.

The groundwork for the new diffusion of Pentecostalism within mainline Christendom had been laid during the 1950s through the activities of (1) the Full Gospel Business Men's Fellowship International and (2) David Du Plessis. The FGBMFI was born in Los Angeles in 1951 as a nondenominational fellowship of Full Gospel (Pentecostal) businessmen and professionals. Supported initially by Demos Shakarian (a wealthy California dairyman) and Oral Roberts (the faith-healing evangelist), local chapters of the FGBMFI emerged throughout America in the 1950s. In 1953, the organization began issuing its monthly "testimony" magazine, now called *Full Gospel Business Men's Voice* (or just *Voice*). Meetings of the fellowship's local chapter and interchapter conventions eventually attracted mainline clergy and laity who had received the Pentecostal experience or who were merely interested in it. These meetings provided an opportunity for fellowship with "respectable" Pentecostals (i.e., businessmen and professionals) without the explicit or even implicit demand of affiliation with any particular Pentecostal denomination or church. Later, *Full Gospel Business Men's Voice* magazine was distributed among mainline laity and clergy—featuring personal testimonies of Christians from the historic denominations who had been baptized in the Spirit.

David Du Plessis, a leader in the Pentecostal movement throughout the world, and then an Assemblies of God (U.S.A.) minister, spent much of the decade of the 1950s participating as a Pentecostal "observer" in the emerging ecumenical movement and, at the same time, sharing the Pentecostal experience with non-Pentecostal clergy and laity alike—some of whom were high-ranking ecumenical leaders. His own irenic stance as a Pentecostal spokesman—in the context of his relationship with non-Pentecostal ecclesiastical officials—did much to "dignify" the Pentecostal experience and message in the minds of an heretofore skeptical and belittling ecclesiastical establishment. By the 1950s, some mainline church leaders had even come to regard Pentecostalism as a "Third Force" in world Christianity—with Protestantism and Catholicism[2]—and Du Plessis himself can be credited with the growth and spread of that attitude during the decade.

By 1960, the historic denominations had had some preparation for the new diffusion of Pentecostalism, which was soon to be felt within their own ranks as Charismatic Renewal.

"OUTBURST OF TONGUES" AT ST. MARK'S

Dennis Bennett, who was born in London, came to the United States with his family at the age of ten. His father, a Congregational minister, settled the family in central California. Following his schooling, Dennis Bennett became briefly associated with an electronics firm as a salesman, but soon decided on a ministerial career and attended the University of Chicago Divinity School, where he received the B.D. in 1949. In 1951, Bennett converted to the Episcopal Church—the Anglo-Catholic wing—and, in 1953, accepted a call to become rector of St. Mark's Episcopal Church in Van Nuys, California. At that time, the church was just recovering from serious financial difficulties and consisted of about five hundred members. Dennis Bennett proved to be a successful pastor. By 1960, St. Mark's membership roll stood at twenty-five hundred, services were extremely well attended, and the rector had three curates on his staff.

During 1959, John and Joan Baker, who were members of another Episcopal church, received the baptism of the Holy Spirit through the witness of Pentecostal friends. They were tempted, at that point, to forsake the Episcopal Church—in which they had, in any case, been only nominal members—and join a Pentecostal assembly where they would be understood. They resisted this temptation, however, and remained in their Episcopal parish. Soon afterward they told their vicar, Frank Maguire, about their Pentecostal experience. He took the news calmly, assuming that other "more balanced" members of the church, would eventually dissuade them from further involvement in this departure from traditional Anglican orthodoxy.

The "problem" with John and Joan Baker, however, was that they seemed to have become *better* Episcopalians after their Pentecostal experience than before. They thrust themselves completely into the work of the church, attended even weekday services, and began to tithe. Moreover, instead of other members of the parish influencing the Bakers, the reverse was true until, with the passage of just a few months, about a dozen members had been baptized in the Spirit and were (quietly) speaking in tongues. Before long, therefore, Frank Maguire found it necessary to seek pastoral advice on the matter.

Since Dennis Bennett was a colleague and personal friend, Maguire consulted him first. Yet, if anything, Bennett was more ignorant about the issue than Maguire—but interested. Soon, Bennett met the Bakers personally and, as a result of this encounter, received the baptism of the Holy Spirit himself in November 1959, followed three days later by Frank Maguire. A Pentecostal prayer group was already functioning in Maguire's parish, and Bennett began sending interested members of his own congregation to the fellowship, which was headed by John and Joan Baker. Within the next four months, eight ministers and nearly a hundred lay people in the diocese (including a number of key members of St. Mark's) were baptized in the Spirit. By April 3, 1960, some seventy members of St. Mark's Episcopal Church had received the Pentecostal experience.

Although these new Anglican Pentecostals tried hard to keep quiet about their experience, news leaked out quickly within Bennett's parish and the city of Van Nuys as a whole. Rumors, dissension, and misunderstanding—centering on alleged excessive Charismatic behavior (i.e., rolling in the aisles)—became commonplace. Certainly, participants in the Pentecostal experience were intensely enthusiastic. Prayer and fellowship meetings often lasted until 1:30 A.M. (even as late as 4:00 A.M.), but *order* was insisted upon from the beginning, and Charismatic activity was not permitted within formal services of worship.

On Passion Sunday 1960, Dennis Bennett explained everything to his parishioners openly. During the sermon, one of his curates took off his vestments and resigned publicly while walking out down the center aisle. Another curate declared that such things simply could not be tolerated in respectable churches, while the church treasurer demanded Bennett's resignation. To keep the peace, the rector of St. Mark's did resign two days later, and sent a long, explanatory, and irenic letter to all members of the parish.[3] In this letter, Bennett made it clear that he was *not* leaving the Episcopal priesthood, and was not encouraging anyone either to leave St. Mark's or cancel his pledge. That, of course, was the crucial decision. Shortly thereafter, Bishop Francis Bloy of the Los Angeles Episcopal Diocese banned any more speaking in tongues under church auspices; and later, the remarkable news of the outburst of tongues at St. Mark's was carried in both *Time* and *Newsweek*.[4]

Dennis Bennett thus found himself without a job and branded throughout the Episcopal Church as a religious fanatic and crank. However, the then bishop of Olympia, Washington, invited him to become vicar of a small mission church in Seattle that was redundant and, in fifty years, had made no noticeable impact on its community. Bennett accepted the call, and arrived on July 1, 1960, at the bankrupt St. Luke's Episcopal Church to lead two hundred confused and disillusioned communicants. Twelve months later, eighty-five of the members of St. Luke's had received the baptism of the Holy Spirit—practically the whole inner core of the church. Attendance had multiplied, and the building could no longer hold all the people. The budget had increased dramatically, and all outstanding debts had been paid. Today, over two thousand people attend a thriving St. Luke's Episcopal Church weekly.[5] Dennis Bennett's "defeat" had turned out to be a victory for the movement he symbolized.

AN INCREASINGLY RECOGNIZABLE MOVEMENT

Dennis Bennett took the Pentecostal experience with him from Van Nuys to Seattle, and the number of Neo-Pentecostals continued to increase in both areas. With the dramatic growth of St.

Luke's Episcopal Church, Seattle, after Bennett's arrival in 1960, the fame of its rector spread accordingly—both locally and nationally. Bennett soon became a very popular speaker in the Episcopal Church itself and in other denominations and interdenominational groups where the Pentecostal message was beginning to attract attention. As a Neo-Pentecostal facilitator, this Episcopal priest became a modern-day Alexander Boddy and was himself responsible for much of the early growth of Charismatic Renewal—especially among Episcopalians, Lutherans, and Presbyterians.[6]

But the focal point of the development of Neo-Pentecostalism remained, oddly enough, in Van Nuys, California, until 1966. Among those who had received the baptism of the Holy Spirit at St. Mark's before Bennett's resignation was Jean Stone, a lifelong Episcopalian whose husband was a prominent corporate officer of Lockheed Aircraft. With the financial assistance of her husband, Donald, Jean Stone organized in Van Nuys the first Charismatic Renewal fellowship, which existed from 1961 to 1966—the Blessed Trinity Society ("Trinity" to emphasize the "newly rediscovered" work of the third person, the Holy Spirit). David Du Plessis was an original member of the board of directors of this organization. In addition to fellowship activities for Neo-Pentecostals, the Blessed Trinity Society offered a sophisticated and expensive quarterly ($1.50 per issue), *Trinity*, to inform its readership of current news of the movement and to introduce Charismatic Renewal to non-Pentecostals in the historic (especially Anglican and Lutheran) denominations. Eventually, *Trinity* magazine was sent to interested clergy and lay people in countries throughout the world (although its cost prevented widespread distribution in some areas—Great Britain, for instance). Then, motivated in part by Ralph Wilkerson (now pastor of Melodyland Christian Center, Anaheim, California), the Blessed Trinity Society launched in 1962 the first interdenominational teaching seminars dealing with Charismatic Renewal—"Christian Advance." These gatherings and conferences were directed at the historic churches and attracted laity and clergy from all parts of the United States. As the movement continued to spread, Jean Stone, editor of *Trinity*, was invited to speak to interested groups throughout the country, including the National Council of Churches' staff in 1964.[7]

By 1963, it was estimated that 200 Episcopalians in the Los Angeles diocese were speaking in tongues,[8] and six out of 225 congregations of the American Lutheran Church in California had been affected by the glossolalia phenomenon.[9] Soon afterward, the Pentecostal experience became known in two of the most prominent Presbyterian churches in Los Angeles—Bel Air, and Hollywood First (then the nation's largest—with 600 speakers in tongues in 1964).[10] Both are still very affluent congregations.

During the first few years of the movement's growth, a number of important leaders emerged who spread the message of Charismatic Renewal throughout America and abroad as well. We have already mentioned Dennis Bennett, Jean Stone, and Ralph Wilkerson. Also included in this group of Neo-Pentecostal leaders were Herald Bredesen, then pastor of the First Reformed Church, Mt. Vernon, New York[11]; Howard Ervin, an American Baptist clergyman, now chairman of the Department of Religion at Oral Roberts University[12]; Larry Christenson, pastor of Trinity Lutheran Church, San Pedro, California[13]; Robert Frost, then professor of biology at Westmont College, Santa Barbara, California[14]; Graham Pulkingham, former rector of the Church of the Redeemer (Episcopal), Houston, Texas, who is now doing Charismatic Renewal work in Great Britain[15]; and Todd Ewald, rector of Holy Innocents Parish (Episcopal), Corte Madera, California.[16] When the Blessed Trinity Society collapsed in 1966, and Jean Stone passed from Neo-Pentecostal leadership, the focal point of Charismatic activity in California moved to the nondenominational Melodyland Christian Center in Anaheim and its pastor, Ralph Wilkerson.

In the early 1960s, Charismatic Renewal became a widespread topic for the secular and religious press, radio, and television, because glossolalia was for the first time in America being practiced by sophisticated, middle-class church members. Neo-Pentecostal leaders and their churches were the subject of numerous interviews and discussions in the media.[17] In October 1962, as a result of two campus visits by Herald Bredesen, the glossolalia phenomenon broke out in the academic community—at Yale University, among members of the evangelical Inter-Varsity Christian Fellowship there. Included in this Neo-Pentecostal revival were Episcopalians, Lutherans, Presbyterians, Methodists, and even one Roman Catholic. Five were members of Phi Beta Kappa, and some were religious leaders on campus (soon called "GlossoYalies").[18] Thereafter, the movement spread to Dartmouth College, Stanford University, and Princeton Theological Seminary (where it was particularly significant). By May 1964, Charismatic Renewal prayer groups had sprung up in colleges and seminaries in at least fifteen states in the Northeast, north-central states, and on the West Coast. Four years after its inception, Neo-Pentecostalism was a clearly recognizable religious movement—affecting both clergy and laity, students and professionals, men and women, in the Episcopal Church and almost all the mainline Protestant denominations in the United States.[19]

RAPID SPREAD TO OTHER PARTS OF THE WORLD

Charismatic Renewal in Europe and the British Commonwealth was profoundly affected by the emerging Neo-Pentecostal movement in the United States during the early 1960s; although in many countries, the stage for further development had been set by the ecumenical visits and activities of David Du Plessis in the course of the preceding decade.

In Great Britain, the second wind of Pentecostalism occurred about 1962—again, primarily (but not exclusively[20]) among clergy and lay people of the Church of England. In the first years of its publication, *Trinity* was circulated in a number of areas of the British Isles. Its coverage of recent Charismatic happenings among Episcopalians in the United States (together with their own accounts and testimonies of those events) certainly helped to attract the initial interest of British Anglicans. As a result of *Trinity*'s circulation at that time, a small number of people received the baptism of the Holy Spirit in 1962. Also, during the same year, Phillip Hughes, editor of *The Churchman* (an Evangelical Anglican periodical), visited America and, at her invitation, met with Jean Stone in California. Upon his return to London, Hughes wrote an important editorial in the September issue of that publication that was very favorable to the new movement—an especially influential essay[21] (sixty thousand copies were sold in 1962–63) because the author was widely respected as a balanced mainline (albeit evangelical) religious thinker and churchman.

In May 1963, Frank Maguire visited Britain and addressed a privately convened ministers' meeting in London where *some* interest was shown. Later, he spoke at the Church Army Training College, where one student was baptized in the Holy Spirit. Yet another gathering was arranged in an Oxfordshire village after which a few more people received the Pentecostal experience. Finally, the Episcopal priest from Monterey Park, California, was invited to preach in a West End (London) Anglican church. But altogether, Maguire's visit represented a mere beginning for the movement in Great Britain.

In August 1963, on his way home to San Pedro, California, from a Lutheran World Federation conference in Helsinki, Larry Christenson spoke at meetings both in Germany and in London. Again, a private gathering for ministers was convened in London, followed the same day by one for interested lay people. Before returning to California, Christenson had been instrumental in leading two curates of an Anglican church in London to the Pentecostal experience. (Later, an Anglo-Catholic vicar who had attended the meeting also received the Spirit baptism—followed before many months by a number of the clergy of his diocese.) One of those two curates influenced by the Lutheran pastor was Michael Harper, then on the staff of the prestigious All Souls Church, Langham Place, London. (Harper eventually became the most prominent Neo-Pentecostal leader in Great Britain—as founder of the Fountain Trust in 1964 and editor of its bimonthly magazine, *Renewal*, in 1966. The Fountain Trust coordinates Charismatic Renewal conferences and fellowship gatherings in Britain, and publishes *Renewal* and books dealing with Neo-Pentecostalism, distributing them throughout the world. In this way, it quickly became the Blessed Trinity Society of the British Isles.) It is perhaps especially significant that Christenson had, sometime before his visit to London, written a booklet, *Speaking in Tongues: A Gift for the Body of Christ*, which was translated into German and was widely circulated in Germany. In the autumn of 1963, with Michael Harper's help, it was first published in Great Britain.

Later in 1963, David Du Plessis visited London en route from Holland to his home in the United States. Once again, a meeting was arranged—this time in a West End hotel. Several hundred invitations were sent out, the room was filled, and the audience gave Du Plessis a very enthusiastic response. After that gathering, a few more individuals received the baptism of the Holy Spirit.

Slowly but surely, the Neo-Pentecostal upsurge continued unabated in Great Britain. In the spring of 1964, Jean Stone accompanied her husband on a European business trip, which included London. By the time she arrived, a rather extensive itinerary had already been worked out—consisting of a press conference, two public meetings in London, a trip to Scotland, and trips to several other places in England. In Scotland alone, nearly fifty people (including several ministers) received the Spirit baptism. The London gatherings, incidentally, were the first ones open to the public and arranged by "non-Pentecostals" since the days of Alexander Boddy and Cecil Polhill. Over fifty persons received the Pentecostal experience as a result of these meetings. Then, in the summer of 1964, David Du Plessis returned to the British Isles, where he spoke at many gatherings in England, and attended the General Assembly of the Church of Scotland in Edinburgh. Interest in Charismatic Renewal increased in various denominations throughout Britain, particularly in the Church of England among Anglo-Catholics no less than Evangelicals. By 1965, over a hundred ministers of the historic churches had the baptism of the Holy Spirit.[22]

During 1965 itself, two further events greatly advanced the cause of Neo-Pentecostalism in the British Isles. The first was Dennis Bennett's visit in October of that year. Bennett freely discussed his own Pentecostal experience, the dramatic growth of a once-dying St. Luke's Episcopal Church in Seattle, and the nature of Charismatic Renewal itself as a contemporary movement within Christendom. He spoke at a number of Anglican (and one Jesuit) theological colleges in London, Oxford, and Cambridge. Bennett spent a fair amount of his time in Cambridge, where his first address was given at Great Saint Mary's, the University Church. He was welcomed there (enthusiastically) by Hugh Montefiore, then its vicar, and spoke to a congregation that included the late Bishop James Pike of California, an old friend of Bennett's. As a guest of the dean of Magdalene College, the rector of St. Luke's also preached at Holy Trinity Church, and addressed a luncheon meeting of college chaplains, a number of whom were impressed. Besides Cambridge, the Charismatic Episcopal priest fulfilled numerous other speaking engagements, including one at Southwark Cathedral in London. Most of these

gatherings were extremely well attended. The curate of Great
Saint Mary's wrote in the *Cambridge Daily News* of October 30,
1965:

> What kind of man is Bennett? A Bible puncher? A fire
> eater? No, he is quiet, sincere, with a great sense of
> humour and a very balanced view of life. And he is a
> High Churchman. But his faith makes me echo that
> comment: "that man has got something, and I want it."[23]

Thus, Dennis Bennett's sojourn added considerably to the respectability of Neo-Pentecostalism in Great Britain thereafter.

The second major happening for Charismatic Renewal in the
British Isles during 1965 was the "airlift" of hundreds of Full Gospel Business Men (and their friends among the clergy) from the
United States to London in November of that year. The
FGBMFI Americans wanted to share in a London convention
with their British brethren (using the London Hilton Hotel as
headquarters), but they also saw the visit as an opportunity for
evangelism. During the first week, meetings were held in and
around the capital city. Then, in the course of the second week,
evangelistic teams went to many other cities throughout Great
Britain—including both Oxford and Cambridge. The final gathering was at Royal Albert Hall in London, which was filled with
people to hear Oral Roberts conclude the convention (among
other participants during the two-week visit were Demos Shakarian, Herald Bredesen, Howard Ervin, and Ralph Wilkerson). By
the end of 1965, Neo-Pentecostalism in the British Isles (including Northern Ireland[24]) had established itself as an important force with which the church would sooner or later have to
make its peace.[25]

Although the United States and Great Britain constitute the
focus of this study, we should also note that the movement spread
rapidly in the mid- and late 1960s to New Zealand (facilitated by
visits of Dennis Bennett and Michael Harper), where developments have been recorded in the periodical *Logos*[26]; and to Australia[27] and South Africa (aided by visits of Michael Harper and,
of course, David Du Plessis), where the situation has been
depicted in *Gift* magazine.[28] (The New Anglican archbishop of

Cape Town, Bill Burnett, is a Neo-Pentecostal.[29]) In Germany, Charismatic Renewal has remained almost totally independent of Classical Pentecostalism (theologically and culturally). Leadership there is centered largely in the Evangelical Sisterhood of Mary in Darmstadt, and in the person of Arnold Bittlinger (a pastor of the United Church of the Palatinate) and his Ecumenical Academy at Scholoss Craheim, near the village of Wetzhausen (not far from the East German border).[30] More recently, Neo-Pentecostalism has also advanced significantly in Scandinavia[31] and in other countries.

ALL ROADS LEAD TO ROME: CATHOLIC PENTECOSTALS

Long before the initial development of Pentecostalism as a movement within Roman Catholicism, there were individual Catholics who had received the Pentecostal experience[32]—often through the influence of Pentecostal friends. But Catholic Pentecostalism as a "movement" emerged only in 1967, in the United States—this time, however, within the academic community itself. From the start, Catholic Pentecostals (a number of whom had already been influenced by the evangelical Cursillo movement in the Roman Catholic Church) were determined both to remain *Catholic* and to reject all the cultural baggage associated with Classical Pentecostalism (especially its ethical taboos and fundamentalism). At the same time, they did not allow this determination to detract from the possibility of fellowship both with Classical Pentecostals themselves and with other Neo-Pentecostals.

In the autumn of 1966, several Catholic laymen, all faculty members of Duquesne University in Pittsburgh, were drawn together in a period of prayer and discussion about the vitality of their Christian lives. All were active churchmen. They prayed "that the Holy Spirit of Christ would renew in them all the graces of their baptism and confirmation. . . ."[33] In August, these men had been introduced by friends to David Wilkerson's book *The Cross and the Switchblade* (1964)—an account of the beginnings of his service among young gang members and dope addicts in the Bedford-Stuyvesant section of New York City (which led, ultimately, to the founding of a ministry to the youth-drug culture throughout the world, Teen Challenge International). The latter part of the book deals with the Pentecostal experience, and this interested the men. Kevin and Dorothy Ranaghan recall,

> In their struggles with the apathy and unbelief among college students they realized they needed the kind of power that Wilkerson seemed to possess in the face of the agony and ugliness of the dropouts, delinquents, and addicts of Brooklyn.[34]

For the next two months, they shared—talked and prayed about —issues raised in *The Cross and the Switchblade*.[35]

One of the men, Ralph Keifer, then an instructor in Duquesne's Department of Theology, also had been led to read John Sherrill's *They Speak with Other Tongues* (1965)—a journalist's account of the emergence of Charismatic Renewal in the United States—and gave it to the others. Eventually, the group decided to become personally acquainted with local Christians who had the Pentecostal experience, and they asked a nearby Episcopal priest for his advice. He introduced them to an active laywoman in his parish who was participating in a Pentecostal prayer group. During their brief encounter, the men were surprised and pleased that this woman did not fit the Classical Pentecostal stereotype.

On January 13, 1967, the academics from Duquesne met with the prayer group—organized by another woman, a Presbyterian. Impressed by the warmth and sincerity of the meeting and its biblical tenor, two of the men attended the next gathering as well. There, Ralph Keifer and his friend asked to be prayed with for the baptism of the Holy Spirit. Keifer prayed in tongues almost immediately. In the following week, he, in turn, laid hands on the other two men, who also received the Pentecostal experience. This event was followed by what they feel was a dramatic interior transformation in their lives and by the reception of numerous *charismata* as well.

By February 1967, four Catholics in Pittsburgh had been baptized in the Holy Spirit. And as Roman Catholics, they could discern no doctrinal problem with what happened to them. Indeed, the men were convinced that the Pentecostal experience could only make them *better* Catholics. The same month, a small group of students arranged a retreat with the faculty members in question. About thirty people attended this "Duquesne weekend" (as it has come to be called) and received the baptism of the Holy Spirit while there. Later, they became the nucleus of the first Catholic Pentecostal "community."[36]

Within a month, what had been born at Duquesne spread both to the University of Notre Dame and to the Catholic student parish at Michigan State University.[37] In January 1967, Kevin Ranaghan (then teaching at St. Mary's College, Notre Dame) and his wife, Dorothy, heard that their good friends at Duquesne had sought the Pentecostal experience, a fact that *shocked* them. In mid-February, Ralph Keifer came to South Bend, Indiana, on business and spent the weekend with the Ranaghans. For two days the discussion was entirely concerned with Pentecostalism, during which time Kevin and Dorothy Ranaghan raised every intellectual, aesthetic, and psychological objection to Keifer, who by this time had actually received the Spirit baptism. Then on March 5, nine people from the Notre Dame academic community met together to seek the Pentecostal experience. That night, there were no manifest *charismata* among the group; but the "blessing" apparently had been received. The Ranaghans describe what happened to themselves and the others as follows:

> In general, we all experienced and witnessed in each other the breakthrough of the love of Christ in our lives. . . . Many were drawn to long periods of prayer, marked by the predominance of the praise of God. Some found themselves opening the Bible anew with a real hunger for the word of God. Just about everyone found a new boldness in faith, a desire to witness about Jesus to friends and to strangers. Divisions, even hatreds, between brothers were healed. . . . It was like this all throughout that first week.[38]

On March 13, the new Catholic Pentecostals met in prayer with members of the South Bend chapter of the Full Gospel Business Men's Fellowship International, where Catholic "intellectuals" and evangelical Protestant lay people discovered quickly that their unity in an experience transcended deep theological and cultural differences. Many of the Catholics who attended the gathering received the gift of tongues that evening.

Through a number of house and campus prayer meetings in the weeks to come, more students and instructors (including Edward O'Connor[39] and Josephine Ford[40] of the Notre Dame Department of Theology), priests and nuns, laymen and laywomen from South Bend came to have the Pentecostal experience. By Easter vacation 1967, about thirty Catholics in the Notre Dame area had received the baptism of the Holy Spirit.

Shortly after spring break, the Notre Dame group decided to join with others from the Catholic student parish at Michigan State University, East Lansing (some of whom had recently been Spirit baptized), for a time of prayer, fellowship, and further inquiry—now known as the "Michigan State weekend." The facilities of Old College, Notre Dame, were reserved for this purpose. About forty people from Michigan State and an equal number from Notre Dame and St. Mary's participated. By the end of that weekend in which numerous Christians received the Pentecostal experience, the Catholic Pentecostal movement was flourishing at Duquesne, Notre Dame, and Michigan State—and spreading elsewhere. Hundreds of Catholics across the country had been baptized in the Spirit by the end of the spring semester.

During the summer session of 1967, about three thousand students came (as usual) to Notre Dame—mostly nuns, priests, and teaching brothers. A number of the Catholic Pentecostals remained on campus that summer and arranged a panel discussion on the topic that interested them most. The previous events at Duquesne, Notre Dame, and Michigan State had been reported in the Catholic press; hence, three hundred attended that discussion. Afterward, interest was such that regular prayer meetings were scheduled once or twice a week for three weeks in which hundreds of people took part; and when the participants left Notre Dame, of course, they took the Pentecostal message and experience with them.[41] Catholic Pentecostalism had become a clearly visible movement.

From Notre Dame and Michigan State, Pentecostalism in the Roman Catholic Church spread quickly to the University of Michigan (where The Word of God community, now led by Ralph Martin, became particularly vigorous),[42] to Cleveland, to the University of Iowa, and to the University of Portland (Oregon). Meanwhile, similar developments were taking place in other parts of the country—outside the academic community as well—in Boston, Orlando, Seattle, Los Angeles, St. Louis, and central New York. By October 1970, there were Pentecostal prayer groups among Catholics throughout the country, and possibly ten thousand Catholics were actively involved in the movement in the United States. In addition, Catholic Pentecostal prayer groups were flourishing in Canada, England, New Zealand, Australia, and in several Latin American countries—with beginnings observed also in continental Europe and in Africa.[43]

The best-known external work of the Notre Dame community in particular (True House was disbanded in 1974 because of leadership problems) was the organization of national (now international) Catholic Pentecostal conferences, which grew out of the Michigan State weekend in 1967. In 1968, attendance was between 100 and 150. The 1969 weekend brought together about 450, including perhaps 25 or 30 priests (David Du Plessis was a participant at this conference). In 1970, the increase was more spectacular. Almost 1,300 people attended the conference from a much wider area of North America than before (including Canada).[44] Then, in 1973, the Charismatic Renewal conference at Notre Dame (June 1–3) brought together 22,000 attendees, who occupied every available room in a 50-mile radius of South Bend. In addition to the multitude of American participants, Catholics from Australia, Germany, Holland, France, Israel, Mexico, Haiti, Colombia, Korea, and India were present to hear Léon Joseph Cardinal Suenens, archbishop of Malines-Brussels, a well-known reformer and Catholic Pentecostal himself, both endorse and encourage Charismatic Renewal—which at this time embraced possibly 300,000 American Catholics or more.[45] The 1974 Notre Dame conference was attended by 30,000 people.[46] And the 1975 international conference, held in Rome, attracted 10,000 pilgrims from fifty countries to hear Pope Paul VI express his warm appreciation for the movement.[47]

The dramatic emergence and growth of Catholic Pentecostalism since 1967 has produced a good deal of rather sophisticated theological literature on Pentecostal phenomena (specifically in the Catholic Church) by those who have been active participants, and has also resulted in the diffusion of Charismatic Renewal into predominantly Catholic countries both in Europe and the Third World—Latin America especially, where it is bringing together former enemies, Roman Catholics and Classical Pentecostals, in a totally unexpected way.[48] Neo-Pentecostalism is growing faster perhaps within Roman Catholicism than in any other denomination—a fact that makes Michael Harper's words early in 1970 particularly relevant at this point: "Catholic renewal could in the end out-space renewal in all other churches."[49]

THE NEW PENTECOSTALISM TODAY

Neo-Pentecostalism has continued to grow. The original purpose and goals of Charismatic Renewal, broadly formulated as early as 1960, have not been changed by the process of its growth. The conviction persisted that the Pentecostal experience, properly understood, was a force powerful enough to renew the church in its full range of contemporary institutional expressions—and potent enough to unify Christians (spiritually) in an experiential and expressive way without requiring organic (institutional) oneness.

Nevertheless, despite its continued character as a movement, a distinct leadership has emerged within Neo-Pentecostalism as a whole. Underlying the movement, in this regard, we can discern a reticulate structure made up of individual leaders and organizations—united in certain ideological or theological themes (notably the baptism of the Holy Spirit and the present-day operation of *charismata*)—which facilitates personal ties between lay "members" and group leaders and between the groups themselves, and justifies Charismatic Renewal's identity as a movement. In this study, we shall distinguish between the characteristics and emphases of Classical Pentecostalism and Neo-Pentecostalism as two basic expressions of the Pentecostal movement more broadly defined; but we must also take into account the fact that the specifically sectarian nature of Classical Pentecostalism itself is gradually changing (more in some denominations than in others), and that Classical Pentecostals and Neo-Pentecostals (including Catholics) increasingly participate *together* in the various organizations fostered by Charismatic Renewal.

In Great Britain, the most important organization associated with Charismatic Renewal is still the Fountain Trust (located near London), which publishes books and *Renewal* magazine, and coordinates conferences (some on an international scale) and other kinds of activities. In the United States, there are a number of especially prominent organizations linked to Neo-Pentecostalism. By means of its local chapters, together with its regional, national, and international conferences and "airlifts," the Full Gospel Business Men's Fellowship International (Los Angeles) remains a pivotal "fellowship" arm of the movement, and, through the publication of its *Full Gospel Business Men's Voice* magazine, it continues to be an important worldwide recruiting organization as well. Like the Foundation Trust in England, it too sponsors gatherings featuring leaders of Charismatic Renewal throughout the globe. Another influential organization associated with the movement is Melodyland Christian Center (Anaheim, California). It not only functions as an interdenominational Pentecostal fellowship center but also organizes annual "charismatic clinics," conducted by prominent Neo-Pentecostals, which serve as a "teaching" and evangelism arm of the movement (succeeding the Blessed Trinity Society's Christian Advance seminars). In addition, Melodyland Christian Center has recently established a school of theology to serve the Charismatic Renewal community in the area of professional ministerial education. Yet another intellectual center for the movement is Oral Roberts University (Tulsa, Oklahoma), founded by the eminent faith-healing evangelist (now a United Methodist minister). For those interested in the scholarly study of Pentecostalism and Pentecostal phenomena, a professional academic association has been formed —the Society for Pentecostal Studies. The chief American publisher of books on Charismatic Renewal is Logos International (Plainfield, New Jersey), which also issues a popular bimonthly magazine, *Logos Journal*. Finally, divine healing as a ministry in the Neo-Pentecostal context is best represented by the Kathryn Kulhman Foundation (Pittsburgh) and the "miracle services" held by its Charismatic Baptist founder and president.

All of the aforementioned organizations (which we shall discuss in some detail later)—except the Fountain Trust—are based in the United States, and they minister largely to Americans. (In addition, we should mention here Christian Growth Ministries, Fort Lauderdale, Florida, as well—and its magazine *New Wine*—especially the ministry of its most prominent teachers, Don Basham, Derek Prince, Bob Mumford, and Charles Simpson, all *men.*) But all of them have an international influence as well. To these leading nondenominational organizations associated with Charismatic Renewal we can also add numerous Pentecostal fellowship communities within (but not apart from) the various Protestant, Anglican, and Catholic denominations affected by the movement —e.g., Catholic Charismatic Renewal Services, Lutheran Charismatic Renewal Coordinating Committee, American Baptist Charismatic Fellowship, Presbyterian Charismatic Communion, and Episcopal Charismatic Fellowship.[50]

Charismatic Renewal appears to be strong enough today— among lay people and clergy, ecclesiastical bureaucrats, and theologians—to have warranted the gradual acceptance of Pentecostal phenomena in most of the historic denominations. Walter Hollenweger says:

> It will become harder and harder to make a clear-cut distinction between American Pentecostals and American non-Pentecostals in the future, now that the experience and message of the baptism of the Spirit have found a way into all [?] the American denominations.[51]

In Catholicism, as we have seen, the growth of Pentecostalism has been especially dramatic—to the point that the Secretariat for Promoting Christian Unity of the Roman Catholic Church is currently engaged in a five-year official conversation with leaders of some Classical Pentecostal denominations and with participants in Charismatic Renewal within Protestant, Anglican, and Eastern Orthodox churches.[52] (Not a great deal has been said about Pentecostalism in Eastern Orthodoxy. But a strong movement is, in fact, taking place there; numerous priests, led by Eusebeius Stephanou, are receiving the Pentecostal experience.[53]) One of the best-conceived statements on the present state of Charismatic Renewal from its leadership was made by Michael Harper late in 1972:

> The charismatic movement is now firmly on the map. All over the world, and in all churches, it is growing fast

and forcing itself by its sheer vitality upon the attentions of the church and the world.

There can be no holding back now. Books, magazines, and television are presenting the movement to wider audiences than ever. It is a talking point everywhere. Its future seems assured, and there are few signs yet of its being bureaucratised into impotence. Its main strength, and for many its attractiveness, lies in its spontaneity, and in the fact that it is so far comparatively unstructured. It is not basically a protest movement, but a positive affirmation of faith in God and His power to change people and institutions. It is a new style of Christian life.[54]

We shall now examine the nature of Charismatic Renewal with respect to its leadership, its characteristic faith and practice (including structure and organization), its relationship both to Classical Pentecostalism and to the church as a whole, reasons for its emergence and success, and its relationship to trends in the wider culture. In so doing, we shall discern to what degree Neo-Pentecostalism's actual function in the church and in society validates its own self-understanding and identity.

CHAPTER FOUR: *The Leadership of Charismatic Renewal*

The principles of Charismatic Renewal leadership must be discerned in the context of Pentecostal organization itself. Luther Gerlach and Virginia Hine have studied the structural character of Pentecostalism as a movement in *People, Power, Change: Movements of Social Transformation.* Beginning with Gerlach and Hine's structural analysis of the Pentecostal movement as a whole, we can proceed to apply their findings to Neo-Pentecostalism in particular.

The Pentecostal movement is first of all, according to Gerlach and Hine, fully *decentralized.* There are widely recognized leaders within Pentecostalism. And, to outsiders, these men and women often appear to be the key individuals without whom the movement would grind to a halt. Yet not one of them could rightly be called *the* leader of the movement in which they work. Pentecostal leaders disagree on matters of theological emphasis. None of them are even aware of all the groups that consider themselves participants in the movement. None of the leaders can make decisions binding on all participants; they cannot speak for the movement as a whole, nor do they have regulatory power over it. (There are, of course, no "real" members of the Pentecostal *movement* as such—only "participants"—although there are members of specific Classical Pentecostal denominations.) Pentecostal Christians recognize each other on the basis of criteria born of a common experience, not because a leader announces that a given person is a legitimate participant in the movement.[1]

Leadership in a decentralized movement is, by and large, based on personal charisma rather than the fulfillment of bureaucratic training requirements and progression up through ranked positions.[2] In Charismatic Renewal, however, individuals who are already bureaucratic leaders in their own denominations (or academic institutions, for instance) can become recognized Neo-Pentecostal leaders far more easily than the rest—once they receive and publicly share the Pentecostal experience. Furthermore, we can distinguish within Charismatic Renewal the development of a largely "organizational" (goal-oriented) leadership rather distinct from (but perhaps derivative of) the leadership based on personal charisma.

"Charisma," a term first used in sociology by Max Weber, was employed by him to signify supernatural or spiritual endowment as acknowledged by others. It was, thus, a social recognition of a claim to supernatural power (as in the case of Jesus Christ himself). In the Pentecostal movement, however, charisma, with reference to leadership, indicates that a given individual (1) is recognized by others as possessing one or more of the spiritual gifts in special degree; (2) has a forceful personality; and (3) is able, through personal qualities, to exercise leadership. This is what we mean when we refer to "charismatic leadership" within Charismatic Renewal.[3]

Second, according to Gerlach and Hine, the Pentecostal movement is *segmentary*. It consists of a great variety of localized groups or cells that are essentially independent but that can combine to form larger configurations or divide to form smaller units. Quite often each segment will tend to recruit from different parts of the total societal population. Each will tend to develop a "religious style" of its own—and its own specific goals and means as well. These groups proliferate rather quickly because of (1) the Pentecostal ideology of personal access to power (any Pentecostal has direct access to the source of spiritual power, wisdom, and authority—"the priesthood of all believers" carried to an extreme), and because of (2) pre-existing personal and social cleavages. Thus, a given class-, culture-, or ecclesiastical-consciousness will probably cause Pentecostals having that particular consciousness to stick together in their own primary groups.[4]

Charismatic leaders in the Pentecostal movement are supported financially (and otherwise) by fellow Pentecostals who believe the recipients have been called by God to do a specific work. The givers believe in the work fully as much as the recipients of financial support feel *obligated* to do the work well.[5]

Third, according to Gerlach and Hine, the Pentecostal movement is *reticulate*. Its structure is weblike; the cells and groups are all tied together, not at a central point, but by intersecting sets of personal relationships and other intergroup linkages. There are personal ties among participants. For instance, a Pentecostal *may* attend Sunday services at one church and Wednesday night prayer meeting at another; or he may hold an interdenominational weekly "house meeting" at his home. Then there are personal ties among the leaders of various groups themselves—even invitational conferences for Pentecostal leaders alone. Furthermore, traveling evangelists link the segments together, as do ritual activities (conferences and the like), where participants gather for expressive rather than formal, goal-oriented purposes. Such gatherings promote religious fervor, intensify commitment, and express the movement's basic unity (even in much diversity). Finally, regional, national, and international associations function to link the various Pentecostal groups together.[6]

The decentralized, segmentary, and reticulate character of the Pentecostal movement assumes a constant supply of leaders and replacements should any be lost. It limits the ability of established opposition to penetrate, gather intelligence about, and counteract the movement. And this structure allows the unifying Pentecostal experience to spread the movement across class, cultural, and ecclesiastical boundaries. Thus, in a sense, there is a Pentecostal church or group for "everyone."[7]

THE TRUSTED AUTHORITY FIGURE

As a result of his ten-year study of glossolalia among Protestant and Anglican Neo-Pentecostals (*The Psychology of Speaking in Tongues*), John Kildahl concludes that speakers in tongues develop deeply trusting and submissive relationships to the authority figures who introduced them to the experience. He discerned that glossolalists have a strong need for external guidance from some trusted authority—someone "more powerful" than themselves who gives them security and direction, even peace and relaxation in their lives. Kildahl also found that speakers in tongues tend to "overinvest" their feelings in their leaders to the point of "idealizing them as nearly perfect parents."[8] Thus, while national and international Neo-Pentecostal leaders (recognized to be endowed with one or more particularly evident *charismata*) command the general respect and admiration of participants, it is the *local* group leaders with a largely personal ministry who come closer to exercising "real" authority over their followers (in the context of specific requirements of the various ecclesiastical traditions to which Neo-Pentecostals adhere).

In the very beginning, a recognizable and influential Neo-Pentecostal leadership emerged almost spontaneously. Among the "first" mainline clergy and lay people who received the Pentecostal experience, certain highly committed individuals soon attracted a following of Anglicans and Protestants to whom the baptism of the Holy Spirit seemed novel and exciting. The former became trusted authorities on the experience—denominational interpreters. These charismatic leaders were, of course, aided both by the positive and the negative comments of the secular and religious press, and by exposure to the media in general. Neo-Pentecostal leaders quickly began seeking each other out for fellowship and mutual support—among them, Dennis Bennett, Herald Bredesen, Howard Ervin, and Larry Christenson, all mainline clergymen. Open Classical Pentecostals who already enjoyed standing in the movement—Demos Shakarian, Ralph Wilkerson, and David Du Plessis (in particular), among others—soon identified themselves with the Charismatic Renewal participants. Jean Stone, an Episcopal laywoman, emerged as a Neo-Pentecostal leader largely through the widespread circulation of *Trinity*, which she edited and her husband financed—and which was the first distinctly Neo-Pentecostal periodical. In Great Britain, Michael Harper, an Anglican clergyman, became a Charismatic Renewal leader partly through his camaraderie with early American Neo-Pentecostal personalities, but mostly by the circulation of *Renewal* and, later, his successful books.

The Full Gospel Business Men's Fellowship International provided early organizational support for the movement; so did the Blessed Trinity Society (while it lasted) and the growing Melodyland Christian Center. In Great Britain, as we have seen, the Fountain Trust functioned in a similar manner to the Blessed

Trinity Society in America. By becoming a United Methodist minister, Oral Roberts, the Classical Pentecostal faith-healing evangelist, identified "officially" with Charismatic Renewal, and his new university added a measure of academic prestige to the movement. The career of "miracle worker" Kathryn Kuhlman, a Baptist minister, was clearly enhanced by her association with Neo-Pentecostalism—as much as the movement itself was aided by her participation. The same can be said about the vocal support of celebrities like Pat Boone and Maria von Trapp. Furthermore, Logos International, the highly successful publisher of Charismatic Renewal literature, has also been a significant asset to the movement's media efforts.

In Catholic Pentecostalism, Maria von Trapp and Cardinal Suenens are perhaps the only persons who come close to being real celebrities. Some of the Catholic Pentecostals in the United States, such as academics Edward O'Connor and Josephine Ford, authors Kevin and Dorothy Ranaghan, and editor-author Ralph Martin, have become international leaders in the movement. But in Catholicism, more than elsewhere, Pentecostals have gathered into church-related communities (some highly disciplined), directed by a local shared leadership that is very submissive to the Roman Catholic Church's hierarchy.

Thus, despite the inherent diffusion of charisma and the presence of local authority figures, Charismatic Renewal does have its widely recognized national and international, charismatic and organizational, leaders who preach, teach, inspire, and provide (through visits, lectures, and publications) an identity for the movement and a measure of cohesiveness to a decentralized, segmentary, and reticulate structure.

PROMINENT CHARISMATIC LEADERS

In a decentralized movement, as we have seen, charismatic leadership predominates. Charismatic leaders have the power of persuasive influence over others. They inspire faith and loyalty (and also aid in the recruitment process). Charismatic Renewal has produced many purely charismatic leaders within its various segments, and some whose "charisma" transcends those cells and groups. The latter include celebrities like Kathryn Kuhlman, Oral

Roberts, and Pat Boone, who aid the movement no less than lesser-known Neo-Pentecostal charismatic leaders who work locally at the person-to-person level.

With the gradual development of structure and organization (without rigid bureaucracy) since 1960, Charismatic Renewal has produced a number of persons who, because of their close ties to specific important organizations associated with the movement, can rightly be termed "organizational" leaders. On the one hand, these individuals do not really function as classically "bureaucratic" leaders who have fulfilled *formal* bureaucratic training requirements (which do not exist in Neo-Pentecostalism), and have progressed up through ranked positions (which, again, do not exist). But neither are they leaders by virtue of personal charisma alone—though most of them, perhaps, *are* endowed with charisma, which has itself aided their advancement to organizational leadership. These men and women quite often are known and respected *because* of their identification with a particular organization, publication, or church (or, as in the case of David Du Plessis, are simply regarded as natural "organizers" in the larger sense) rather than merely by virtue of personal charisma. Demos Shakarian is a leader because he founded and directs the Full Gospel Business Men's Fellowship International. Ralph Wilkerson, as a leader, is identified with the church he founded and pastors, Melodyland Christian Center. Michael Harper is highly regarded as a Neo-Pentecostal leader in Great Britain and elsewhere by virtue of his association with *Renewal* (and his widely circulated books). Ralph Martin is a leader because he is editor of *New Covenant*; and Eusebius Stephanou, since he edits *Logos*. Jean Stone, of course, was also an editor. Even before his formal identification with Charismatic Renewal, David Du Plessis (who still considers himself a Classical Pentecostal) had already "progressed through the ranks" of denominational Pentecostalism to the point that he was the primary organizer (and secretary) of the early Pentecostal World Conferences. Thus, Neo-Pentecostals, from the beginning, regarded him as "Mr. Pentecost" and solicited his help as an organizing facilitator (e.g., he was among the first directors of the

Blessed Trinity Society). Respected participant clergy-become-lecturers (and world travelers) easily fall into organizational leadership within the movement as it manifests itself in those leaders' own denominations—aided by whatever bureaucratic standing such ministers enjoyed prior to their participation in Charismatic Renewal. Hence, Dennis Bennett is a leader in the Episcopal Church and among Anglicans in general; Larry Christenson, in the American Lutheran Church and among Lutherans as a whole; Rodman Williams, in the Presbyterian Church in the United States and among the larger body of Presbyterians; Edward O'Connor and Cardinal Suenens, in the Roman Catholic Church; and Eusebius Stephanou, among Eastern Orthodox Christians. All of them, of course, had the requisite ecclesiastical standing before they identified with Neo-Pentecostalism.

EDITORS AND PUBLISHERS

In a decentralized movement—especially in its beginning, before a pattern of ideological consensus and a definite structure of leadership arise—the periodical editor (aided, perhaps, by a measure of personal charisma) can rather easily become an organizational leader in that movement, influencing its emerging identity. He or she, of course, has the power to select authors and news items (and screen manuscripts) for exposure to participants and the public at large. This editor defines the parameters of ideological acceptability. If the periodical in question is indeed acceptable to participants in the movement, its circulation will increase with the growth of the movement itself. Thus, the editor achieves notoriety, which is further enhanced by widespread circulation of the periodical. Almost automatically, then, the editor becomes a spokesperson for the movement in his editorial comments. A typical modern religious movement is greatly helped (if not "carried" almost entirely) by the mass media. Yet, as a movement's ideological consensus develops (to whatever degree it does) and becomes recognizable, and as a definite pattern of leadership emerges, it becomes less likely that the editor of a *new* periodical will rise to organizational leadership simply by virtue of who he is (and his "breakthrough" journal)—unless he has already achieved leadership status by other means. For if that editor's publication merely reflects commonly publicized and accepted ideology and the views of already widely recognized leaders, it functions merely as a support and reinforcement for such ideology and leadership previously established. The editor can no longer actually help formulate and set ideology (in an "authoritative" sense). If he contradicts the underlying consensus, the editor and his journal may well get nowhere.

(One paradox in Neo-Pentecostalism is that here is a movement very largely organized around the experience of "speaking" —a very primitive form of communication. Yet one has to be impressed with the importance of the printed word in the movement, which reflects a dependence on literacy, and which itself indicates a reliance on subsidiary channels of communication. "Speaking" and "communicating" are basic means of establishing "community." For modern man, however, community depends on other techniques too. Early Classical Pentecostalism probably had much less dependence on journals than does Neo-Pentecostalism.)

In Charismatic Renewal, Demos Shakarian's leadership and the strength of his Full Gospel Business Men's Fellowship International have been aided enormously by the success of *Full Gospel Business Men's Voice* magazine (1953–). Shakarian himself is not the journal's editor; nevertheless, he directs the organization for which *Full Gospel Business Men's Voice* is the official mouthpiece. The magazine itself strengthens the organization and, with it, Shakarian's personal prestige as well; it aids the recruitment process by introducing the Pentecostal experience to people (especially businessmen and professionals), and then directing them to FGBMFI activities for further information and fellowship. Jean Stone, of course, emerged as an organizational leader in the movement almost entirely because of the participant acceptance (and recruiting success) of *Trinity*, the first exclusively Neo-Pentecostal periodical to be published (1961–66). Wide-spread circulation of the magazine that she edited (and that her husband financed) made her an authoritative spokeswoman for the movement. In Great Britain, likewise, Michael Harper became an organizational leader (even theoretician) largely because of his editorship of that nation's first Neo-Pentecostal journal, *Renewal*, which was received by participants with enthusiasm. In the same way, Ralph Martin, editor of *New Covenant,* and Eusebius Stephanou, editor of *Logos,* have also become organizational leaders.

From the movement's beginning in 1960, Charismatic Renewal has employed the mass media very effectively. Especially important has been its distribution of published literature—not only periodicals, as we have seen, but also pamphlets and books. At first, books and pamphlets by Neo-Pentecostal authors and their sympathizers were most often (but not always) printed privately or by small, relatively unknown "publishers." These works were then distributed to the various Charismatic Renewal communities, churches, and conferences by the authors themselves (often charismatic leaders) or by traveling evangelists, teachers, and lecturer-preachers. Meetings of one kind or another (for expressive purposes) have always been a characteristic mark of Neo-Pentecostalism, and they provide a natural outlet for the relevant literature. Invariably, there is a "bookstall" (at least) connected with each Charismatic Renewal community. And in recent years, many of the larger, growing communities have transformed their bookstalls into full-fledged bookstores specializing in Pentecostal titles. But specialized Charismatic Renewal bookstores, independent of any particular Neo-Pentecostal group, have also arisen; for books and pamphlets on the topic in question are marketed easily, and not infrequently become religious best sellers.

In the course of the past several years, specialized Charismatic Renewal publishers have emerged to supply even secular bookstores with their increasingly marketable book, and now also cassette tape titles. Of these publishing houses, the largest and most famous is Logos International, Plainfield, New Jersey, founded by Dan Malachuk (who still directs the operation). Logos not only publishes and distributes its own titles, but also has taken over the publication and distribution of numerous well-received titles previously published and distributed privately or by nonspecialized houses.

Dan Malachuk, a high school dropout and jeweler in Plainfield, New Jersey, has long been an active participant in and board member of the Full Gospel Business Men's Fellowship International. While traveling in Europe with the FGBMFI during the sixties, he came into the notion of publishing. Malachuk discovered an old work by Raphael Gasson, a medium who turned from spiritualism to Christianity and wrote about his experience. Gasson's *The Challenging Counterfeit* was the first title to be published under the Logos imprint. But Malachuk's first great success was *Run Baby Run*—the story of Nicky Cruz, a Puerto Rican gang leader who had been converted to Christ from gang warfare in Harlem through the influence of David Wilkerson's Teen Challenge organization. Cruz is now a popular youth evangelist.

Since 1968, some of Logos International's titles have sold over a million copies. In 1972, Malachuk expected to sell five million books that year alone—many of them his own acquisitions.[9] And among religious periodicals, *Logos Journal*, a bimonthly published by Logos International, is also doing well. In 1973, that magazine had an over-all circulation of about a hundred thousand copies per issue.[10]

There is no question but that the success of Logos International and other exclusively or primarily Neo-Pentecostal publishing houses (such as Whitaker Books, Monroeville, Pennsylvania; Bethany Fellowship, Publishers, Minneapolis; Ave Maria Press, and Charismatic Renewal Services, Notre Dame, Indiana, in the United States; and the Fountain Trust, East Molesey, Surrey, in England) is a good indication of Charismatic Renewal's strength more generally.

PREACHERS AND LECTURERS

In addition to editors and publishers, ordained ministers of the various historic denominations represented in Charismatic Renewal often become organizational leaders of the movement. Once a minister has received the Pentecostal experience and makes the fact known publicly, he will probably win immediate recognition from one or more Charismatic Renewal organizational segments, and will most likely become associated with a Neo-Pentecostal community, possibly within his own denomination, and, perhaps, take on particular leadership responsibilities in that group. A minister's ecclesiastical standing makes him a desirable lecturer within the Charismatic Renewal movement as a whole; for, through lecturing and/or writing, he can help recruit participants from his denomination while he adds respectability to the movement more generally. In time, the Neo-Pentecostal minister may come to "represent" his denomination within the larger Charismatic Renewal.

We have said that certain individuals within Neo-Pentecostalism are recognized as leaders simply by virtue of an easily discernible personal charisma. These persons rise to positions of leadership without regard to bureaucratic training requirements or upward mobility through the ranks. We have also seen that some Charismatic Renewal leaders function in more strictly organizational roles (e.g., in denominations or other ecclesiastical structures or the religious media). Many such leaders are, in fact, endowed with a degree of personal charisma, which helps them; but it is really their standing (ecclesiastical, intellectual, or social) that enhances the emergence of these clergy and lay people in organizational leadership circles. Unlike Classical Pentecostalism, Neo-Pentecostalism understands itself for the most part as a movement of the *respectable*—in whatever context. Hence, the respectability attached to one who has previously achieved social, intellectual, or ecclesiastical standing is a great asset to his participation in the movement. Certain attainments related to status are indeed desirable as prerequisites of organizational leadership.

For clergy, a college or university education, plus formal theological training, including (in the United States) a seminary degree, increases a minister's respectability in Neo-Pentecostalism. Education at "prestigious" institutions is also beneficial, since a Charismatic Renewal leader's academic credentials are always emphasized (if they *are* respectable). Then, clergy are also helped in this context by regular ordination and standing within a historic denomination; and it is even better if the clergy in question already have attained positions of bureaucratic leadership within their denominations or within the institutional ecumenical movement. In this regard, we can also say that academics, simply by virtue of their education and resulting social status, make good organizational leaders within Neo-Pentecostalism—especially theologians who have *both* academic and ecclesiastical standing. The Charismatic Renewal stress on respectability of leadership is in sharp contrast to Classical Pentecostal requirements for ministerial organizational leadership—Spirit baptism, spiritual gifts, and "the call" (often omitting higher education as a requisite altogether). Of course, there are *some* ordained Neo-Pentecostal organizational leaders without benefit of higher education and mainline ecclesiastical standing; but their rise to the ranks of leadership often has more to do with personal charisma or previous Classical Pentecostal standing than anything else.

For lay people, other criteria are also beneficial in the context of desirable "requisites" for Charismatic Renewal organizational leadership. These include formal higher education (as in the case of clergy), but also public esteem, participant lay membership in one of the historic denominations, and financial success. For especially wealthy Neo-Pentecostals (e.g., Full Gospel Business Men), leadership in one or more of the Charismatic Renewal organizational segments is predicated on the degree of generosity they exhibit toward the movement's sometimes very ambitious activities and projects (Pentecostals, like other evangelicals, are admonished to tithe—at least). Rich lay leaders of the various Neo-Pentecostal organizations are often called upon to help support the evangelistic efforts of Charismatic Renewal minister-lecturers-become-world-travelers who cannot finance such trips themselves. Within Neo-Pentecostalism, lay people do rise both to charismatic and organizational leadership; but their active participation is more often "in the background" and quieter than that of ordained ministers, whose vocal leadership in preaching and teaching is *expected* by virtue not only of their recognized spiritual gifts, but also because of their training and ecclesiastical standing.

KATHRYN KUHLMAN: DIVINE HEALING IN THE 1970S

With the rise of Kathryn Kuhlman, divine healing (or "faith-healing") in Christian orthodoxy has increased in respectability. Even *Time* magazine says:

> Joyfully middle-class, fiftyish [?], a lady who likes fine clothes, Kathryn Kuhlman looks for all the world like dozens of the women in her audience. But hidden underneath the 1945 Shirley Temple hairdo is one of the most remarkable Christian charismatics in the U.S. She is, in fact, a veritable one-woman shrine of Lourdes. In each of her . . . services . . . miraculous cures seem to occur.[11]

It is only since the mid-1960s or thereabouts that Kuhlman has been identified with the Pentecostal movement at all. (Most scholarly studies of Pentecostalism, including Hollenweger's, do not even mention Kuhlman's name as being associated with the movement.) Previously, she was very much an "independent" phenomenon—an ordained Baptist minister through whom, her followers believe, God works to perform miraculous healings. We have already said that Kuhlman's identification with Charismatic Renewal has enhanced her popularity as well as the fortunes of the movement she supports. In 1972, Oral Roberts himself invited her to speak to the graduating class of Oral Roberts University.[12]

Kathryn Kuhlman's style contrasts sharply with that of the stereotyped American revivalist faith-healer. There are no healing lines, prayer cards to be completed beforehand (alleged to sort out "hopeless" cases), prayer cloths, or special talismans; nor is there the traditional "miracle touch" ("point of contact," as Oral Roberts called it, between the faith-healer and his subject).[13] Kuhlman holds her miracle services in numerous places in the United States (rarely elsewhere)—regularly at the First Presbyterian Church, Pittsburgh; Stambaugh Auditorium, Youngstown, Ohio; and the Shrine Auditorium, Los Angeles. Chartered buses (offering guaranteed reserved seats) make the trip to these locations whenever services are held. Once the buses have emptied into a given auditorium, people outside who may have waited several hours are allowed inside until the hall is filled—just a few minutes after the doors are opened. Hundreds, even thousands, are regularly turned away or forced into "overflow" space connected to the live service by closed-circuit television. Kuhlman seems to prefer "limited access" to her meetings, for she *could* hire larger facilities.

Services, as James Morris describes them, are "folksy, friendly, and charming."[14] There is often musical entertainment at the beginning, followed very frequently by a sermon. Charismatic activity is noticeably curtailed, though participants practice the Pentecostal (and very ancient) *orans* prayer posture (hands uplifted), and are almost always "slain in the Spirit" (falling backward into an usher's arms) when Kuhlman touches them *after* their testimonies to an alleged or verified healing. At the conclusion of her sermon (if there is one), the charismatic leader points to various places in the audience where she discerns healings have already occurred prior to that moment. She cites the ailment—everything from terminal cancer to allergies (though amputated limbs never reappear; teeth are not miraculously filled with gold)—and asks those who feel they are healed to come forward to the platform to testify about what has happened. (Trained ushers try to screen cases and verify healings as much as possible beforehand.) Quite often, there are physicians on the platform who themselves may be asked for confirmation; and everyone is urged to confirm an apparent cure with his or her own doctor. Some individuals, of course, testify, but are not healed; others seem to get better, but later regress; probably most in attendance are not cured at all. Nevertheless, the media and various respected authorities attest that a small number of people, at least, do receive an apparently miraculous cure. Some of these appear on Kuhlman's daily radio and weekly half-hour television programs, which span the country.[15] Other spectacular cases are "documented" in her three books.[16] Unlike most traditional faith-healers, people who experience healings in the Kuhlman services are generally mainline Protestants and (increasingly) Roman Catholics—not Classical Pentecostals. In addition, even "nonbelievers" (Jews, agnostics, and atheists) are healed ("mercy healings," according to Kuhlman), while highly committed Christians may continue to suffer.[17] Yet, Kathryn Kuhlman refuses to take the credit for any of the healings that take place in her presence. She often says, "I have nothing to do with these miracles."[18]

Born in Concordia, Missouri, the daughter of a Methodist mother and Baptist father, Kuhlman underwent an evangelical conversion during her early teens (her age is a "classified" secret—estimates range from "fiftyish" to eighty-four; sixty-four probably the most acceptable[19]). She dropped out of high school after her sophomore year to take up preaching (Kuhlman is sensitive about her lack of education[20]) and was ordained by the Evangelical Church Alliance (Missouri) after two years of informal Bible study.[21] Four years after an unhappy marriage, Kuhlman was divorced by her husband,[22] and she spent over two decades as an itinerant preacher in Idaho and the Midwest. After her Spirit baptism in 1946, a woman claimed to be cured of an ailment during a Kuhlman service in Franklin, Pennsylvania. In 1947, the charismatic leader moved to Pittsburgh, and the healing aspect of her ministry began to grow. She is still based in Pittsburgh, where the Kathryn Kuhlman Foundation (which aids foreign missions, drug addicts, and college students) has its offices in the Carlton House Hotel. She has no membership organization, no magazine or newsletter; and, of course, she urges persons healed in her services to remain in their own churches. Kuhlman travels five hundred thousand miles annually[23]; and, in 1970, she drew a salary of twenty-five thousand dollars from her foundation.[24]

In 1972, twenty-two hundred persons gathered at the Pittsburgh Hilton Hotel to help Kathryn Kuhlman celebrate the twenty-fifth anniversary of her ministry in that city. Dan Malachuk of Logos International was there; and Carl Albert, Speaker of the House of Representatives, sent special congratulations.[25] Kuhlman has earned the respect of city leaders of Pittsburgh as well.[26] Robert Lamont, former pastor of Pittsburgh's prestigious First Presbyterian Church, where the Kathryn Kuhlman Foundation holds meetings every Friday, insisted that he examine the charismatic leader's finances before granting her permission to use his church sanctuary for services. Having scrutinized her financial records closely, he stated in 1972, "I've been doing this for the last four years and can report that her finances are cleaner than the United Presbyterian Church."[27] On October 11, 1972, Kuhlman was invited by Pope Paul VI to a private audience with him in the Vatican—during which time he assured her of his personal blessing on her work and his continual prayers[28]—thus guaranteeing an even larger Roman Catholic following for this remarkable woman.

Within Neo-Pentecostalism, Kathryn Kuhlman is clearly a prominent charismatic leader. She is now *the* representative of the movement's healing ministry; but more than that, as we have said, Kuhlman's miracle services have increased the respectability of divine healing in Christian orthodoxy (Protestantism especially).

ORAL ROBERTS: FROM FAITH TO UNIVERSITY PRESIDENT

For two decades, Oral Roberts was the most prominent Pentecostal in the United States. Pentecostal preachers were proud to have him as a champion, and the popular faith-healing evangelist's crusades attracted as many as twenty-five thousand people at a time in America, and up to sixty thousand in other countries.[29] Unlike Kathryn Kuhlman, Roberts always had a significant ministry abroad. His healing crusades took place under the great "cathedral tent," where services were conducted in the American revivalistic tradition—with the focus on prayer for the sick who generally stood in "healing lines" waiting for the evangelist to "touch" them and pray for them. But Roberts' style was never so sensational as many of his Pentecostal counterparts, his financial dealings were apparently more open to inspection and honest, and he integrated his crusades early.[30] Oral Roberts' personal charisma and success as a faith-healer (he disliked the term[31]) made him Classical Pentecostalism's most prominent leader long before he identified with Charismatic Renewal.

The faith-healing evangelist's parents dedicated Roberts to the service of God while he was a young child. His father was a Pentecostal Holiness minister, and the family was very poor. Roberts played basketball in high school (one reason why Oral Roberts University has had one of the best basketball teams in that collegiate sport); but, during tournament play, at the age of sixteen, he collapsed on the court, and was later diagnosed as having tuberculosis in both lungs. Defeat turned into victory, however, for Oral Roberts' family took him to a Pentecostal faith-healer in his native Oklahoma, and young Roberts experienced a dramatic healing, which changed the course of his life. Two months after his miraculous cure, Oral Roberts began preaching—an unusual feat for someone who had once been extremely fearful of crowds and a chronic stutterer. Like his father, Roberts became a Pentecostal Holiness pastor, first in Georgia and then in Oklahoma. In the course of time, his own gift of healing became manifestly apparent to many who attended his services. While pastoring, Oral Roberts spent several semesters at Oklahoma Baptist University and Phillips University, but never graduated. In 1947, a highly successful evangelistic effort in Tulsa, Oklahoma, led the faith-healing evangelist to make that city his headquarters. A year later, in Durham, North Carolina, Roberts began his healing crusades in earnest; and it was only a matter of time before Pentecostalism, divine healing, and Oral Roberts became synonymous.[32]

After two decades of healing ministry both in the United States

and abroad, Roberts pulled down the big tent permanently in
1967. An unsuccessful crusade in Anaheim, California, that year
had been the final blow. He says:

> I could see that the tent was ceasing to be an asset. Peo-
> ple were no longer attracted by its novelty. They had be-
> come used to cushioned chairs and air-conditioning and
> to watching television.[33]

The day of preaching from a platform with a a backdrop of pastors followed by a healing line had come and gone. The day of the
gospel tent was over.

But Oral Roberts had already been moving in another direction. By the early 1960s, the Oral Roberts Evangelistic Association
held substantial assets—chiefly in real estate (Roberts himself for-
sook "love offerings" for a regular salary paid by the association in
1960).[34] With the additional help of numerous Pentecostal supporters and Full Gospel Business Men,[35] the faith-healing evangelist realized his long-standing dream in 1965—to found a distinctively Christian university with high academic standards. Oral
Roberts University (ORU) is a four-year liberal arts institution in
Tulsa, Oklahoma, with a forty-million-dollar campus—one of the
most modern in the world. It educates about two thousand students from every state, and from many races and denominations.
At the center of campus stands a twenty-story "prayer tower,"
which is staffed twenty-four hours a day by persons who take telephone calls from all over the world (Roberts started his telephone
prayer-request ministry in 1958). ORU was formally dedicated in
1967, with Billy Graham as featured speaker; and it won full regional accreditation in 1971—only the second private college or
university to receive this distinction so soon after its opening. It
had been a long way for Oral Roberts from Pentecostal Holiness
faith-healer to president of his own university.[36]

Roberts' intention to educate young people intellectually and
physically as well as spiritually[37] was hardly in keeping with the
Classical Pentecostal Bible school tradition. A recognized liberal
arts university with faculty members trained at some of the leading institutions of higher education in the United States and
abroad simply was not compatible with the Classical Pentecostal

ethos and emphasis on "spiritual" (i.e., Bible) education alone. So, in 1968, Oral Roberts left the Pentecostal Holiness Church, joined Boston Avenue United Methodist Church in Tulsa, and was received as an ordained minister (through transfer of credentials) by the Oklahoma Conference of the United Methodist Church. Although the university president had been a Methodist as a young child and had numerous friends and colleagues in that denomination (including several faculty members and the chaplain of ORU), Roberts' sudden change of ecclesiastical affiliation seemed dramatic at the time. It was something a Pentecostal leader "just didn't do." He says, "I was charged with having gone liberal, turning Communist, and being a backslider."[38] From April to December 1968, income received by the Oral Roberts Evangelistic Association (now the Oral Roberts Association) and ORU decreased by more than one third. His Classical Pentecostal supporters thought Roberts had left the faith.[39]

The prominent charismatic leader never intended to change his basic theology—only his style. As a respectable United Methodist university president who was deeply involved in the transdenominational Charismatic Renewal, Oral Roberts would have a much broader appeal to mainline Christian parents of prospective students and to qualified academics who were potential faculty members than he would as a Classical Pentecostal who was still associated with the denominational Pentecostal cultural milieu. The United Methodist Church would allow Roberts to work for spiritual renewal as a Neo-Pentecostal within its ranks. Thus, he declares:

> I began to feel that God was leading me to transfer to the Methodist Church. To my mind, the Methodist Church was more than a denomination. It represented all the diverse elements of historic Christianity. In its membership and ministry were deeply committed evangelicals. Yet it had radical liberals, too. More importantly, it had maintained a free pulpit; Methodist ministers could preach their convictions.[40]

Oral Roberts had explicitly rejected the sectarian notion of a "pure church" in favor of a very inclusive ecclesiastical structure that could embrace lay members and ministers of considerable theological diversity. His "conversion" to the United Methodist Church—from leadership within Classical Pentecostalism to leadership in Charismatic Renewal—almost signaled the (symbolic) conversion of Pentecostalism itself. James Dunn, writing in the *Scottish Journal of Theology*, suggests:

> The fact that the well-known Pentecostal evangelist Oral Roberts joined the Methodist Church in 1968 is a significant indicator of the new direction of Pentecostalism, and may mark a turning point for the whole movement, old and new.[41]

By projecting a new radio and television image, Roberts had also forsaken Classical Pentecostal's rejection of the wider society and culture. The faith-healing evangelist first appeared on television in 1954[42] with a traditional Pentecostal image, and continued successful programming until 1967, when he dropped the use of this medium. In 1969, however, he returned to the air with a very different format. Roberts' television sermons took on an "existential" character—*focusing* on "the NOW" more than the hereafter; but more important than that, talented and carefully selected students at ORU (where the weekly half-hour shows are taped) began to offer regular musical entertainment and highly sophisticated choreography. These "World Action Singers" now offer both religious and secular popular music—from gospel to folk to rock—and interracial coupling (with hand-holding, even) is a notable characteristic of the show. Furthermore, Roberts also schedules quarterly prime-time television specials, usually filmed at NBC studios in Burbank, California (but as far as Honolulu and London as well), which have featured celebrities from the entertainment industry such as Pat Boone, Johnny Cash, and Dale Evans Rogers (all prominent Christians), and other stars such as Jimmy Durante, Kay Starr, Sarah Vaughan, and black "soul" vocalist Lou Rawls. This inclusion in his television programming of celebrities from the "worldly" show-business industry, together with a culture-affirming interracial group of student entertainers from his own university who dance as well as sing, is another mark of the new Oral Roberts and a new style of

ministry that still, however, emphasizes the Pentecostal experience.[43]

Even if the larger healing ministry has indeed been transferred
from Roberts to Kathryn Kuhlman, Oral Roberts remains a prominent charismatic leader within Neo-Pentecostalism no less than
his female "successor" and present colleague in the movement.[44]

DAVID DU PLESSIS: AN ECUMENICAL ODYSSEY

No single person is more responsible for Neo-Pentecostal
growth throughout the world than David Du Plessis, whose rise to
leadership within the Pentecostal movement came about largely
through his own organizational ability. Speaking for Neo-Pentecostals in general, Michael Harper calls him "our Pentecostal
father-in-God."[45] Du Plessis terms himself a Pentecostal "ecu-
maniac," and he is widely known in Charismatic Renewal circles
simply as "Mr. Pentecost."[46] Although David Du Plessis still
considers himself a Classical Pentecostal, there is good reason for
all these titles.

Born in South Africa of French Huguenot stock in 1905, Du
Plessis experienced an evangelical conversion in 1916, and received
the baptism of the Holy Spirit in 1918. He describes himself as "a
little white heathen saved by the life and ministry of black
Christians."[47] In 1927, Du Plessis was married, and the following
year was ordained to the ministry of the Apostolic Faith Mission
of South Africa.[48] Like most Pentecostals of the time, he had no
formal theological education.[49] Reared in the typically sectarian
Pentecostal tradition, Du Plessis relates how his parents were
turned out of the Dutch Reformed Church for their Pentecostal
activity. This fact, of course, shaped the course of his early ministry;

> I began preaching at a very youthful age. In those days
> there was much preaching against the Pentecostals. I
> used to listen to Dutch Reformed ministers preach
> against us and call us false prophets standing on street
> corners. Then I would promptly go back to the street
> corner and preach against "these blind leaders of the
> blind." How we attacked one another.[50]

From 1928 to 1949, David Du Plessis gradually emerged into bureaucratic leadership within the Apostolic Faith Mission—from evangelist, pastor, youth leader, Sunday School director, and chief editor, to general secretary of the denomination.[51]

As we have seen, after World War II, the characteristically sectarian traits of Pentecostalism began slowly to abate. In 1947, the first Pentecostal World Conference was called in Zurich. Du Plessis attended this meeting as a delegate from his denomination; and in 1948, he was asked to convene a second such conference in Paris and to serve as its secretary—an office he held also at the third and fifth Pentecostal World Conferences, in London (1952) and Toronto (1958), respectively.[52] His position as an important organizational leader of world Pentecostalism was now firm. In 1949, David Du Plessis became a permanent resident of the United States, and in 1955 gained ministerial standing in the Assemblies of God.[53]

The "ecumenical odyssey of Mr. Pentecost" began in 1951. Du Plessis says: "In 1951 the Lord spoke to me and clearly told me to go and witness to the leaders of the World Council of Churches."[54] Introducing himself as "world secretary" of the Pentecostal movement, he was warmly received by members of the WCC New York office.[55] In 1952, Du Plessis was invited to the International Missionary Council assembly at Willingen, Germany—his first experience as a Pentecostal at an ecumenical convention. As the guest of John Mackay, then president of Princeton Theological Seminary and an eminent leader in the ecumenical movement, Du Plessis talked about the dramatic successes of Pentecostalism on the mission field, and related the Pentecostal message to numerous WCC officials in attendance. Then, in 1954, "Mr. Pentecost" attended the second WCC assembly in Evanston, Illinois, at the invitation of General Secretary Willem Visser 't Hooft (the former also held staff status). This was followed in 1961 by his participation as a Pentecostal observer at the third WCC assembly in New Delhi.[56] Du Plessis' once sectarian attitudes had now changed dramatically:

> Instead of the old harsh spirit of criticism and condemnation in my heart, I now felt such love and compassion

for these ecclesiastical leaders that I would rather have
died for them than pass sentence upon them.[57]

As a result of his new ecumenical contacts and the recognition
he was accorded in the ecumenical movement, David Du Plessis
lectured at Princeton Theological Seminary, Yale Divinity School,
Union Theological Seminary (New York), and at other mainline
Christian theological schools in the years just before Neo-Pentecostalism emerged as a movement in 1960.[58] Since then, "Mr.
Pentecost" has continued his strong ecumenical ties. He was
Pentecostal observer at Vatican II,[59] and is currently co-chairman
of a five-year "dialogue" between the Secretariat for Promoting
Christian Unity of the Roman Catholic Church and leaders of
Classical Pentecostalism (a few of them, at least) and Charismatic Renewal—which meets annually.[60] Du Plessis has lectured
and preached in more than forty-five countries,[61] and he travels
throughout the world almost without a break.

But "Mr. Pentecost's" ecumenism cost him his standing in the
Assemblies of God. In 1962, he was "disfellowshiped" by the governing board for his fraternal contacts with the WCC (though
Donald Gee continued to back his efforts).[62] Du Plessis is supported by no denomination and admits that he now has no "official" standing in the worldwide Pentecostal movement (though
he obviously remains an "organizational" leader):

> Recently a group of Episcopal ministers in America
> asked me who sponsored me in this work and what my
> position was now in the Pentecostal Movement. I had to
> explain that this was a faith venture. No one hired me
> and no one can fire me. I have resigned from every posi-
> tion I held, and so I have become just a great "has been"
> insofar as positions are concerned. I am a good will am-
> bassador for Christ.[63]

Because of his ecumenical ties, David Du Plessis has encountered much opposition both from Classical Pentecostals and from
fundamentalists and evangelicals more generally. Yet he continues
to act as a Neo-Pentecostal facilitator and liaison between Classi-

cal Pentecostalism and Charismatic Renewal—again, still calling himself a Classical Pentecostal. Responding to his critics, Du Plessis declares:

> There are many today who make a study of the Ecumenical Movement to find out what is wrong with it. Diligently they seek out men and statements that appear liberal and socialistic, and then seek to blanket the whole Movement with the few "exceptions" that they have discovered. On this basis I have every reason to blanket the Ecumenical Movement with a "conclusion" that they are Pentecostal. Not only does their published literature propagate strong Pentecostal teachings, but there are now many Spirit-filled, yes indeed, "tongues-speaking" ministers in the National and World Council of Churches. I shall not be surprised when our fundamentalist friends who attack the Pentecostals as severely as they do the World Council, begin to "expose" the Pentecostal trend with the ranks of the Ecumenical Movement.
>
> The Holy Spirit has never recognized barriers.[64]

David Du Plessis does not speak publicly about the action taken against him by the Assemblies of God in 1962. And it would appear that, given the increased level of communication and fellowship between Classical Pentecostals and Neo-Pentecostals, he will eventually be vindicated, and again recognized by the Assemblies of God. In 1974, Du Plessis was listed among "the eleven most influential Christian thinkers of today" by Interchurch Features (an advisory group of editors of various religious magazines in the United States and Canada).[65]

MICHAEL HARPER: EDITOR AND THEORETICIAN

As former editor of *Renewal* and director of the Fountain Trust, Michael Harper is the foremost organizational leader of Charismatic Renewal in Great Britain. His numerous books—dealing not only with the Pentecostal experience itself, but also with its function as a force of Christian *renewal* more generally—have put Harper in the position of one of Neo-Pentecostalism's leading theoreticians as well.

Unlike Dennis Bennett, another Anglican, Michael Harper came out of a strong evangelical rather than Catholic tradition. In 1950, he took up residence at Emmanuel College, Cambridge, as a law student. Later that year, Harper experienced an evangelical conversion at a very unlikely place—Sunday morning communion at King's College Chapel—and thereafter affiliated with Cambridge's evangelical establishment, the Cambridge Inter-Collegiate Christian Union (CICCU).[66] He says:

> I became deeply affected by the ethos of evangelicalism. Most of my friends came from this "set." My books were "sound." My vacations were patterned for me by my friends. There was little time for "cultural" education. Nearly all the vacations were taken up with conferences, house parties, missions and camps. The first flush of inspiration, when I really did know the imprint of the Holy Spirit upon my life, was gradually lost.[67]

In 1952, Harper changed his course from law to theology, became a candidate for Holy Orders, and, in 1953, entered the (strictly Evangelical) Ridley Hall Theological College in Cambridge. He was ordained in 1955, married in 1956, and assigned as a curate of All Souls Church, Langham Place, London, in 1958, under its rector, John Stott. (Stott and All Souls Church have been synonymous with established evangelicalism in Great Britain.) Harper's specific responsibility during his six-year curacy there was chaplain to the Oxford Street department stores; he was only one of six curates assisting Stott at the prestigious church in London.[68] All seemed settled—until 1962.

While preparing to speak at a weekend parish conference at St. Luke's Church, Hampstead, in September, Harper experienced something that changed his life dramatically. He felt liberated from his "legalistic" background, discovered a new sense of freedom in preaching, and his attitude toward *people* was transformed.[69] Shortly thereafter, Harper's wife had the same experience (thus remedying the dilemma of a "distracted wife" and an "impossibly enthusiastic husband").[70] But neither of them knew exactly *what* had happened—or what to call it. At first, Harper and his wife appeared to equate their recent experience with a "second blessing" or entire sanctification made popular by the Holiness movement. As yet, neither had spoken in tongues.[71]

During 1963 an architect, a member of Michael Harper's "lunch-hour congregation" of London business people, related his recent Spirit baptism to the department store chaplain—how he had suddenly spoken in tongues while in the bath one evening.[72] The architect had become interested in the emerging Charismatic Renewal in the United States, and had heard David Du Plessis talk about the experience behind it at a meeting in the City of London. Harper was willing to accept everything but glossolalia. The architect gave him a copy of *Trinity*, which deeply impressed the All Souls curate, since the magazine described the same experience he and his wife shared as a recent occurrence among Episcopalians in the United States. Priests and lay people had become loving and caring, and were worshiping with new enthusiasm; there was a new freedom to express the faith, a new conviction of truth. Even more important, these Episcopalians were staying in their own churches. Yet, the Harpers were troubled, because this was an experience which, except for glossolalia, was entirely similar to the one that they had had.[73] Gradually, they came in contact with others who were involved in Charismatic Renewal.

In May 1963, Michael Harper and his wife met with Frank Maguire (Dennis Bennett's colleague) in London. A private gathering was arranged at All Souls Church, and Maguire told the Harpers that Larry Christenson would be visiting London later that year. As it happened, Christenson and his wife stayed with the department store chaplain during their visit to London, and the Harpers first spoke in tongues at that time.[74] The latter was pleased that their Neo-Pentecostal friends had not doubted the authenticity of their previous experience because they had not yet spoken in tongues (in the typical Classical Pentecostal fashion)—but had still encouraged them to seek this gift also.[75]

In October 1963, David Du Plessis came to London again, and Michael Harper and his wife were able to meet him personally then. Harper himself arranged to have Larry Christenson's booklet *Speaking in Tongues: A Gift for the Body of Christ* printed privately at about the same time. Two thousand copies were quickly distributed throughout the British Isles.[76] The All Souls curate had natural organizing ability. Soon his flat at the corner of Harley Street became the center of Charismatic Renewal activity in Great Britain. The phone rang continually. A bookroom from which tapes could also be borrowed was started. Letters arrived at an increasing rate, and the Harpers' dining room became an office. One publication had already come off the press, and a Neo-Pentecostal conference was planned for early 1964.[77]

It is not surprising that Michael Harper's new activities would conflict with his parish duties—especially since John Stott himself did not share the Pentecostal experience, and was rather unhappy with what was happening in his church.[78] Thus, Harper resigned from his post, effective June 1964 (without pressure to do so), in order to pursue his Charismatic Renewal interests on a full-time basis. From the beginning, it was recognized that some kind of organization would be necessary to facilitate further publication of books (and, beginning in 1966, *Renewal* magazine). Hence, the Fountain Trust was established by a group of Neo-Pentecostals in October 1964 as a registered charity. Harper was immediately appointed secretary on an agreed salary, and he directed the Fountain Trust's publications, regional, national, and international conferences, and other fellowship activities. Although finances posed a difficulty at first, funds gradually began to flow in as Charismatic Renewal continued to grow, and Michael Harper came to be recognized as its foremost leader in Great Britain.[79]

From 1964 to 1970, the Harpers traveled over a hundred thousand miles in the British Isles alone and made their first overseas visit in 1965—to the United States as guests of the Full Gospel Business Men's Fellowship International.[80] During 1967, the then secretary of the Fountain Trust traveled around the world, speaking in New Zealand, Australia, and South Africa.[81] After that, international travel became an integral part of Michael Harper's Neo-Pentecostal ministry; for he was soon to be regarded throughout the world as Charismatic Renewal's most articulate British spokesperson and as a leading theoretician of the movement as a whole. Like David Du Plessis, Harper is currently a member of the international "dialogue" between Classical Pentecostals and Neo-Pentecostals and the Roman Catholic Church, sponsored by the latter's Secretariat for Promoting Christian Unity.[82] The world scope of his Charismatic Renewal ministry has recently forced the former chaplain to Oxford Street's department stores to curtail his Fountain Trust duties. A new secretary was appointed in 1972, but Michael Harper remained editor of *Renewal* and chairman of the executive board (as "director" of the trust)[83] until 1975 when he resigned these posts to write and travel more extensively.[84]

We have offered brief biographical sketches of a few of the most prominent Neo-Pentecostal charismatic and organizational leaders. Others, such as Demos Shakarian, Ralph Wilkerson, Pat Boone, and Rodman Williams, will be mentioned later in a different context. It now remains for us to look at some of the important organizations themselves that have facilitated the emergence and growth of Charismatic Renewal not only in the United States and Great Britain, but also in other parts of the world. Of course, behind each of these organizations stands a specific leader who more or less "directs" its general operation. Yet the basic principles of Neo-Pentecostal leadership remain "democratic"; and within any of the prominent Charismatic Renewal organizations (and through their publications and activities), new (and old) participants may gain exposure and thus take on leadership at any time.

DEMOS SHAKARIAN:
FULL GOSPEL BUSINESS MEN'S FELLOWSHIP INERNATIONAL

We have already observed the extent to which the Full Gospel Business Men's Fellowship International has contributed to the growth of Charismatic Renewal in the United States and in other countries throughout the world. Demos Shakarian, a wealthy Armenian-American one-time dairyman in California, is the leading figure behind the FGBMFI organization, which is based in Los Angeles.

The Shakarian family left Armenia for the United States (California, ultimately) in 1905 as a result of prophetic warnings (during World War I, every person in their village was slaughtered when the Turks overran Armenia).[85] Having settled in Los Angeles, the Shakarians witnessed the Azusa Street revival in 1906 firsthand (they had been among those Presbyterians in Armenia who were practicing glossolalia long before the beginnings of the Pentecostal movement[86]), and became Pentecostals. Demos' father, a dairy farmer, started his business with three cows, but by 1943 owned a herd of three thousand.[87]

Demos Shakarian himself did not feel called to the ministry, although he began sponsoring Pentecostal evangelists in 1940. At a 1951 Oral Roberts campaign, Shakarian shared his idea concerning the establishment of a Pentecostal layman's organization for evangelism with the faith-healing evangelist, who later publicized the fellowship in the course of his crusades.[88] (Walter Hollenweger maintains that Shakarian's idea arose because of the Assemblies of God's decision not to accept into their leadership those who were not full-time pastors.[89]) Later, in 1951, the wealthy dairyman called an initial meeting of Pentecostal laymen to the "upper room" of Clifton's Cafeteria in Los Angeles (twenty-one persons attended[90]); that was the beginning of the Los Angeles chapter. In 1953, five directors were appointed (including Lee Braxton, first chairman of the Board of Regents of Oral Roberts University), and articles of incorporation were drawn up. That year, the FGBMFI also published the first issue of *Full Gospel Business Men's Voice* magazine (five thousand copies), which was intended to be distributed throughout the world.[91]

Begun by and for denominational Pentecostals, the FGBMFI never had any official ties with Pentecostal ecclesiastical structures. Thus it became a natural vehicle to facilitate the growth of Charismatic Renewal. Mainline Christian ministers and laymen from the historic denominations who identified with the Full Gospel Business Men were not pressured to leave their churches; they could enjoy expressive Pentecostal fellowship (without formal membership) at the regularly scheduled and relaxed breakfast and dinner meetings of the FGBMFI in downtown restaurants and prestigious hotels.[92] David Du Plessis calls the organization truly ecumenical in that the "Full Gospel Business Men's Fellowship has been bridging the gap between Pentecostals and 'mainliners.' "[93] This fact is especially true with respect to Roman Catholics, who are particularly responsible for the FGBMFI's dramtic growth in recent years.[94] Discussing opposition to his organization, Shakarian says that it "comes mainly from those we believe should support us [i.e., fundamentalists, evangelicals, and many Classical Pentecostals]. None from liberal Christians."[95] Of those who attend FGBMFI gatherings in some American cities, as many as 80 per cent are non-Classical Pentecostal (women and young people are now invited too, but do not share organizational leadership).[96]

Demos Shakarian, FGBMFI president, is over sixty. Six thousand delegates took part in the nineteenth world convention of the FGBMFI in San Francisco in 1972, and there are now over eleven hundred active chapters of the organization in fifty-two countries—more than seven hundred of them in the United States and Canada—with about four hundred thousand attending monthly, and an annual operating budget in excess of one million dollars. The FGBMFI also produces a half-hour weekly television broadcast, which is viewed on numerous stations in the United States, and finances (through wealthy businessmen who pay their own way and help participants who cannot) "international airlifts" for evangelism throughout the world. *Full Gospel Business Men's Voice* magazine presently has a monthly circulation of six hundred thousand, and is translated into seven languages.[97] International directors include corporation presidents, attorneys, distributors, surgeons, real-estate developers, building contractors, owners of insurance agencies, and retailers[98] (hence the predominant FGBMFI philosophy that God "prospers" people [financially] who are committed to him).[99]

Organization is highly decentralized, and kept to an absolute minimum. The executive committee approves applications for affiliation submitted by a prospective FGBMFI local chapter. Apart from the fact that the same committee also has the power to "disfellowship" a local chapter (it rarely exercises that authority), most organizational authority rests with the individual chapters themselves and their own officers. Steve Durasoff says that "a great stress is placed upon love as the true basis of unity, rather than doctrinal agreement"[100]—while the organization's chief purposes are (1) evangelism (especially the spread of the Pentecostal message) and (2) interdenominational fellowship for Classical Pentecostals and Neo-Pentecostals. FGBMFI regional, national, and international conventions offer an important platform to eminent charismatic and organizational leaders of Charismatic Renewal—Kathryn Kuhlman, Oral Roberts, David Du Plessis,

Michael Harper, and the like. Thus we can discern the degree to which the Full Gospel Business Men's Fellowship International provides evidence of the prominent role of laymen in the emergence and continued growth of Charismatic Renewal as a movement in various parts of the world.[101]

JEAN STONE: BLESSED TRINITY SOCIETY

The Blessed Trinity Society (so named to re-emphasize the work of the third person of the Trinity in a "high church" context) was founded in 1961 by Jean Stone, a well-to-do Episcopal laywoman and communicant of St. Mark's Episcopal Church, Van Nuys, California, while Dennis Bennett was its rector. Walter Hollenweger says of this affluent housewife and mother (whose husband, Donald, was a corporate director of Lockheed Aircraft):

> Though she assiduously prayed in the way that is required in the Anglican church, went to all the services and gave a good deal of money to the church, she "felt a void in my life, which nothing but more of him could fill." Because she was a woman she could not be ordained in the Anglican church, because she was a mother she could not become an Anglican nun and because her husband had no vocation on the mission field, she could not become a missionary. So she saw no possibility of active work in the church. But when she was filled with the Holy Spirit, she saw that it was not her destiny to waste her life with aimless conversations at parties with the "high society" of California. Her home became a meeting place for clergy and laity from the upper levels of society who sought the baptism of the Spirit.[102]

Thus, the Blessed Trinity Society was organized in Jean Stone's living room as the first distinctively Neo-Pentecostal organizational structure for fellowship, teaching, evangelism, and, most of all, publication. (While the Full Gospel Business Men's Fellowship International welcomed and encouraged Mrs. Stone,[103] she could never have assumed leadership in that men's organization.) Although fellowship and teaching *were* important functions of the society (e.g., the "Christian Advance" seminars to acquaint people with Spirit baptism[104]), it was formed primarily to publish *Trinity* magazine (1961–66), a Charismatic Renewal quarterly aimed at "the well-educated, conservative suburbanite from the denominational church."[105] Her editorship and her husband's major financial support of *Trinity* made Jean Stone one of the first organizational leaders of Neo-Pentecostalism (however, by 1963 the Blessed Trinity Society had enrolled fifty-nine "patrons" who had contributed at least one hundred dollars, and nine "sponsors" who had given at least one thousand dollars for its support).[106] With the magazine's increased circulation, Mrs. Stone became a recognized authority and lecturer on Charismatic Renewal.[107] Writing in 1965, Michael Harper said of *Trinity*:

> It seems to find its way sooner or later on to the desks of most ministers in the Western Hemisphere and seldom ends up in the wastepaper basket. It gets more and more dog-eared as it passes from vicarage to manse, and usually dies of sheer exhaustion at a ripe old age. Anglican bishops (publish it not in Gath) have surreptitiously read it and passed it on to their chaplains.[108]

Until 1966, the Blessed Trinity Society in Van Nuys was the unofficial "headquarters" of Neo-Pentecostalism; *Trinity*, its leading periodical voice; and Jean Stone, its most important spokeswoman. But Mrs. Stone's travels and organizational leadership in the movement destroyed her marriage that year. The divorce was quiet and unpublicized; the Blessed Trinity Society and its magazine suddenly ceased to exist; and Jean Stone disappeared from the Charismatic Renewal scene[109] (though she subsequently married her associate editor, Richard Willans, and together they went to Hong Kong as independent "faith missionaries" for the movement[110]). Melodyland Christian Center, Anaheim, California, later became one of Neo-Pentecostalism's new American "headquarters"; Christian Advance re-emerged as Melodyland's "charismatic clinics"; and in 1971, *Logos Journal,* Plainfield, New Jersey, and *New Covenant,* Ann Arbor, Michigan, succeeded *Trinity* as the leading American Charismatic Renewal periodicals.

FOUNTAIN TRUST

In 1964, as we have seen, Michael Harper resigned his curacy under John Stott at All Souls Church, Langham Place, London, to work full-time with the emerging Neo-Pentecostal movement in the British Isles. Without benefit of patronage, Harper and a circle of Charismatic Renewal participants established the Fountain Trust as a registered charitable organization for the advancement of Neo-Pentecostalism in Great Britain. (Its name comes from the Fountaingate in Jerusalem—illustrating the work of the Holy Spirit. But originally, the organization's designation was the "Watergate Trust" after the old riverside gate at Charing Cross, London, which was reclaimed from the river.[111]) Michael Harper became the Fountain Trust's first director; and from the beginning, there were no real "members." Persons who had been baptized in the Spirit were encouraged to stay in their own churches. Meetings arranged by the Fountain Trust were until recently advertized only in its official literature and are held on an irregular schedule so as to avoid "regular customers" who could regard the organization as a "church."[112]

Harper's chief aim has been to enable Christians (through the Fountain Trust) to receive the power of the Holy Spirit and the full benefits of Charismatic Renewal while safeguarding them too. A fourfold purpose, according to Michael Harper, guides the operation of the Fountain Trust as follows:

> 1. CHRIST CENTERED. It recognizes that the fundamental work of the Holy Spirit is to glorify Jesus Christ, who should be the center and pattern of all renewal.
> 2. CHARISMATIC. It sees the world-wide charismatic movement as one of God's ways of renewal for the whole church. It regards the recovery of the power and gifts of the Spirit as an essential part of this renewal.
> 3. CORPORATE. It sees renewal chiefly in corporate rather than merely personal terms. Its main concern is to

see churches of all denominations rather than individuals renewed by the Spirit, while recognizing that God brings renewal through individuals.

4. COMPASSIONATE. It believes that love is the heart of renewal, and that the intention of God is that church renewal should overflow to the world in terms of evangelism and social action.[113]

The Fountain Trust does not establish its own "groups," but has contact with sympathetic churches and other religious organizations. In 1975, Michael Harper resigned as director of this Neo-Pentecostal organization and has been succeeded by Thomas Snail, but remained its director and editor of *Renewal* until then. Very recently, the Fountain Trust moved from London to East Molesey, Surrey, where it hopes to establish a "charismatic library" for the British Isles, and a "fellowship house" suitable for counseling, prayer meetings, and other small Charismatic Renewal gatherings.[114] Since its inception in 1964, the Fountain Trust has remained the British headquarters for Neo-Pentecostalism; and Michael Harper, as we have said, has become one of the movement's foremost theoreticians.

RALPH WILKERSON: THE "CHARISMATIC CLINICS" OF MELODYLAND

In 1960, Ralph Wilkerson, a former Assemblies of God pastor, now minister of Melodyland Christian Center, Anaheim, California, had led two successful Charismatic Renewal Christian Life Advance meetings. At a standing-room-only gathering in Berkeley, California, eighty ministers of various denominations reportedly received the baptism of the Holy Spirit, and most went on to speak in tongues. Using Wilkerson's model, Jean Stone established her Christian Advance teaching seminars sponsored by the Blessed Trinity Society—designed to introduce Spirit baptism to denominational ministers and lay people. But when the Blessed Trinity Society died in 1966, Ralph Wilkerson again took on this teaching and evangelism function in Charismatic Renewal by instituting at his church annual "charismatic clinics" since 1967. The first clinic attracted eight hundred participants in August 1967; five thousand converged at Melodyland in August 1973 for the sixth annual conference. Speakers for the charismatic clinics regularly include such Neo-Pentecostal leaders as Dennis Bennett, Herald Bredesen, Larry Christenson, Michael Harper, Kathryn Kuhlman, Kevin Ranaghan, and Oral Roberts, and Classical Pentecostal David Du Plessis. Clinics are now videotaped; and "spin-offs" have taken place in cities like Mexico City, Toronto, and London. The avowed purpose of this organizational effort of Ralph Wilkerson is to "instill maturity" in persons newly baptized in the Spirit, and to provide "healing" for churches disrupted by the often sudden emergence of Charismatic activity among their members. In recent years, moreover, there has been a new emphasis in the clinics themselves—a shift of stress from miracles, healings, and speaking in tongues to "mind gifts" such as knowledge, wisdom, and "discernment of spirits." Furthermore, in 1973, Wilkerson and his staff made a significant effort to include as leaders and participants more blacks and Mexican-Americans; and the week-long charismatic clinic was this time preceded by a new three-day institute for pastors, which was attended by 350 clergy—an institute intended to relate the operation of *charismata* to the particulars of parish life and to supplement the Charismatic ministerial fellowships within at least six historic denominations. So successful have been Melodyland's charismatic clinics that the church has also established an annual winter conference along similar lines, but focusing on the *theology* of the Pentecostal experience.[115]

We have now discussed some of the most important Charismatic Renewal organizations and leaders in the context of a fully decentralized, segmentary, and reticulate Pentecostal movement. Charismatic and organizational leadership have facilitated Neo-Pentecostal growth; but it is a personal *experience* rather than leadership per se that continues to hold the movement together. We shall now consider Charismatic Renewal faith and practice as it has developed from that experience.

CHAPTER FIVE: *Faith and Practice*

Given the heterogeneous character of Neo-Pentecostalism with respect to issues of faith and practice, we must be content at this point to speak of observable tendencies rather than *all-pervasive features* of the movement. Apart from specific theological and behavioral expectations a given church or fellowship group *may* impose on its own adherents, Charismatic Renewal as such has no mandatory or even optional statements of faith, and does not require compliance with any set code of conduct. Neo-Pentecostal unity is unity in a great deal of diversity.

In the Pentecostal movement as a whole, ministry has been democratized. Kilian McDonnell suggests that although Classical Pentecostal groups tend to be "minister oriented" and often "leader dominated," ministry itself is conceived as "body ministry"—the whole body of Christ witnessing. This is true in worship, evangelism, and service. Ideally, what distinguishes a minister from a layman or laywoman is a specific charism, a special gift and call of the Holy Spirit. Rather than thinking of the priesthood of all believers, Classical Pentecostals focus on a related concept—gifts of the Spirit. The lay person has his own gift, his ministry. Gifts and ministries differ, but all have received one Spirit, and all have a voice in witnessing. Everyone is a speaker; everyone has a message. Everyone is involved in worship, evangelism, and service.[1]

In Charismatic Renewal, as in Classical Pentecostalism, each denomination or independent congregation sets its own requirements and standards for ordination (e.g., Melodyland Christian Center has on its staff duly ordained ministers with standing in a historic denomination, but it ordains ministers independently as well[2]). Neo-Pentecostalism as a movement cannot of itself ordain and sanction clergy. Yet all ministries are recognized. Thus, Michael Harper declares "that this movement is the most unifying in Christendom. . . . [For] *only in this movement are all streams uniting, and all ministries being accepted and practised.*"[3]

PROMINENCE OF THE LAITY

Even though, as we have seen, the laity have been prominent at all levels of Charismatic Renewal participation and leadership from its beginnings,[4] the distinctive (e.g., sacramental) functions of ordained ministers and priests—and their special "calling"—are nevertheless clearly recognized. Throughout the movement in general, priests and ministers predominate in leadership. They are almost always referred to by their ecclesiastical titles (e.g., "the Reverend" or "Father") rather than by the typical Classical Pentecostal designation, "Brother." Furthermore, laymen who rise to leadership in Charismatic Renewal but who are not educationally or otherwise qualified for ordination in the historic denominations *may* be ordained by a local, independent Neo-Pentecostal congregation such as Melodyland Christian Center.

Perhaps the best expression of the cooperative role of clergy and laity in the movement has been articulated by George Martin, a Catholic Pentecostal layman. Although Martin speaks of the specific situation in the Roman Catholic Church, his comments reflect a widespread feeling within Charismatic Renewal more generally:

> It is clear that the charismatic ministries do not replace the ordained ministry; priests need not worry about becoming obsolete . . . Christian communities cannot be formed by the work of either clergy or laity alone. . . .
> The charismatic renewal of the Church holds promise for a much more balanced state of affairs. The maturing of the charismatic ministries holds promise of a fuller involvement of every member of the Church in building

up the body of Christ without jeopardizing anyone's role. It holds this promise because its primary focus is not on the differences between clergy and laity, but on the gifts of service that every follower of Christ receives.[5]

YOUNG PEOPLE AND WOMEN

The "outburst of tongues" within the Inter-Varsity Christian Fellowship at Yale University in 1962 heralded the beginning of visible participation of young people (i.e., students) in Neo-Pentecostalism.[6] Accounts of similar events in other colleges and universities in the United States followed shortly thereafter.[7] As we have seen, Catholic Pentecostalism first emerged among academics and students at Duquesne, Notre Dame, and Michigan State universities, and at the University of Michigan in 1967. Today, some of the most vigorous communities of Catholic Pentecostals are still centered in the university environment.[8] For a while, even the Full Gospel Business Men's Fellowship International tried to encourage youthful involvement in Charismatic Renewal by instituting teaching seminars by and for young people—students and academics[9]—and by publishing a scholarly journal appealing to serious thinkers (first called *View*, then *Charisma Digest*—1966–69). But the businessmen soon tired of catering to the intellectual interests of scholars and students; yet, they continued to welcome their participation in the movement.[10] With the advent of the Jesus movement in 1969, it became clear that many American young people had embraced the Pentecostal experience; for most of the Jesus People (and their various groups) stressed—or at least tolerated—Pentecostal phenomena (especially glossolalia and divine healing) within their ranks. Although Neo-Pentecostalism is a movement largely within the institutional church, and the Jesus movement was not, most Neo-Pentecostals were quick to affirm and support the Jesus People anyway simply because of the latter's Pentecostal leanings and practices.[11] Today, many of the Jesus People have joined existing Classical Pentecostal or Neo-Pentecostal churches or have established similar structures of their own.[12] In any case, the active participation of young people in Protestant and Catholic Charismatic Renewal continues unabated, while their actual leadership within the movement as a whole appears (by and large) confined to their own distinctive groups and communities.

Women are also prominent participants (active ones) in Neo-Pentecostalism. But they generally have not risen to prominent leadership in the movement. Among the exceptions are a few highly respected "healers" such as Kathryn Kuhlman and, to a lesser degree, Agnes Sanford[13] in the United States, and Jean Darnall[14] in England. There was Jean Stone, of course, a notable exception. And one may also mention Catherine Marshall, the novelist, who is a Presbyterian laywoman.[15] Unlike some Classical Pentecostal denominations (e.g., Assemblies of God, International Church of the Foursquare Gospel, and Pentecostal Holiness Church) and churches, the foremost Charismatic Renewal church—Melodyland Christian Center—neither ordains women nor permits them membership on its governing board.[16] One of the most prominent women within Catholic Pentecostalism, Josephine Ford, an eminent New Testament scholar at Notre Dame University, has been especially vocal in recent years criticizing the "sexist" character of the Pentecostal movement in the Roman Catholic Church.[17]

SPIRITUAL AUTHORITY

In fundamentalism and evangelicalism as a whole, Scripture *itself* functions as the final authority in matters of faith and conduct. Generally speaking, biblical "inerrancy" as a doctrine is the "test" of fellowship whereby individuals and groups are either accepted as "true believers" or rejected as heterodox or heretical. Thus, liberals (who may not accept the full and final authority of Scripture) and Roman Catholics (who accept the authority of tradition as well) are rarely admitted into fellowship with evangelicals and fundamentalists. For the latter, there can usually be no (institutional or even "spiritual") Christian unity apart from doctrinal agreement (on certain essential "truths") based upon the propositional authority of the Bible. In Charismatic Renewal, however, it is felt that the truth of Scripture is available to the reader or hearer *only* through the power (action) of the Holy Spirit, who himself is understood as the (experiential) source of all Christian unity. Neo-Pentecostals maintain that biblical authority (the word written) must always be subservient to the authority of the *living,* "dynamic" word of God made known through the present activity of the Spirit himself. Michael Harper says:

> Christians are finding in their experience of the Holy Spirit a new unity in Christ, and that is exactly what Christ prayed for.
>
> But there are some who, while agreeing with the doctrine of the baptism of the Spirit, are looking askance at this. They cannot yet accept the movement among Roman Catholics, for example, as being a genuine work of the Holy Spirit. They are suspicious of liberals, who now speak hopefully of a revival of the Holy Spirit. They stress the need for unity in truth rather than unity in experience.
>
> . . . it is of the greatest significance that in the Acts of the Apostles Jesus gave the experience of the Holy Spirit to men as a uniting factor *before* they were united in truth. Christians then, as now, made the mistake of thinking that men had to believe as they did before they could experience the Holy Spirit. . . . Complete unity and agreement in the truth is impossible in this life and age. In this life "we see through a glass darkly." We live in a fallen creation, and our mental processes are not infallible. But we can trust the Holy Spirit to lead us all immeasurably closer to one another in the truth.[18]

This open stance, whereby the Holy Spirit is seen to lead people to theological truth *following* (rather than prerequisite to) a common experience, is clearly ascendent throughout Neo-Pentecostalism; it is one reason why evangelicals, liberals, and Roman Catholics have been joined together (spiritually, at least) for the first time.

The subservience of Scripture—the word written—to the Holy Spirit's authority is also illustrated by the acceptance in Charismatic Renewal of the validity of the gift of prophecy in the life of the contemporary Church. For the Neo-Pentecostal (no less than his Classical counterpart), God speaks today just as authoritatively as he spoke to the biblical authors. This existential under-standing of the Word of God (in which revelation did not cease with the closing of the canon) is articulated by Rodman Williams, president of Melodyland School of Theology:

The Bible truly has become a fellow witness to God's present activity. What happens today in the fellowship and in individual lives also happened then, and there is the joy of knowing that *our* world was also *their* world. If someone today perhaps has a vision of God, of Christ, it is good to know that it has happened before; if one has a revelation from God, to know that for the early Christians revelation also occurred in the community; if one speaks a "Thus says the Lord," and dares to address the fellowship in the first person—even going beyond the words of Scripture—that this was happening long ago. . . . If one speaks in the fellowship of the Spirit the Word of truth, it is neither his own thoughts and reflec-tions . . . nor simply some exposition of Scripture, for the Spirit transcends personal observations, however in-teresting or profound they may be. The Spirit as the liv-ing God moves through and beyond the records of past witness, however valuable such records are as a model for what happens today. For in the Spirit the present fel-lowship is as much the arena of God's vital presence as anything in the Biblical account.[19]

Catherine Marshall puts its another way:

Jesus's promise of "further truth" gives us clear reason to believe that not all the truth and instruction Christ has to give us is contained in the canon of the Old and New Testaments. . . . He who *is* Truth will never find the people of any given century able to receive everything He wants to give. Because the Holy Spirit is a living, al-ways-contemporary Personality, down all the centuries there must be an ever-unfolding manifestation of Jesus, His personality, His ways of dealing with us along with new, fresh disclosures of the mind of the Father.[20]

In Neo-Pentecostalism, then, spiritual authority rests ultimately in the present activity and teaching of the Holy Spirit at least as much in the Bible itself, whose essential truth is made known to individuals only by the power of the Spirit. Thus Charismatic Renewal rejects "bibliolatry."[21]

HUMAN AUTHORITY

The belief that the Holy Spirit speaks and acts today in the same way he did in biblical times (as recorded in Scripture)—through the *charismata*—obviously sanctions a widespread diffusion of gifts (and related authority) in the local church. As we have seen, all Christians who are baptized in the Spirit see themselves and each other as endowed with certain gifts and ministries for worship, evangelism, and service. The "charismatic congregation" functions as the primary human authority base in Neo-Pentecostalism. Here, God does not restrict his revelation to the Bible (i.e., a closed canon) or to an ordained ministry. Anyone with an authentic gift of prophecy may speak the very word of God (accepted or rejected as such by the given community of faith in which it is spoken). Thus, in Charismatic Renewal, as we have seen, there are no leaders holding *absolute* authority. Submission to authority, ideally, is *mutual* submission, although individuals differing in recognized Charismatic endowment also differ with respect to the degree of "actual" authority they wield (or following they have) in a specific segment of the movement or in the movement as a whole.

The charismatic congregation itself is a reflection of the widespread diffusion of charisma in the wider society today. It is almost a truism to say that traditional patterns of absolute or "legitimate" authority in every quarter of contemporary society are increasingly questioned and rejected. Furthermore, the consequent alternative stress on "reasonable" authority has been reinforced both by the secular Human Potential movement and by the various social "liberation" movements focusing on personal freedom and fulfillment, self-worth, and growth (discovering and developing inherent abilities, talents, and "gifts"). Thus it is perhaps only logical that this trend toward charismatic diffusion in the wider society should of itself enhance the general attractiveness of a religious movement motivated and led by the charismatic congregation in which every participant has a vital function —a unique ministry.

EVANGELISM

Luther Gerlach and Virginia Hine suggest that a major factor in explaining the spread of a modern religious movement is face-to-face recruitment along lines of pre-existing significant social relationships. Whatever motivation for "joining" that is verbalized by the participant or imputed by the social scientist using his deprivation, disorganization, or maladjustment models, they declare, it cannot occur without the catalytic agent—another human being.

In Classical Pentecostalism, Gerlach and Hine say, recruitment is most successful among relatives. But kinship ties are apparently more important at lower socio-economic levels; hence, in Neo-Pentecostalism, recruitment is most often undertaken among close friends, especially fellow church members, and among neighbors, business associates, fellow students, and the like, where previous significant interaction has already occurred. Furthermore, these anthropologists stress the fact that Pentecostals in general do not do well by recruiting loners or drifters who would have difficulty in bringing in others; they fare much better recruiting those who have an "automatic" influence over friends, family, associates, or admirers (thus we can understand why Neo-Pentecostals emphasize and affirm as leaders prominent denominational pastors and ecclesiastical officials, academics, celebrities, and wealthy businessmen).

Gerlach and Hine also tend to reject the sociological notion that "deprivation" of some kind is the prime reason individuals join sectarian or enthusiastic churches or movements.[22] They have found in their research repeated examples (both among Classical Pentecostals and Neo-Pentecostals, for instance) where economic or social status deprivation is clearly nonexistent, and disorganization or maladjustment simply is not observable.[23] John Kildahl, however, in his ten-year study of Neo-Pentecostal speakers in tongues, concludes "that a personal crisis of some kind preceded the initial experience of speaking in tongues in 87 per cent of the cases examined."[24]

In Charismatic Renewal, the sociological concept of recruitment is expressed by the theological word "evangelism"—the proclamation (and demonstration) of the good news, the *full* Gospel. Rooted in modern evangelical piety, evangelism here means proclaiming (1) the necessity of a *personal* commitment to Jesus Christ as Savior and Lord (conversion), plus (2) the *subsequent* (but related) need for Spirit baptism or infilling. There can be no Spirit baptism *prior* to conversion. In this respect, it is likely that many seemingly nonevangelical Neo-Pentecostals (e.g., Catholics and "liberals") actually have experienced an evangelical conversion closely linked to their Spirit baptism. Such is particularly apparent in testimonies of Catholic Pentecostals who try to integrate the "saving efficacy" of the sacraments with their new "personal relationship with Jesus."[25]

Most Neo-Pentecostal fellowship organizations are also evangelistic. Charismatic Renewal participants often invite their non-Pentecostal friends to FGBMFI gatherings, for example, where specially gifted speakers and others tell of their own Pentecostal experience in such a way as to attract the interest of prospective candidates for Spirit baptism. This evangelism is usually very "low key" in character, and *emphatically* does not require a convert to leave his or her present church. And, although literature published by these organizations (or Kathryn Kuhlman telecasts, for instance) advertises Charismatic Renewal meetings, face-to-face recruitment is still the most important factor in attracting converts. John Kildahl says of the Neo-Pentecostal evangelistic zeal:

> The happy effects of this phenomenon [glossolalia] were testified to by tongue-speakers from coast to coast of the United States. . . . The glossolalist noted first that there had been a maturing of his own religious life, which then expressed itself through an intense concern that one's friends and fellow church members should share the same experience.[26]

Again, new participants in Charismatic Renewal are urged by the movement's leaders not only to remain in their churches, but also to become *better* church members as a result of their experience. They are told to expect at least *some* opposition, but to avoid all "spiritual pride" that might develop as a result of this opposition. The hope, obviously, is to attract recruits by a changed life and "a gentle witness, filled with love."[27] Don Basham, a Disciples of Christ clergyman, engaged in "deliverance" ministry, writes on the matter in question:

> Let your experience of the Holy Spirit draw you into deeper and more loving participation in the life of your church, not only with some charismatic group you may join, but in the church's worship and service as well. Other church members having heard your testimony, will be waiting—and rightly so—to see the fruit of your experience in your actions, and they will be far more impressed with what you share if the experience leads you into a deeper love for the church and its people, than if they see you deserting the church to start off on some tangent of your own.[28]

At first, Neo-Pentecostals called their emerging movement a "Charismatic revival"—heralding the restoration of the *charismata* to the life of the contemporary church.[29] Soon, however, the term "revival" was generally replaced with "renewal" to (1) dissociate the movement from revivalistic fundamentalism and (2) link it with a larger goal of not only reintroducing spiritual gifts to the historic denominations, but also of relating the *charismata* to spiritual and institutional Christian renewal more inclusively and comprehensively.

Renewal here is not a hysterical reassertion of religious truth by investment in strong emotions. While a case can be made that Charismatic Renewal does provide some evidence of the power of emotion in a highly routinized society in which technology seems to dominate, it is also true that—in contrast to much of Classical Pentecostalism—emotional expression in Neo-Pentecostalism has been greatly subdued. Michael Harper argues that the "present-day charismatic movement, generally speaking, is not . . . a movement of unthinking fools floating on a wave of emotional experience."[30] Nor is Charismatic Renewal necessarily a side-stepping of critical theological onslaught, or the alternative legitimation of religion from Scripture to *experience* confirmation (though experiential legitimation does appear to be a frequent tendency, especially among Protestant Neo-Pentecostal lay people). Harper goes on to castigate unequivocally the anti-intellectualism of Classical Pentecostalism and to declare that an "unthinking old-fashioned fundamentalism will always be a hindrance to the forward surge of the Holy Spirit."[31]

In Neo-Pentecostalism today, renewal is a *positive* concept related to Christian unity and "wholeness" (*full* Gospel) more generally, and is linked to the present operation of the Holy Spirit in the church. To quote Michael Harper again:

> Our aim has been to be positive. The Church needs restoration, not demolition. It needs encouragement, not condemnation. It needs divine inspiration, not a new set of human instructions. Many Christians are battered and bruised. Others are disheartened. Is this the time to draw attention to their faults and failings, which they are all too well aware of, or is it not time to point them to the Lord Jesus Christ, who is ready to forgive, and to fill them with the Holy Spirit?[32]

Furthermore, going beyond mere *Christian* renewal, Rodman Williams envisions Charismatic Renewal as ultimately "a renewal and advancement of the whole human situation." His understanding of renewal marks the most comprehensive and idealistic yet expressed by a Neo-Pentecostal theologian; but such a visionary assessment is not at all out of keeping with Protestant and Catholic Charismatic Renewal thinking as a whole:

> Again, this new world of the interpenetration of the spiritual and the natural not only brings into play spiritual powers but also enhances natural capacities and functions. By no means does the natural become less important, but it is given fuller power and direction under the impact of the Holy Spirit. The mind takes on keener awareness of the true shape of reality; the feelings become more sensitive to the moods, the concerns, the

hopes of the world and of people; the will finds itself strengthened to execute with more faithfulness and determination those ethical actions to which it gives itself. Thus through the conjoining of the spiritual and the natural, in which strange powers penetrate and invigorate the natural realm (the vast area of the intellectual, the aesthetic, the moral), there is a renewal and advancement of the whole human situation.[33]

FELLOWSHIP

The small group is the center of Charismatic Renewal life. Even in churches where the minister or priest and a majority of members are Neo-Pentecostal participants, Charismatic activity is most often confined to small prayer groups in which members reinforce each other in their faith and experience. Formal services of worship tend to remain rather untouched, except in preaching emphases.

PRAYER MEETINGS

Although Charismatic Renewal groups are of different kinds (e.g., study, fellowship, or testimony), prayer with Charismatic expressions tends to be the central feature of any given group. Don Basham says:

In every town of any size there is at least one charismatic prayer group—usually interdenominational [sponsoring church members bring friends from other churches]— meeting in a home or church. Such groups not only offer inspiration and fellowship, they also help keep us "aglow with the Spirit,"[34] giving us confidence to speak the quiet word of witness where we work or in our own church and among our friends and neighbors.[35]

At the same time, it is recognized by Neo-Pentecostal leaders that such small groups easily become "in-groups," and thus have a divisive function in the more inclusive congregation. Larry Christenson, a Lutheran pastor, speaks about the small-group principle in general, and the tendency toward divisiveness or fragmentation in particular:

> We do not encourage speaking in tongues during the regular Sunday worship service. . . . It seems more appropriate . . . at an informal meeting or a prayer group.
> We prefer to have these prayer groups meet either in the church, or in the home of one who is clearly recognized as a responsible leader in the congregation.[36]
> Seek fellowship with others who share your joy and enthusiasm in this blessing. But guard against any "cliques" within the congregation. Prayer meetings and group get-togethers should generally be open to any member of the congregation. Beware of spiritual pride.[37]

Michael Harper elaborates further on the problem of divisiveness, and the related issue of the Charismatic fellowship group becoming a "substitute" for parish church membership and participation (something the Fountain Trust tries to prevent by irregular scheduling of its own events):

> It is an almost universal feature of the present wave of new blessing coming to God's people that there is an intense longing for deeper fellowship than is sometimes possible in our churches. . . . There is surely no harm in such meetings, as long as the dangers of divisiveness are remembered. If such a group develops in a local church, it should do so with the knowledge and permission of the minister and elders. There are few things more dangerous in a church than a secret society. . . . Sometimes people may meet together who are members of different local churches. Again, there is nothing wrong, and indeed much blessing can flow from these meetings. But the dangers should not be forgotten. This kind of group can become a substitute for a local church, and would, therefore, sap rather than strengthen the churches. They can easily develop into "holy huddles," concerned only with a narrow aspect of truth, instead of fellowships

where Christians can rekindle the gift of the Spirit within them, and go back to their local church with greater strength than they had before.[38]

Although small groups constitute an important feature of Protestant and Anglican Charismatic Renewal, they have taken on an even greater significance within Catholic Pentecostalism. Of prayer meetings among Roman Catholic Pentecostals, Edward O'Connor says:

When the Pentecostal movement began at Duquesne and Notre Dame, it took root first among people who already belonged to prayer groups, and the prayer meeting was spontaneously and unquestionably adopted as the natural vehicle of the movement. In fact, it has proved to be an ideal vehicle, to such an extent that wherever the movement has spread, the prayer meetings have gone with it.[39]

In such prayer meetings (not unlike those conducted by Protestant Neo-Pentecostals), someone is usually called upon to be a leader—a *facilitator* rather than one who dominates. Each member, in the context of *order*, is free to pray in any manner he or she wishes (respecting the demands of "love and faith"). The focus is on people praying *together*, not simultaneously. Content of the meetings may include, in addition to prayer, Scripture readings, testimonies, hymns, and various Charismatic expressions (e.g., glossolalia, prophecy, and divine healing). Participants commonly gather together for long periods of time at regular intervals (four to five hours not being uncommon), but informality is a key feature; coffee breaks are part of the general practice of such fellowship gatherings.[40]

Out of Catholic Pentecostal prayer meetings have emerged strong "communities" (as well as distinctively Charismatic parishes[41]) focusing on every aspect of life as it pertains to Christian "renewal" in the Charismatic context. One of the strongest of these communities (The Word of God, with over one thousand members) is based in Ann Arbor, Michigan, near the University of Michigan. Corporate prayer meetings attract hundreds of people at a time, and these gatherings are supplemented by numerous well-attended teaching seminars. Membership in the community requires a high degree of commitment to its purposes and goals, and a willingness to submit to the discipline it imposes. By 1970, the Ann Arbor community also consisted of nine sub-communities, including living groups. Each living group has a "head" or co-ordinator who facilitates activities, and each also conforms to its own statement of purpose. One subcommunity, for instance, functions as a guest house for women visitors to the larger community. Another engages in evangelism of the campus and its environment. A third engages primarily in the life of prayer and sharing of the various responsibilities of Christian community life. All groups meet regularly for worship, retreats, and social activities. It is clearly apparent, moreover, that members of Catholic Pentecostal communities in general—because of the rather strict (but not necessarily ascetic) discipline they follow—separate themselves to a large degree from the everyday concerns of the wider society. In fact, one sees in this community phenomenon a concrete expression of the typically Catholic notion that to really be *religious*, one must set himself apart with others having the same goal (quasi-monasticism, perhaps); Roman Catholic Charismatic Renewal communities function as the epitome of small-group consciousness within Neo-Pentecostalism as a whole.[42]

INTERCHURCH GROUPS

We have already discussed the largest interdenominational Charismatic Renewal fellowship and publication organizations—the Full Gospel Business Men's Fellowship International (based in Los Angeles) and the Fountain Trust in Great Britain. Of course, other such organizations exist in numerous places on a far smaller scale. Some of these actually might be better termed "interchurch" (focusing on local congregations) rather than inter-denominational with respect to their activities—fellowships of churches in which Pentecostal phenomena are widely diffused. But there are also purely denominational associations of ministers and/or laity who share the Pentecostal experience. Of these, perhaps, the most important are Catholic Charismatic Renewal

Services[43] and the Presbyterian Charismatic Communion (once headed by Rodman Williams). The latter, like counterparts in the American Baptist Churches, the Episcopal Church, and among Eastern Orthodox Christians in the United States,[44] conducts national and regional retreats and conferences on the Pentecostal movement as it bears upon the problems of individual congregations affiliated with a Presbyterian denomination. In October 1972, a Lutheran Conference on the Holy Spirit brought together eight thousand people in Minneapolis for a wide variety of teaching seminars (led by Neo-Pentecostal leaders) and for fellowship more generally.[45]

MELODYLAND CHRISTIAN CENTER

Independent, nondenominational churches have become increasingly prominent Charismatic Renewal organizations. Applicants are accepted for membership, but formal membership is not solicited to the degree it is in traditional churches. Many persons who attend these "Christian centers" and contribute to their programs are already members of a historic Protestant, Anglican, Eastern Orthodox, or Catholic church—and have *two* religious affiliations. The institutions themselves actually understand their function as a fellowship "center for all Christians" rather than a church.

Founded in 1960, Melodyland Christian Center, Anaheim, California, has been the model for other Christian centers established since then. Ralph Wilkerson, a former Assemblies of God, "Bible belt" preacher, left his previous parish in Palo Alto, California, to found an independent congregation in Southern California (Orange County) that would be receptive to and supportive of the emerging Charismatic Renewal. Anaheim's Christian Center began in Wilkerson's home with 68 participants. Its budget grew from about $7,500 annually in 1960 to nearly $1,000,000 in 1971. During the early 1960s, Christian Center moved to a traditional suburban church campus but rapidly outgrew those facilities. In 1969, therefore, the center bought the bankrupt Melodyland Theater across the street from Disneyland for $1,125,000; and Wilkerson justified the popular resort location "because history shows that the church is the center of community life."[46] Melodyland

Christian Center's sanctuary-in-the-round holds approximately 3,700 people, and several services are scheduled each Sunday and on weeknights as well. In addition to services, the center's program includes a School of the Bible (for lay people), a School of Theology (for ministerial candidates—men *and* women), a national telephone "hotline" (chiefly for drug addicts and alienated youth seeking help), a large bookstore emphasizing Neo-Pentecostal literature and cassette tapes, and annual international teaching conferences ("charismatic clinics" and winter conferences, as we have seen). Wilkerson has a number of ministers on his staff who hold standing in historic denominations, and a "theologian in residence," Rodman Williams, president of Melodyland School of Theology. The center, as a recognized headquarters for Charismatic Renewal throughout the United States and the world, continues to grow in membership while it acquires additional facilities —aided, of course, by the affluence of California's almost totally suburban Orange County and by the personal qualities of Ralph Wilkerson himself.[47]

UNITY IN DIVERSITY

The foundation of Charismatic Renewal theology, and ethics is the *experience* of the baptism of the Holy Spirit, however interpreted. We have seen that Neo-Pentecostals accept as normative for the Christian church in every age the historical narratives of the Book of Acts—which, in the words of Michael Harper, relate how "Jesus gave the experience of the Holy Spirit to men as a uniting factor *before* they were united in truth."[48] Thus, close doctrinal agreement is not a prerequisite for unity or "fellowship."

"Feeling" is an important part of the Pentecostal experience. Theologically, biblical doctrine becomes almost existential, as Leonard Evans, writing in *View* magazine, suggests:

> So speak a growing host of people today, Pentecostal and denominational, of a God we not only "think" but a God whom we can "feel," as a wonderful child of God put it. Then we discover that God not only loved us in the past, in the provision of a marvelous atonement for our sins, but loves us today in His desire to minister

directly to our person and corporate hunger for Him and His real presence.[49]

The existential "encounter" with Christ rather than correct doctrine intellectually accepted becomes, in Charismatic Renewal, the only basis for Spirit baptism and the unity it effects. Ralph Wilkerson, therefore, has said:

> We're too busy in Anaheim winning people to Jesus to get involved in arguments over doctrine. The most important thing is to get our spirits right with one another, and this can only be done through the crucified life.[50]

While Neo-Pentecostalism does place its chief emphasis on experience, Michael Harper warns that, taken in isolation—apart from Scripture, the sacraments, and the church—experience alone is dangerously subjective and tends to cause division and breakdown. It must be "harnessed properly" to the point where Spirit baptism allows Christians to discern the reality and vitality of the sacraments and Scripture in the context of their experience.[51]

Steve Clark, a prominent Catholic Pentecostal layman, praises the Pentecostal movement for having brought Catholics into contact with other Christians "through a sense of common sharing in the life of the Spirit" and into communication with "a group of Christians who never spoke with Catholics on a Christian level before—members of the pentecostal denominations."[52] Donald Gelpi, a Jesuit theologian, considers this Roman Catholic-Classical Pentecostal rapprochement especially remarkable in view of the fact that the Pentecostal churches, by their very diversity, embody "just about all the enthusiastic tendencies that the Catholic Church over the centuries has judged to be heretical and divisive"—an intellectually inflexible and dogmatic fundamentalism that confuses piety and theology, revivalistic tendencies characterized by a suspicious religious emotionalism, almost neurotic fears and self-righteous certainty about personal salvation, and a piety so Charismatic that it becomes anti-institutional and antisacramental in principle.[53] He then accounts for such an unlikely feeling of unity among seeming belligerents by his understanding of the qualitative unity and diversity of the Charismatic experience:

> The charismatic experience is an experience which from generation to generation admits a wide variety of historical expressions. The experience, therefore, has both qualitative unity and diversity. Moreover, both the qualitative unity and the qualitative diversity of the experience possess a discernible historical background. The qualitative unity of the charismatic experience is grounded in the normative character of Jesus' own charismatic experience of divine sonship. Since his charismatic experience was a human experience of what it means to be by nature the Son of God, his charismatic experience of divine sonship is the limit toward which the charismatic experiences of those who share his Spirit by adoption must converge. Hence, the qualitative unity of the charismatic experience is teleological. It is produced by the convergence of a variety of charismatic experiences toward the same normative limit.[54]

So intense is the unity in diversity felt in Charismatic Renewal that even those ministers and lay people who have been pressured or forced to leave their historic churches are being encouraged by the movement's leadership to be reconciled. David Du Plessis suggests:

> Nothing formulates error as fast as isolationism. . . . I am praying desperately that we will not do anything to stop the move of God by our lack of love or harsh criticism of those who have hurt us in the past.[55]

GENERAL THEOLOGICAL ORIENTATION: ORTHODOX, EVANGELICAL, REFORMIST, AND ECUMENICAL

Edward Carnell, the late president of Fuller Theological Seminary, Pasadena, California, defines historic orthodoxy as "that branch of Christendom which limits the ground of religious authority to the Bible."[56] By and large, Charismatic Renewal is orthodox in that sense of the word. Of course, there is in Neo-Pentecostalism the implicit if not explicit belief in continuing revelation (a dynamic understanding of the Word of God); and, among Catholic Pentecostals, Scripture stands as authoritative only in the context of the whole Christian tradition, as stated by Kevin Ranaghan:

> There is no question that the Bible is affirmed to be the inspired Word of God. As it has been given by the Holy Spirit to the people of God . . . it is a testimony to the authentic faith and a primary source of spiritual direction and nourishment. Scripture, however, from a Catholic point of view stands at the heart of, or at the core of, the whole Christian tradition. It stands very much *within* the Church; it was inspired and written within the Church, is proclaimed in the Church. . . .
>
> To the Catholic mind, since it is believed that the inspiration of the Holy Spirit is operative in the life of the Church as a whole as well as in Scripture (which is nevertheless uniquely inspired), the Holy Spirit acts authentically in a variety of ways: in teaching, in sacramental celebration, in prayer, and in the ordinary life of the Catholic people.[57]

Neo-Pentecostalism also tends to be evangelical—concerned with the proclamation of the Gospel to bring nonbelievers into the Christian faith (conversion), and Spirit baptism. It is reformist in its desire to *renew* existing ecclesiastical structures, and ecumenical in its search for Christian unity across denominational lines. Speaking of Neo-Pentecostals, Walter Hollenweger, the eminent authority on Pentecostalism, describes these people as follows: "Most of them, but not all, are rather evangelical. All of them want to stay within their churches."[58] Among Charismatic Renewal leaders who do not necessarily portray themselves as traditional evangelicals are Arnold Bittlinger of Germany (a Lutheran theologian)[59] and John Hinkle, pastor of Christ Church, Los Angeles, a congregation formerly related to the Unity School of

Christianity. There are now even a few Unitarian-Universalist Charismatics.[60]

Howard Ervin, as a chief theological spokesman for Neo-Pentecostalism, sees Charismatic Renewal as the alternative to both antisupernaturalist ("liberal") theology on the one hand, and to doctrinaire orthodoxy on the other:

> An anti-supernaturalist "theology" has no solution, only theories, for the human predicament, which is basically man's alienation from God. Instead, it acknowledges its redemptive sterility by its unabashed capitulation to the human predicament, and by its frenetic pursuit of "relevance" to the contemporary mood. . . . It is captive by consent to modern society's ego-centric humanism. . . .
>
> On the other hand, a doctrinaire theological orthodoxy is not a serious option. It is essentially a refurbished scholasticism whose concept of metaphysical reality has congealed in abstract definitions and propositions. It is too prone to confound definition with essence. . . . Its continuing strategy is largely retrenchment, rather than dynamic involvement. Intimidated by apostasy, it has largely surrendered all hope of revival, charismatic or otherwise. Characteristically, its ethic is a platitudinous legalism. . . . Its strategy is fundamentally "trench warfare" waged from dogmatic bastions. . . .
>
> If the book of Acts bears witness to normative Christian experience—and it undubitably does—then by every Biblical standard of measurement contemporary Church-life is subnormal. As a consequence, it does not speak meaningfully, much less authoritatively, to our fragmented modern world. . . .
>
> It is precisely at this point that the Holy Spirit through the present charismatic awakening of the fragmented Christian Community, speaks urgently to the whole Church on the ecumenical, the denominational, the congregational, and the personal levels of a unity of Spirit and of Life. Only out of the plenitude of its own charismatic "fulness" can the modern Church plunge into redemptive confrontation with an alienated world. . . .[61]

THE BAPTISM OF THE HOLY SPIRIT

Central to Pentecostal theology is the doctrine of Spirit baptism. Don Basham describes the baptism of the Holy Spirit as a *second* encounter with God (after conversion) in which the Christian begins to receive the supernatural power of the Holy Spirit into his life.[62] Walter Hollenweger defines Spirit baptism as a "religious crisis experience subsequent to and different from conversion."[63] Hollenweger goes on to say that the baptism of the Holy Spirit is "generally but not always identified with speaking in tongues."[64] With respect to this issue, Basham declares:

> What is significant for us to remember is that the baptism in the Holy Spirit, which Jesus Himself bestows, includes speaking in tongues. . . .
> The baptism in the Holy Spirit with speaking in tongues was normative in the early church. We pray it will become normative in the church today.[65]

Furthermore, in Classical Pentecostal theology, the distinction has been made between Spirit baptism with the *initial* evidence of speaking in tongues, and the *gift* of tongues (continuing glossolalia). For Dennis and Rita Bennett, however, the initial experience of glossolalia should always be cultivated so that the first "utterances" grow, ultimately, into a "language" for prayer:

> If it were true that most believers only prayed in tongues once, at the time of receiving the Holy Spirit, and perhaps never again, or very rarely, it would be of paramount importance to be sure that those first "utterances" were totally inspired by the Spirit, and not human effort. We are teaching, however, what we know to be true, that these first efforts at obeying the Spirit are only the beginning. It doesn't matter if the first sounds are just "priming the pump," for the real flow will assuredly come. . . .
> Keep on with those sounds. Offer them to God. . . . As you do, they will develop and grow into a fully developed language.[66]

The Bennetts feel that there are two ways speaking in tongues may be manifested. The most common, in their view, is glossolalia as a devotional language for private edification, needing no interpretation. Less common but still important is the *public* manifestation of tongues—always with interpretation—in which it is felt that God is speaking to the unbeliever (as a "sign" to him), or to the believer, or in which the speaker is offering a public prayer to God.[67]

Exactly what *is* glossolalia? William Samarin, a prominent linguistics scholar, suggests that glossolalia consists of strings of generally simple syllables that are not matched systematically with a semantic system. Moreover, it is clearly "learned behavior"—a linguistic phenomenon that can occur independently of any participating psychological or emotional state. Then, speaking in a religious context, Samarin goes on to say that for Neo-Pentecostals glossolalia both signals and symbolizes transition (similar in character to an evangelical conversion). It is a "linguistic symbol of the sacred—a symbolic, pleasureful, expressive, and therapeutic experience." He concludes his argument (which runs counter to the older notions that speaking in tongues indicates psychological pathology, suggestibility, or hypnosis, or is the result of social disorganization and deprivation[68]) by declaring that people practice glossolalia because it is "part of a movement" that offers them the fulfillment of aspirations their previous religious experience created in them.[69]

Walter Hollenweger defines speaking in tongues as a

> meditative non-rational form of prayer, wrongly confused by non-specialists with ecstatic experiences [as commonly defined], highly valued by Paul for private prayer (I Cor. 14:4,39), but regulated for liturgical use (I Cor. 14:27).[70]

Pentecostals often insist that glossolalia is a "real language" in the linguistic sense. While not denying this notion, Larry Christenson attempts a more adequate definition in the face of various linguistic evidence to the contrary:

> Speaking in tongues is . . . speaking in a language [not "gibberish"]—a language which expresses the deep feel-

ings and thoughts of the speaker, a language which God
understands.[71]

If speaking in tongues expresses the meaning of the speaker, then,
for Christenson, it is a language.

For almost all Neo-Pentecostals, Spirit baptism is linked
directly to the glossolalia phenomenon. Don Basham, as we have
seen, describes the dual experience as "normative,"[72] and Larry
Christenson affirms that the "baptism with the Holy Spirit, with
the manifestation of speaking in tongues, was for *all* believers
(Acts 2:4; 10:44–46; 19:6)."[73] In Catholic Pentecostalism, however, there appears to be a greater openness to the possibility of
Spirit baptism *without* the gift of speaking in tongues. Thus, Edward O'Connor can say: "Some people begin speaking in tongues
at the moment of the baptism. Others do not begin until hours,
days, or even weeks later, and some never do."[74]

Finally, we should also be reminded that glossolalia is not the
only gift of the Spirit in Charismatic Renewal theology. Other
spiritual gifts most often mentioned by Neo-Pentecostals are
those listed in I Corinthians 12, for instance, and categorized by
Dennis and Rita Bennett as follows: (1) inspirational or fellowship gifts: tongues, and interpretation of tongues and prophecy;
(2) gifts of power (power to *do*): healings, working of miracles,
and the gift of faith; and (3) gifts of revelation: discernment of
spirits, the "word of knowledge," and the "word of wisdom."[75] Arnold Bittlinger, however, insists on a much broader understanding
of the *charismata* (which has yet to be recognized within Charismatic Renewal as a whole, however):

> To *each* one gifts are given. The possession of spiritual
> gifts is therefore in no sense a measure of Christian ma-
> turity. Spiritual gifts are received as presents from God
> by every Christian who will accept them in childlike
> faith. The sinner who comes before God in his help-
> lessness with the words "God have mercy on me a sin-
> ner" receives, to begin with, the *charisma* of eternal life
> (Rom. 6:23).
>
> There are a number of places in the New Testament
> where the gifts of divine grace are listed (e.g., Rom.

12:5–8; I Cor. 12:8–10; I Cor. 14:26f; Eph. 4:11). The great multiplicity of gifts makes it clear that the activity of Jesus extends to the whole range of human experience. The list of gifts in I Corinthians 2:8–10 is concerned especially with the controversial gifts, those that were often misused or misunderstood.[76]

WATER BAPTISM AND CONFIRMATION

One of the most difficult problems in Neo-Pentecostalism (especially in Catholic Pentecostalism) is the relationship between Spirit baptism (or infilling) and water baptism (as well as conversion and confirmation). For the evangelical Protestant, a second definite "work of grace" after conversion—Spirit baptism—does not pose great theological difficulties except with respect to the question of whether the Holy Spirit enters a person at the time of conversion (or water baptism, in Catholic theology) or only in the baptism of the Holy Spirit itself. This problem, then, is also related to the exact nature of Spirit baptism. Are receiving the Spirit and becoming a Christian identical?

Pentecostals base their doctrine of two steps to the "fullness of the Spirit" on Luke-Acts (Hollenweger, contrary to Dale Bruner and James Dunn,[77] both evangelical New Testament scholars, feels that they are right in doing so). Following the argument of Eduard Schweizer, the eminent New Testament authority, Hollenweger maintains that Luke does in fact favor the two-stage approach—first, water baptism or becoming a Christian, and second, baptism of the Spirit with recognizable signs—while Paul appears to have a different understanding of the Holy Spirit. For Paul, it would seem that becoming a Christian and receiving the Spirit are identical. Though much has been written about the Pauline and Lukan views of the Spirit—and how to reconcile them—Hollenweger, believing that the Bible is not necessarily a "unified system," is prepared to accept both the Lukan and Pauline doctrines as not fundamentally contradictory. (Pentecostals, however, try to solve the problem by positing two modes of the Holy Spirit's operation—a primary mode, essential for regeneration [Paul], and a secondary mode, providing additional equipment for service [Luke].)[78]

Catholics understand Spirit baptism differently from other Pentecostals. Edward O'Connor accepts the reception of the Spirit as a twofold experience, but in a sacramental context. In the first stage, at the moment of water baptism, the Holy Spirit comes to dwell in a person's life; but his presence there remains "hidden" until the second stage of reception occurs. This stage is the baptism of the Spirit by which the Holy Spirit becomes "manifest" in an individual.[79] Kevin and Dorothy Ranaghan compare the Catholic and Protestant Pentecostal views as follows:

> To evangelical pentecostals, baptism in the Holy Spirit is a "new" work of grace. In the life of a Catholic it is an "old" work, yet practically "new" because the phrase as used by Catholic pentecostals is a prayer of renewal for everything that Christian initiation is and is meant to be. In practice it has come to be an experience of reaffirmation rather than of initiation. Among Catholic pentecostals this baptism is neither a new sacrament nor a substitute sacrament. Like the renewal of baptismal promises, it is a renewal in faith of the desire to be everything that Christ wants us to be. . . . For Catholics this experience is a renewal, making our initiation [into the church] as children concrete and explicit on a mature level.[80]

Thus, for Protestant Neo-Pentecostals, the baptism of the Holy Spirit is generally a second work of grace (after conversion) in which the Spirit is actually "received" for the first time or in which the Spirit's supernatural power is initially received (e.g., Basham). For Catholic Pentecostals, Spirit baptism is non-sacramental. In it, the Holy Spirit, present in an individual (in a hidden state) since water baptism, becomes manifest. Here the baptism of the Holy Spirit functions as a renewal of water baptismal initiation rather than as a second, literal baptism. This renewal, moreover, is similar to (but not identical with) the renewal of baptismal vows in confirmation, and is a spiritual renewal which, in the words of Rodman Williams, "seems to have little or no relation to . . . [a person's] confirmation—or lack of it."[81]

SACRAMENTAL INTERCOMMUNION

In Charismatic Renewal, celebration of the sacraments (or ordinances) is most often confined to the formal services of worship of whatever denominations and churches are represented in the movement. Ecumenical conferences, however, may include an interdenominational service of communion—particularly at their conclusion. As in the ecumenical movement more generally, Neo-Pentecostal ecclesiastical leaders do occasionally participate together in sacramental celebration (or "concelebration"). In this regard, Rodman Williams relates a few of his experiences:

> I can look back over the past several months and recall occasions of *full* participation at the Lord's supper in traditions as widely different as Roman Catholic and Assembly of God, Episcopal and Church of Christ. As a Presbyterian minister it has been my privilege to concelebrate Mass, jointly to officiate at the Eucharist with an Episcopal priest, and perhaps the most amazing of all, to participate in a service of Holy Communion presided over by an Assembly of God minister assisted by a Roman Catholic priest and myself![82]

NEO-PENTECOSTAL CULTURE: SPIRITUALIZATION AND "SOCIALIZATION" OF HOLINESS

Classical Pentecostal culture is rooted in American revivalism, which emerged in the late eighteenth century, became a major national religious movement during the first two thirds of the nineteenth century, and was radicalized in the Holiness movement of the last third of the nineteenth century. Although the "cultural baggage" of revivalism in general and Classical Pentecostalism in particular has certainly found its way into the Pentecostal movement in the historic denominations, it has been resisted—especially by those churches (e.g., Roman Catholic, Episcopal, Lutheran, and Presbyterian) that are not grounded in the revivalist-fundamentalist tradition. One result of this rejection of cultural baggage in large segments of Neo-Pentecostalism has been the spiritualization or "socialization" of holiness. In Charis-

matic Renewal, it is increasingly the case that holiness has more
to do with an attitude of the heart and interpersonal relationships
than it does with the traditional ethical rigorism and negativism.
Thus, Robert Frost, a highly respected Neo-Pentecostal teacher,
can say:

> True holiness can never be cataloged as a list of do's
> and don'ts. Rather it is an attitude of the heart that lov-
> ingly recognizes the Lordship of Jesus Christ. . . .
> So often we have a tendency to logically construct an
> artificial list of worldly do's and don'ts as if holiness of
> heart could be measured by men's minds. . . .[83]

Kevin Ranaghan is particularly firm about his rejection of Classical Pentecostal cultural baggage:

> Often with the revivals came a simplistic and individ-
> ualistic Christian ethic. The righteous life [i.e., holiness]
> was characterized by clean living; therefore no smoking,
> drinking, dancing, makeup, theater-going or other
> amusements were allowed. While it was considerably
> tempered over the last several decades, the revivalistic
> culture continues to pervade denominational pen-
> tecostalism. . . . In its own cultural setting and devel-
> opment, this religious style is quite beautiful, meaningful
> and relevant. But it is not essential to or desirable for the
> baptism of the Holy Spirit, especially among people of
> far different religious backgrounds.[84]

In Catholic Pentecostalism especially, but also in Neo-Pentecostalism more generally, there is very little desire to forsake the
affirmation of the wider culture for the culture rejection that is
characteristic of Classical Pentecostalism and sectarian religion as
a whole. Spiritualization and socialization of holiness—of sanctification—make possible a more balanced view of life, of the
relationship between the "sacred" and the "secular." To quote
Kevin and Dorothy Ranaghan again:

> The men and women, clerics and lay people who have
> sought and received the baptism in the Holy Spirit are

by and large ordinary Catholic people from every walk of life, profession and socio-economic bracket. . . . Serious about their religion, concerned for the spiritual welfare of others, anxious for constructive renewal in the Church, they have been equally involved in their civic communities and employment, entering fully into all the normal activities which mark this period of our national life—human rights, law, justice, good government, peace.[85]

This culture affirmation in Catholic Pentecostalism is also described in Walter Hollenweger's account of the prayer meetings typical of the Pentecostal movement in the Roman Catholic Church:

It was not the uneducated but the intellectuals, not the uncritical but the critical exegetes, not frustrated Puritans, but quite normal Christians who took part in the meetings. There is not only speaking in tongues but critical discussion of theological and social problems; not only the singing of hymns but the composition of new hymns, not only praying, but eating, drinking and smoking.[86]

We have already mentioned the new television image of Oral Roberts since he joined the United Methodist Church. Another Pentecostal celebrity who became well known in the entertainment industry is Pat Boone. Boone's popularity as a vocalist during the late 1950s and early 1960s rivaled that of Elvis Presley. Formerly an active Churches of Christ layman, Boone was always regarded as "the nice clean all-American boy who lived next door and wore white buck shoes"[87]—but his singing and acting career was also the target of criticism by fellow American fundamentalists and evangelicals. After a family and business crisis experience in 1969, and through the influence of Oral Roberts, Herald Bredesen, David Wilkerson, and George Otis, a millionaire businessman, Pat Boone (and his wife and four daughters) received the baptism of the Holy Spirit. Having been "disfellowshiped" by his Church of Christ congregation as a result, he identified with the emerging (noninstitutional) Jesus movement, but finally joined a "progressive" (almost Neo-Pentecostal) assembly of the International Church of the Foursquare Gospel ("The Church on the Way," Van Nuys, California), and is now active in Charismatic Renewal leadership circles. Boone's religiosity is well known in the entertainment industry, where he has many "secular" friends. He writes:

> Dean Martin and I have hacked up some songs and golf courses together. Not long ago, in his mock-serious 100 proof way, Dino cracked a new one.
>
> "That's Pat Boone! He's so religious! Y'know, I shook hands with him the other day and my whole right side sobered up!"
>
> My friends in the entertainment profession are colorful, vital people! We have a great time together.[88]

Pat Boone clearly does not believe in "separation from the world" in the Classical Pentecostal sense; he does not reject the wider culture per se. Recently, the entertainer appeared on a "Dick Clark rock 'n' roll television special" (Clark has been a leading rock promoter for many years) in which Boone sang a number of his "hit" records and discussed his positive view of rock music with Clark. When his business schedule permits (Boone is now a millionaire and lives in Beverly Hills, California), Pat Boone travels extensively to keep concert engagements with his wife and four teen-age daughters, who together sing both secular and religious songs—even at the major hotels in Las Vegas, Nevada.[89]

If the spiritualization of holiness allows culture affirmation, its socialization (from a rigorous personal moral negativism to a concern for the healing of interpersonal relationships and humanity as a whole) represents a departure from the focus on "pious words and practices" typical of the Holiness movement and fundamentalism to a newly emerging interest in social morality. Hence, Kevin and Dorothy Ranaghan express their hope for a "humanly concerned" Christian witness within Charismatic Renewal:

> Men today are not interested in pious practices or abstract virtue. Where Christianity is part of the fiber of

the society as an establishment, where the nation goes to church but the Sunday dose of spiritual medicine wears off in Monday's marketplace, faith is dead. A God may indeed be worshipped here, but he is faceless and abstract. He is not the Father of our Lord, Jesus Christ.

The idealistic young, the "secular" theologians . . . the "man in the street" all seem to be crying out: "Down with pretty music and pious preaching; let us love one another right now!" Christian witness if it is to survive, if it is to be Christian, must be humanly concerned. It must be truly loving. It must be Christ.[90]

PERSONAL VS. SOCIAL MORALITY: DEVELOPING SOCIAL CONSCIENCE

To what degree, we might ask at this point, has there been a shift within the Pentecostal movement from an emphasis on personal morality to social morality ("human concern")? Kilian McDonnell rightly suggests that Classical Pentecostalism has most often been associated with indifference to social conditions and political issues—until World War II, a reflection, in part, of the political and social apathy common to the lower socio-economic levels[91] (although *some* Classical Pentecostals were pacifists during World War II). This apathy was reinforced by the socio-political conservatism inherent in American fundamentalism.[92] McDonnell also insists that there is nothing innate in the Pentecostal experience to change a person's political and social attitudes. He says that although

the Pentecostal experience does seem to elicit a new openness and generosity toward others it does not endow people with a new passion for political and social justice. If socio-political awareness were present before one became involved in Pentecostalism, the Pentecostal experience supports and reinforces it. But the Pentecostal experience will not, by and of itself, supply one with socio-political awareness.[93]

Nevertheless, among the leadership of Charismatic Renewal (in contrast to Classical Pentecostalism), there does appear to be an increasing interest in social concern, which is sometimes understood as an appropriate result of Spirit baptism. For instance, Michael Harper discusses this issue:

> True pietism . . . has in the past been deeply concerned with social matters, and . . . its prophets have attacked social injustice and exalted social righteousness. The roots of modern British Socialism stretch down to the seed-beds of Methodism, for instance.
>
> Every one of us should be passionately concerned about justice, public morality, and the plight of the under-nourished and under-privileged, and a balanced spirituality should reflect really deep commitment to the cause of man's physical as well as spiritual well-being. The Holy Spirit in the Acts of the Apostles was constantly destroying racial barriers, and reconciling deeply entrenched prejudices. It is important to notice too that in I Cor. 12:13 the baptism in the Spirit is seen in this context.[94]

Given the fact that Catholic Pentecostalism emerged originally within the academic community and within a church which, compared to its evangelical and fundamentalist Protestant counterparts, is not inherently "middle class" nor associated with the social and political status quo, it should not be surprising that Catholic Pentecostals (within Charismatic Renewal more generally) seem to have a greater social conscience than most Protestant Neo-Pentecostals. Yet, according to Edward O'Connor, there is a strong feeling within some quarters of Catholic Pentecostalism, at least, that more socio-political involvement is desirable. He speaks of the ill-fated Notre Dame community:

> The members of the Notre Dame community are involved in many different forms of social action. . . . A group of young families on the West Side of South Bend are actively working to improve race relations between blacks and whites. . . .
>
> While the members of the community are . . . active

in a multitude of ways, there is no . . . work proper to
the whole community. . . . This has disturbed some,
who feel that the community as such ought to have a
ministry. "God does not form a Christian community
just to hold prayer meeting," they sometimes declare.[95]

Kevin and Dorothy Ranaghan address the problem of social morality with a sense of urgency:

> We have before us the task of being Christ in the world.
> That means that in, with, and through him, by the
> power of the Spirit we are to worship, love, and adore
> our Father, just as Jesus did. It also means that we, the
> corporate Body of Christ, must communicate the experi-
> ence of the saving love of Jesus to the world. To the
> world means to mankind; not to men's feelings or emo-
> tions, not to men's disembodied spirits, but to human
> people in human societies and man-made institutions.
> The world that needs Jesus' love is shackled with poverty
> and disease, with racism and war, with lust for power
> and just plain indifference to the "other guy." This is the
> world we are sent to transform with Jesus' love, not so
> the world will be condemned but that it will be saved.[96]

We can indeed point to a *few* rather significant practical projects relevant to an emerging concern about social morality in Neo-
Pentecostalism. One is the drug addiction prevention center associated with Melodyland Christian Center. This center was
established during the emergence of the Jesus movement to rehabilitate youthful drug addicts through counseling, education, and
referral to residential therapeutic communities. It now operates a
national telephone "hotline," which allows troubled young people
to telephone the center toll-free from anywhere in the United
States for counseling and referral to similar centers in their own
areas; and the Orange County Municipal Courts have designated
Melodyland center to receive convicted youthful drug offenders
for education and counseling as an alternative to further court
proceedings and a jail sentence.[97]

Another prime example of social action within Charismatic Renewal is the new "communalism" that has emerged in the Episcopal Church of the Redeemer, Houston, Texas, a once-dying inner-city parish whose former rector, Graham Pulkingham, received the baptism of the Holy Spirit in 1964. In 1963, parish enrollment stood at 900, with one third of that number inactive (most had moved to the local suburbs). But by 1971, parish enrollment had risen to 1,400, average weekly attendance had reached 2,200, and "pledging" to meet the church budget was discontinued. As an experiment, Pulkingham and thirty parishoners (all Neo-Pentecostal) established a residential community in the inner city near the church that was patterned after the second chapter of Acts. The rector describes that initial community as follows:

> For six months thirty-one people all but lived together. In order to include wives and children in this fellowship, husbands continued [to meet] at the early morning hour and returned at 7:30 in the evening for a family gathering. All day Saturday, and Sunday after church, were spent together in one of the member's homes. Although nothing formal was put forward and no covenants were signed, each family let me know that everything they had or could command was at the disposal of the ministry [the community]—savings, insurance, earnings, possessions, borrowing power, themselves; we relinquished everything in a literal way. It was made available to help the needy.[98]

Somewhat similar to the Catholic Pentecostal communities, numerous other communes were founded within the Church of the Redeemer parish. Suburbanites returned to the inner city until, by 1972, there were 40 communities with 350 people—ranging from groups of working people to homes for parentless children. Thus, Graham Pulkingham comments on his church's Charismatic Renewal communalism as a positive expression of social concern:

> The fellowship members have not turned their backs on society. On the contrary, they are trying to make changes

in society at large and particularly in the Houston area by setting an example for others to follow.[99]

PATTERNS OF WORSHIP

Set largely in the contest of middle-class Christianity—and in historic ecclesiastical structures where liturgy is regulated—the Pentecostal experience of worship has been greatly subdued in Charismatic Renewal. Kilian McDonnell describes Classical Pentecostal speech patterns, prayer postures, mental processes, and expectations as part of the cultural baggage that must be rejected in Neo-Pentecostalism. Though these practices may have validity in one religious culture, they do not in another, since baggage is culturally determined and not transferable.[100] In this regard, David Du Plessis advises Neo-Pentecostals:

> Do not conform to Pentecostal patterns, for example, clapping one's hands out of imitation of the (classical) Pentecostals, or raising one's arms in prayer.[101]
> Let me say right here that I consider it heresy to speak of shaking, trembling, falling, dancing, clapping, shouting, and such actions as manifestations of the Holy Spirit. These are purely human reactions to the power of the Holy Spirit and frequently hinder more than help to bring forth genuine manifestations.[102]

Charismatic Renewal, as a rule, emphasizes the praise of God (see the works of Merlin Carothers, a United Methodist minister), but in the context of liturgical order and, as Kathryn Kuhlman calls it, "the quiet Spirit" in the formal services of worship where uplifted hands in prayer and being "slain in the Spirit" (falling backward "under the Spirit's power"), however, are often permitted. Neo-Pentecostal Charismatic activity tends to be relegated to small prayer groups of believers only, so as not to frighten and thus deter newcomers who are present during formal worship; and it is always well regulated. Addressing the matter in question, Larry Christenson speaks of Charismatic activity in his Lutheran congregation:

> We do not encourage speaking in tongues during the regular Sunday worship service, although it surely is not

forbidden. It seems more appropriate, however, at an informal evening meeting or a prayer group. . . .

We discourage the copying of any set of traditions, customs, or mannerisms in our prayer groups. We have nothing against these traditions from other Christian groups, but we do not feel that they are essential to the manifestation of the gifts of the Spirit in our setting. It is unnatural for our people to pray in loud voices, or to intersperse another person's prayer with frequent "Amen's" or "Hallelujah's."[103]

Michael Harper, likewise, is explicit about the regulation of *charismata* both in the context of formal worship and otherwise:

Just as we hand presents graciously to those we love . . . and do not thrust them rudely at them, so we should manifest spiritual gifts "decently." This means we shall not shout unnaturally words of prophecy, nor speak so quietly that no one can properly hear us. It means we will not lay hands violently on people for healing, but gently and reverently . . . and the laying-on-of-hands should be carefully ordered in the churches. The minister and other leaders in each church should specify who should have this ministry. . . .

We should also observe the principle of orderliness. "God is not a God of confusion but of peace," Paul reminds the Corinthians (I Cor. 14:33). We may receive, for example, an anointing to manifest a gift during a service, but that does not mean that we have to do so there and then. We can wait until an appropriate opportunity presents itself. . . .

In some churches it is customary to punctuate prayers or sermons with loud "amens" and "hallelujahs," etc. This can be very distracting to the one who is leading in prayer or exhortation, as well as to the congregation, each member of which should be following what the one leading is saying. . . . Another tradition to avoid is the practice of speaking in tongues during a meeting, without interpretation and in concert. This contradicts the command of Paul in I Cor. 14:28.[104]

We shall now delineate the specific differences between Classical Pentecostalism and Charismatic Renewal that have already been briefly mentioned—cultural and social differences, and differences in theological belief and practice.

CHAPTER SIX: *Classical Pentecostalism and Charismatic Renewal in Contrast*

In contrasting Classical Pentecostalism with Charismatic Renewal or Neo-Pentecostalism, we are immediately reminded of the characteristic pattern of sect development into a church or denomination. Classical Pentecostalism has usually been regarded as illustrative of the sect-type religious organization in sociological typologies; while Charismatic Renewal, so it seems, because it is a movement largely *within* the historic Protestant, Anglican, and Eastern Orthodox denominations and the Roman Catholic Church, should be identified with the church- or denomination-type religious organization. Indeed, specific differences between Classical Pentecostalism and Neo-Pentecostalism (to a degree, at least) are reminiscent of the general variances between sect and denomination or church as ideal types.

Bryan Wilson, reader in sociology at Oxford University, suggests the following as typical characteristics of a *sect*: (1) a voluntary association; (2) membership by proof to sect authorities of some claim to personal merit such as knowledge of doctrine, affirmation of a conversion experience, or recommendation of members in good standing; (3) exclusiveness, and exercise of expulsion against those who dispute doctrinal, ethical, or organizational precepts; (4) self-conception of a special elect; (5) personal perfection (however this is judged) as the expected standard of aspiration; (6) belief (at least as an ideal) in the priesthood of all believers; (7) high level of lay participation; (8) opportunity for spontaneous expression of commitment by members; and (9) hostility, or indifference to secular society and the state. By way of elaboration on these points, Wilson then goes on to say that the commitment of the sectarian is always more total and well defined than that of the member of other religious denominations. Sect ideology is clearer than that of church or denomination, and behavioral expectations serve to keep sect members apart from the wider society—"the world."[1]

In Wilson's typology of religious sects, Classical Pentecostalism is described as reflective of the "conversionist" sect model. A conversionist sect centers its teaching and activity on evangelism or recruitment. It is typified by extreme bibliolatry (including literalism), and the demand for conversion as the test of fellowship. Much emphasis is placed on individual guilt for sin, and the need for redemption through Christ. The conversionist sect precludes no one, and revivalist techniques are employed in evangelism. It is distrustful of denominations and churches it feels have diluted or betrayed "authentic" Christianity. This sect is hostile to clerical learning, and especially to liberalism. It is opposed to modern science, particularly to geology and theories of evolution. And finally, the conversionist sect disdains culture and the artistic values accepted in the wider society.[2]

In the course of the decades following 1901 (and especially since the end of World War II), however, Classical Pentecostalism as a whole has undergone a transformation that has caused it to lose some of its sect characteristics and to take on (to a degree, at least) various traits of the church or denomination type of religious organization (though not without internal tensions leading to the establishment of numerous more conservative "split-off" groups and independent churches). Increasingly, Classical Pentecostalism can no longer be *uniformly* identified with the disadvantaged and deprived often associated with sect membership. John Nichol makes the point well:

> Pentecostals have become property owners rather than being property-less. They have risen economically, and their churches have become more elaborate, their worship more dignified. There is a greater demand for music of a professional quality and for an educated ministry. The groups have grown in influence and numbers, and, in the process, they have developed an increasing amount of ecclesiastical "machinery." Prior concerns of

meeting the needs of an adult membership have been subordinated to a stress on the religious education of the young. Those cultural standards which the fathers condemned, the children have embraced. The stress on the future, on preparing for the next world, have given way very largely to a principle of accommodation to the surrounding culture.[3]

In a sense, the likelihood of Classical Pentecostalism being denominationalized was always high, because in so many ways it came out of a tradition that was in direct continuity with evangelical Protestantism. Only Spirit baptism and the *charismata* (speaking in tongues, particularly) stood out as *manifestly* separatist and sectarian; they were the *raison d'être* of the movement's separate existence. This element of what Max Weber would call the ecstatic was clearly not part of the old Protestantism as received through the historic denominations, and it was in some ways a threat to the old ascetic—a type of spiritual indulgence. Hence, Classical Pentecostalism was sectarian because it pitched the balance of ascetic and ecstatic at a different point and sought scriptural warrant for so doing. (It was the doctrinal underpinning and strict scriptural basis, of course, that made Pentecostalism so much more respectable than earlier glossolalic movements, and it could fit the spiritual gifts into a received ecclesiology too.)

Neo-Pentecostalism, as we have said, is a movement of renewal mainly within the historic denominations identified with the denomination- or church-type of religious organization. Bryan Wilson characterizes the *denomination* as follows: (1) formally, a voluntary association; (2) acceptance of adherents without imposition of traditional prerequisites of entry and with purely formalized admission procedures; (3) stress on breadth and tolerance; (4) laxity of enrollment leading to a lack of interest in the expulsion of the apathetic and wayward; (5) unclear self-understanding, and de-emphasis of doctrine; (6) satisfaction of being one movement among others; (7) acceptance of the values and standards of the prevailing culture and conventional morality; (8) an educated professional ministry; (9) restricted lay participation; (10) formalized services without spontaneity; (11) more concern for education of the young than for evangelism; (12) nonreligious character of "additional" activities (apart from worship); (13) weak individual commitment; (14) acceptance of the values of the secular society and the state; and (15) membership drawn from any section of the community, but with a stress on social compatibility.[4]

Since Charismatic Renewal is a decentralized movement, there are no "real" members—only participants. But when the Pentecostal experience becomes dominant in a given local church that is part of a historic denomination, certain traits inherent in the denomination-type religious organization are often transformed into attributes more typical of the sect type. For instance, "first class" membership requires evidence of the Pentecostal experience, which is certainly a prerequisite for leadership in the church. The congregation's self-conception is very clear, and doctrinal issues become relatively more important (especially those relating to the Holy Spirit). The congregation sees itself as more generally a part of Charismatic Renewal, which it does not regard as merely one movement among others. It espouses more transcendent values and a "higher" sense of morality than the prevailing culture. Lay participation is greater and less restricted than in the denominational model. Spontaneity does, at times, occur in services of worship—and very often during meetings of prayer groups (a common feature of Neo-Pentecostal churches). Evangelism (particularly as it relates to the Pentecostal experience) is at least as important as religious education of the young. Finally, most additional activities tend to be religious in nature, and individual commitment is very intense indeed.

Charismatic Renewal is primarily a middle- to upper-middle-class movement within the "respectable" historic denominations. Already in 1964, Stanely Plog, then a psychologist at UCLA, said of the Neo-Pentecostals he interviewed that "they're determined to fit the gift of tongues—and the gift of healing, too—into a 'normal,' calm, middle-class way of life, and that's definitely something new."[5]

THEOLOGY: FUNDAMENTALISM VS. "PROGRESSIVE EVANGELICALISM"

Since 1901, biblical literalism has reinforced dispensational (theological and cultural) fundamentalism[6] as the basic theology of Classical Pentecostalism. This is easily discerned in the doctrinal statements and moral demands of the major Pentecostal denominations.[7] Historically, the fundamentalist label has been attached to those individuals and groups that accept what have become known as the five fundamentals of the faith: the virgin birth of Christ, his substitutionary atonement for human sin, his bodily resurrection from the dead, and his literal and imminent second coming in glory, together with the inspiration and authority of Scripture as the only infallible rule of faith and conduct. But fundamentalism has also become associated with (1) a total rejection of (nontextual) biblical criticism, (2) complete separation from nonfundamentalists (theological liberals, especially) and the wider society more generally, and (3) the moral negativism and cultural taboos of American revivalism.

Charismatic Renewal, however, seems to be moving from rigid fundamentalism ("The Lord appears to be making a lot of Episcopalian Fundamentalists in these end time days!," Jean Stone, 1962[8]) to a "progressive evangelicalism" that affirms the authority of Scripture, the necessity of a personal commitment to Christ as Savior and Lord, and the mandate for evangelism, but rejects and repudiates fundamentalist cultural excesses and theological extremes.[9] Although dispensational expectations are still widespread among Neo-Pentecostals, *some* prominent Charismatic Renewal leaders such as Larry Christenson, Howard Ervin, Josephine Ford, Donald Gelpi, Michael Harper, Edward O'Connor, Kevin and Dorothy Ranaghan, and Rodman Williams (as we have seen) are firm in their disavowal of dispensational fundamentalism. Michael Harper summarizes the characteristic Charismatic Renewal stance on this key issue as follows:

Pentecostalism in some people's minds is equated with a belief in the verbal inspiration of Scripture (usually the King James version only), a kind of proof textualism, whereby chapter and verse answers every question irrespective of context. It seems to require a belief in the pre-millennial view of the Second Coming, and an almost complete distrust in theology. . . .

The present-day charismatic movement, generally speaking, is not . . . a movement of unthinking fools floating on a wave of emotional experience. . . . But the danger is still there. An unthinking old-fashioned fundamentalism will always be a hindrance to the forward surge of the Holy Spirit.[10]

WORSHIP: "SPIRIT OF CONFUSION" VS. "THE QUIET SPIRIT"

Influenced deeply by the black religious experience,[11] worship in Classical Pentecostalism has ordinarily been noted for its radical enthusiasm and spontaneity (which includes the exercise of *charismata*), on the one hand, and its almost total disregard for "liturgical order," on the other (less so in Great Britain than in the United States, however, and increasingly less so with the passage of time and the greater upward mobility in Pentecostal denominations).[12] "A Pentecostal meeting where you know what is going to happen next is backslidden," Donald Gee declares.[13] Typical of a Church of God (Cleveland, Tennessee) service (in many places, still), for instance, might be the following:

7:40 P.M.—Our Annual Saturday Evening Testimony and Praise Service, V. R. Sherill in charge. Charles, Harper, Davis and Ted sang, "I shall Ride on the Cloud." Brother Sherill called on the different sections in the balcony to praise the Lord, starting on one side and going all around. This ended in a shout of praise on the platform. The quartet sang, "I see the light house." The congregation stood and clapped hands. A march was started on the platform and continued on the main floor of the building. The blessings of the Lord were upon the people and they danced, shouted and rejoiced in the Lord. One clerk described the outpouring thus: "A march of victory is started on the large platform with leaping, shouting and praising the Lord. Now they move down and make their way through the shouting congregation. Such unity of the spirit I have never felt. The large congregation is aflame with the fire and power of the Holy Ghost and almost everyone is shouting. The large platform is quaking from the impact of hundreds of feet striking the surface as God continues to shower blessing after blessing upon His people. The people on the main floor testified by sections, one after the other. The praises rang out around the balconies again and then all praised the Lord together. At the close of this praise service, Clayton Sherill, his wife and Louise Sherill sang, 'I'm So Glad He Found Me.' "[14]

Like many other scholars, Walter Hollenweger associates this general pattern of worship with liberation from psychological stress caused by various kinds of deprivation (e.g., economic and social).[15]

Wade Horton, a Church of God (Cleveland, Tennessee) overseer, criticizes Charismatic Renewal for subduing the Classical Pentecostal manner of enthusiastic worship. He speaks against the voice that

> accepts the mechanical, quiet, sophisticated tongues speaking, but rejects the emotional, unspeakable joy, spiritually intoxicated, rushing-mighty-wind kind of Pentecostal experience. This group wants to be sure that the multitudes are not confounded and amazed at their actions, and most certainly that they are not accused of being drunk as were the first Pentecostal believers. They want to steer their ship clear of the Pentecostal pattern as recorded in Acts 2. This voice says, "I will accept glossolalia, but, please, not as the Pentecostals do."[16]

Neo-Pentecostals, as we have seen, reject what they sometimes regard as the (non-middle-class) "spirit of confusion" typical of traditional Pentecostal worship (part of Classical Pentecostalism's cultural baggage—"adiaphora," not belonging to the center of the Pentecostal experience). They tend, rather, to stress order ("the quiet Spirit," in Kathryn Kuhlman's words) within formal services of worship. Although uplifted hands in prayer (the ancient *orans* posture) and being "slain in the Spirit" (falling backward "under the Spirit's power") are generally permitted in such services, most Charismatic activity is relegated to small prayer groups of *believers* (and others seriously interested in Spirit baptism) so as not to frighten and deter newcomers attending worship. Furthermore, exercise of the spiritual gifts is *always* regulated (e.g., speaking in tongues only with interpretation, and one person at a time). Again, Charismatic Renewal has adopted the *charismata* to a framework of "ordered respectability" suitable for educated, middle-class Christians who are members of the historic denominations. In 1964, Jean Stone suggested the following rules of conduct for glossolalia and related phenomena in a group context. Her words reflect the normative Neo-Pentecostal position today:

> Speaking in tongues is not spooky; it's wholesome, good, clean, beautiful. We use no weird positions, no peculiar gymnastics. Don't add your own little goodies to it. If you make it sound peculiar, you'll scare people pea-green. I remember one pastor's wife moaned, and it scared my husband to death! Don't moan or shriek. Remember, the gift is to edify and shrieking isn't edifying. And beware of personal prophecy, or prophecy about catastrophic happenings. If we seem too strange to outsiders, we're not going to get many outsiders to become insiders. You'll only attract desperate people. Don't develop separatist tendencies. Instead we are trying to save souls and be witness for Christ in what we say and in the way we live. And don't make the Bible a magical thing; be grounded in the Bible, but don't be a Bible thumper.[17]

ECCLESIASTICAL STANCE: SECTARIANISM VS. ECUMENISM

With their new experience, the first Classical Pentecostals were not welcomed in their own "respectable" churches. This fact—together with the typically fundamentalist attitudes most of them shared (e.g., noncooperation with Roman Catholics and with denominations that included theological liberals)—led these Christians to form other churches and denominations according to the characteristic sectarian pattern.[18] But by the early 1940s, some influential Pentecostal leaders began to question the isolationist stance that their movement had taken during the preceding two decades, at least. Thus, in 1943, a number of the major American Pentecostal denominations joined the National Association of Evangelicals[19]; and in 1947, the first triennial Pentecostal

World Conference was held in Zurich[20]—both events indicating that Pentecostals were ready to strengthen ties with their own denominations and to extend their fellowship to non-Pentecostal evangelicals. Then, in the early 1960s, two Chilean (and later one Brazilian) Pentecostal denominations took the "ultimate" step by joining the World Council of Churches (an action vigorously denounced by American Pentecostals).[21] And since the advent of Charismatic Renewal in 1960, it has become increasingly difficult for Classical Pentecostals as a whole to continue separating themselves altogether from the historic denominations, many of which include large numbers of Neo-Pentecostals within their ranks who share the same experience.

When Dennis Bennett, the Charismatic Renewal pioneer, then rector of St. Mark's Episcopal Church, Van Nuys, California, was put under pressure to resign from his pastorate in 1960 as a result of his recent Pentecostal experience, he told his parishioners that he was *not* leaving the Episcopal Church—that "no one needs to leave the Episcopal Church [or any other church] in order to have the fullness of the Spirit."[22] Among Pentecostals, that nonsectarian position was at the time revolutionary and still prevails today in Neo-Pentecostalism.

As we have said already, Charismatic Renewal participants understand the Pentecostal experience as transcending denominational and ideological walls while it clarifies and underscores what is authentically Christian in each tradition without demanding structural or even doctrinal changes in any church body. They are usually friendly in their attitude toward the World Council of Churches, its regional counterparts, and other ecumenical structures. Furthermore, the Protestant-Catholic encounter within Charismatic Renewal is so intense and heartfelt that it is probably unparalleled in contemporary ecclesiastical experience. Protestants and Catholics, conservatives and liberals, do not automatically discard their own theological and ecclesiastical differences when they come together in this movement. Nor do the movement's leaders themselves agree on the precise definition of baptism in the Holy Spirit or the exact nature of the *charismata* and their operation as outlined in I Corinthians 12–14, for instance. But whether one is theologically liberal or conservative, it is felt that he will almost inevitably come to have a more vivid sense of God as a *person*, since by the baptism of the Holy Spirit God has *demonstrated* his reality to him in a personal way. Likewise, it is felt that the Pentecostal experience may well initiate or restore a person's interest in serious Bible study and give him a fresh awareness of the efficacy of prayer. Regardless of his theological outlook, the Neo-Pentecostal *must* develop a genuine openness to other Christians and the church as a whole if he is to continue successfully as a participant in Charismatic Renewal.

The very unconcern in Neo-Pentecostalism about doctrinal formulations is in contrast to most sects—and in some considerable contrast to traditional Christianity, which has been an intensely "intellectual" (in the sense of being concerned about intellectual distinctions) and doctrinally oriented religion. Charismatic Renewal reflects other currents in our times in being reluctant to create boundaries or to establish firm and objective criteria. There is a powerful subjectivist element in it all.

MIND AND SPIRIT:
ANTI-INTELLECTUALISM VS. INTELLECTUAL MOTIVATION

Classical Pentecostalism was born in the Bible school tradition among people with very little formal education. Fundamentalist in character, it has tended to distrust "modernist" (i.e., nonfundamentalist) theology and the academic world in general, discouraging (for the most part) its prospective ministers from university and seminary education. Training at Pentecostal Bible schools has been primarily training in piety—education geared to the study of the English Bible and fundamentalist exposition of the text. But with the increasing middle-class nature of the major Pentecostal denominations, more Classical Pentecostal young people are being educated—and educated in non-Pentecostal church-related colleges and in purely secular colleges and universities.[23] Also, some of the traditional "Bible institutes" (of the Assemblies of God [U.S.A.], the Church of God [Cleveland, Tennessee], and the Pentecostal Holiness Church, for example) have gradually been transformed into "respectable" (sometimes fully accredited) liberal arts colleges.[24] (The Assemblies of God and the Church of God [Cleveland, Tennessee] are even considering the establishment of a graduate theological seminary.) Furthermore, in 1971, the Society for Pentecostal Studies was formed. This professional organization (of scholars, chiefly) is open to anyone interested in the study of Pentecostalism—with or without a faith commitment—and its leadership is dominated by Classical Pentecostal academics including Russell Spittler (Assemblies of God), Vinson Synan (Pentecostal Holiness Church), and Hollis Gause (Church of God [Cleveland, Tennessee]). Spittler, dean of Southern California College (Assemblies of God), Costa Mesa, California, and a Harvard University Ph.D. in New Testament, was president of the Society in 1973; while Synan, a prominent historian of Pentecostalism and general secretary of the Pentecostal Holiness Church, succeeded him. Participant speakers at the 1973 meeting included Martin Marty of the University of Chicago and *The Christian Century*, a Lutheran church historian; Basil Meeking of the Vatican's Secretariat for Promoting Christian Unity; Edward O'Connor of Notre Dame University, a Catholic Pentecostal; Timothy Smith of The Johns Hopkins University, a Church of the Nazarene minister and eminent historian; and Thomas Zimmerman, long-time general superintendent of the Assemblies of God (U.S.A.).[25] The theme for the 1974 Society of Pentecostal Studies gathering was "The Third Force and the Third World." Various black Pentecostal leaders and Walter Hollenweger were featured speakers at this fourth annual meeting.[26]

Despite the lack of formal higher education of a number of Neo-Pentecostal leaders (e.g., Oral Roberts, Kathryn Kuhlman, and Ralph Wilkerson), Charismatic Renewal (unlike Classical Pentecostalism as a whole) tends to be intellectually motivated. For example, Neo-Pentecostals always emphasize the academic background and respectability of their educated leaders.[27] Oral Roberts University (its somewhat revivalistic ethos notwithstanding) boasts exceptional facilities and a reputable faculty, and has adopted the novel policy (within Pentecostalism) of "educating the whole person for a whole life—spirit, mind, body" (not the spirit alone, as in the Bible school tradition).[28] Melodyland Christian Center has recently established a Neo-Pentecostal "School of Theology" and "Ecumenical Research Academy."

Headed by Rodman Williams (a Columbia University-Union Theological Seminary Ph.D. and former professor of theology at Austin [Texas] Presbyterian Theological Seminary), the School of Theology does not yet *require* a baccalaureate degree for admission, but is clearly developing a standard graduate seminary curriculum for both men and women.[29] Finally, in this connection, Catholic Pentecostalism experienced its initial thrust within the university itself—at Duquesne, Notre Dame, and Michigan State, and at the University of Michigan; and some of the most sophisticated Charismatic Renewal literature to date has been penned by participant Roman Catholics. Michael Harper's assertion that Neo-Pentecostalism is *not*, generally speaking, "a movement of unthinking fools floating on a wave of emotional experience" is, in fact, justified.

RELIGION AND SOCIETY: SOCIAL UNCONCERN VS SOCIAL CONSCIENCE

Classical Pentecostalism has most often been associated with indifference to social conditions and political issues. Kilian McDonnell, as we have seen, attributes this stance (until World War II), in part, to the political and social apathy common to the lower socio-economic levels. But with the increasingly middle-class character of Classical Pentecostalism (after World War II), its continued widespread social unconcern might be linked more properly to the socio-political and cultural conservatism inherent in fundamentalism and evangelicalism as a whole since the latter part of the nineteenth century.[30]

Within Charismatic Renewal, however (again, as we have already seen), there are at least a few strong indications of an emerging social conscience and a mandate for social involvement. For instance, the once-dying inner-city Episcopal Church of the Redeemer, Houston, Texas, was transformed and revitalized—through the Pentecostal experience of its former rector, Graham Pulkingham—into a successful experiment in communal living, and a force for social good in its community. Melodyland Christian Center's support of a national toll-free telephone "hotline," and its alcoholic and drug addict rehabilitation programs, have become well known as effective social action projects; while numerous Catholic Pentecostals (especially) have shown themselves to be deeply involved in political life and social change.

Rodman Williams insists that the Pentecostal experience *ought* to motivate human feelings to

> become more sensitive to the moods, the concerns, the hopes of the world and of people; the will finds itself strengthened to execute with more faithfulness and determination those ethical actions to which it gives itself. . . . Here truly is the transcendence of ancient walls of creed and tradition, race and nationality, cultural, economic, and social differentiation by the overarching Spirit of love.[31]

Michael Harper is even more specific about the issue:

> When we are filled with the Holy Spirit there should be an immediate concern for the world in every area of its life. . . .
> Let [Charismatic Renewal] . . . lead Christians in a war against racism, the exploitation of the environment, inflation, property speculation, and other evils of our age.[32]

Thus Neo-Pentecostalism offers evidence that it is beginning to repudiate the socio-political apathy characteristic of Classical Pentecostalism. Only time will tell if and how fast Charismatic Renewal as a whole will move toward a *significant* sense of social and political concern.

CHRIST AND CULTURE:
CULTURE REJECTION VS. CULTURE AFFIRMATION

Classical Pentecostalism shares with American fundamentalism in general the rejection of participation in the wider culture—"the world." Emphasizing to an almost gnostic degree the spiritual life over against "the desires of the flesh,"[33] Classical Pentecostalism enforces the usual taboos against the (even moderate) use of alcohol and tobacco in any form, social dancing, gambling and card playing, attendance at the theater and cinema, (secular) rock music, "immodest dress," and sometimes even "mixed bathing."[34] Legitimate recreation (escape?) is to be provided by the church ("in the Spirit") and, really, nowhere else. But since these taboos are part of the cultural baggage of revivalism, and have been traditionally enforced only within those churches deeply rooted in the revivalistic culture (e.g., Baptist and Methodist churches, and their offshoots, including Classical Pentecostal bodies), Neo-Pentecostal Catholics, Eastern Orthodox Christians, Anglicans, Lutherans, Presbyterians, and the like are often quite shocked when such taboos are introduced as binding upon them after their Pentecostal experience. Given the presence within Charismatic Renewal of former Classical Pentecostals and others of the fundamentalist-revivalist tradition, together with numerous fellowship contacts between Neo-Pentecostals and Classical Pentecostals, the nontransferable baggage of Classical Pentecostalism piles up in Charismatic Renewal and is often not easily sent away.[35] It is most difficult for a typical Classical Pentecostal (or Baptist Neo-Pentecostal, for instance) to accept as one who shares the same experience a Catholic Pentecostal who drinks, smokes, dances, and gambles—though such acceptance *is*, in fact, becoming increasingly common.

Despite inherent difficulties, however, there is within Neo-Pentecostalism, as we have seen, a noticeable trend in the direction of culture affirmation (as a new or continuing attitude). Holiness is still an important concept; but in Charismatic Renewal circles, Classical Pentecostal legalism is officially shunned, and holiness is being spiritualized and socialized as an attitude of the heart, having more to do with healthy relationships with people and "the life of discipleship" and less to do with moral privatism and negativism—more with what you *do* than with what you don't do.

CONSTITUENCY: WORKING-CLASS VS. MIDDLE-CLASS STANDING

Classical Pentecostalism began as a movement of the poor, the uneducated, the minorities, the disenfranchised, and the socially and economically deprived. To a large degree—but not universally —the same basic kinds of people are attracted to it today (hence, its special strength in the American South and Midwest among rural folk, in the West among "migrants" from the South, in black and Latin ghettos in urban centers, among women, and in the Third World, in Latin America especially).[36] Yet, Walter

Hollenweger points to the relatively large proportion of Pentecostal pastors in his own survey research with middle-class and historic-denomination backgrounds.[37] Furthermore, like Luther Gerlach and Virginia Hine, Hollenweger insists that attempts to understand the Classical Pentecostal subculture as "an inferior culture, as the expression solely of social, intellectual and economic deprivation" are contradicted by the most recent sociological and psychological research.[38]

Charismatic Renewal, however, as we have seen, has always been predominantly middle-class in nature. It first emerged in a "fashionable" suburban Episcopal church in Southern California. (An early sampling of monthly prayer groups that gathered at Jean Stone's home in 1964 showed about equal numbers of men and women, an average age of 42 years, a median monthly income of $630 [with persons earning in excess of $1,600 also present], a large proportion of men in the "professional and technical" occupational grouping and women in the "housewife" category, and Republicans outnumbering Democrats seven to one.[39]) Until Neo-Pentecostalism became a force within Roman Catholicism, the movement seemed very much in continuity with the assumptions of white Anglo-Saxon Protestant traditions as they are stereotyped.[40] Even at the present time, Charismatic Renewal appears chiefly among the white, middle-class, suburban populations of the Western world—North America, Great Britain (including present and former Commonwealth countries such as [white] South Africa, New Zealand, and Australia), Germany, and Scandinavia. It is Classical Pentecostalism, rather, that is experiencing phenomenal growth in the underdeveloped Third World.[41]

CHAPTER SEVEN: *From Opposition to Acceptance*

There are a number of reasons why the Pentecostal experience tends to rouse opposition. First, popular ideas of psychology lead to suspicion when any kind of pressure is put upon people. Thus, when a "second encounter with God" is encouraged, fear is roused that feelings of inadequacy or deprivation will be caused without justification. Second, it is argued that the Pentecostal experience disturbs the life of the church by creating a schismatic group, while the established leaders or members of a given congregation are often unwilling to concede that their own doctrine or experience is lacking in anything. Hence, the latter reject the new teaching, and the former group must either deny or "cover up" its experience or leave the church. Third, the intellectual climate of even the most orthodox church may encourage coldness and conservatism and reject "irrational enthusiasm." The "new thing" is seemingly unmanageable, and that which may appear "supernatural" within it is reduced to whatever categories are at hand to explain it. These categories may include mental imbalance, heresy, or that such things cannot happen now (a favorite dispensational fundamentalist argument). Fourth, the churches from which (Classical) Pentecostalism originally emerged, as well as those that have been most bitter in their opposition to the Pentecostal experience, have frequently been those that *emphasize* what they feel to be the biblical foundation of their doctrine and practice. This is the very "charter" that validates their existence. Thus, when Pentecostals claim their *own* practice as the biblical pattern, it is an obvious challenge to the former (commonly fundamentalist) groups and churches. Finally, among some theological liberals (and skeptics)—not fundamentalists and evangelicals here—one finds offense that "in this day and age" even theologically educated individuals can still "take the Bible in that way" and gain public notoriety by so doing.[1]

Shortly after Dennis Bennett's forced resignation as rector of St. Mark's Episcopal Church, Van Nuys, California (reported by *Newsweek*, July 4, 1960, and by *Time*, August 15, 1960), opposition within affected denominational hierarchies became apparent. Francis Bloy, then Episcopal bishop of Los Angeles, immediately banned any more speaking in tongues under church auspices.[2] In 1962 and 1963, various rather negative reports on glossolalia were prepared and circulated within the American Lutheran Church (ALC)[3]; and in July 1964, Herbert Mjorud was dismissed from the ALC's evangelical staff for promoting speaking in tongues.[4] Also, Everett Palmer, then Methodist bishop of the Seattle area (where Bennett had moved), called glossolalia "a perversion."[5] Such initial reactions all manifested a basic unhappiness with the appearance of the phenomenon within the churches in question. Furthermore, in the early years of Charismatic Renewal, all negative appraisals seemed to identify Pentecostalism with tongues alone.

The late Bishop James Pike's Easter 1963 pastoral letter to the Episcopal diocese of California is the most negative of the early documents on the matter.[6] He says, in part,

> while there is no inhibition whatsoever as to devotional use of speaking with tongues, I urge that there be no services or meetings in our Churches or in homes or elsewhere for which the expression or promotion of this activity is the purpose or of which it is a part. Nor do I believe that our clergy should lead or take part in such gatherings under whatever auspices.[7]

None of the early reports categorically condemns the Pentecostal experience (Anglicanism, of course, has a rich tradition of divine healing and exorcism—both associated with Pentecostalism), although the formulators of these documents were profoundly disturbed by the confusion and division that seemed to attend the appearance of Pentecostalism in their denominations. This concern was clearly not dictated merely by a reluctance to accept what was strange and new. Charismatic Renewal did pose serious pastoral problems, not the least of which was the tendency of the early Neo-Pentecostals to take over uncritically the cultural baggage, exegesis, and doctrine from Classical Pentecostalism rather than integrating the experience into their own theological traditions.[8]

With respect to the distinctively fundamentalist and evangelical denominations, opposition was initially firm (though not well formulated, and rarely published) and, by and large, continues today—a fact that has caused David Du Plessis to remark:

> I shall not be surprised when our fundamentalist friends who attack the Pentecostals as severely as they do the World Council [of Churches], begin to "expose" the Pentecostal trend within the ranks of the Ecumenical Movement.[9]

In Great Britain, however, opposition to Charismatic Renewal from within the historic denominations was apparently never so strong as it was in the United States. By the time the Pentecostal experience had emerged in the Church of England (and later in the Free Churches), it no longer was a "shocking" phenomenon on the world scene. The Anglican hierarchy seemed open from the beginning, while both Evangelical and Anglo-Catholic clergymen became participants in the Pentecostal movement without undue criticism or threats from their superiors.[10]

GRADUAL, CAUTIOUS ACCEPTANCE
BY HISTORIC PROTESTANT AND ROMAN CATHOLIC BODIES

In the course of the late 1960s and early 1970s, most of the historic denominations gradually made peace with the growing Pentecostal movement within their own ranks. But few have as yet issued official pronouncements about Charismatic Renewal. Of those that have (e.g., United Presbyterian Church, U.S.A.; Presbyterian Church in the United States[11]; and Lutheran Church in America[12]), the United Presbyterian Church, U.S.A., has been one of the most positive and helpful. Its very thorough 56-page report was accepted by the 182nd General Assembly of the denomination (1970).[13] The United Presbyterian study committee had the advantages of considerable hindsight and of a rather mature Neo-Pentecostal tradition. Furthermore, it purposely included among its members individuals of professional competence who were themselves Charismatic Renewal participants. As the committee deliberated, it was quickly discerned that Pentecostalism is not merely the exercise of glossolalia (a false assumption present in previous reports of other denominations). And a sincere attempt was made to consider exegetical and psychological evidence presented by persons both within and outside the Pentecostal movement. The committee's final report (which allows for further research and ongoing discussion) welcomes the new ecumenical contacts with Classical Pentecostalism; requests tolerance on the part of ministers, sessions, and presbyteries toward Neo-Pentecostalism in their churches; urges that *charismata* always be practiced "decently and in order" (the Pauline injunction); and expresses its approval of the renewing work of the Holy Spirit wherever such activity is to be found.[14] It also provides specific guidelines on how churches ought to deal with the Pentecostal experience when it arises in their midst.[15] Under the rubric of "guidelines for all" (the "general" category), the United Presbyterian committee suggests the following:

1. Be tolerant and accepting of those whose Christian experiences differ from your own.
2. Continually undergird and envelop all discussions, conferences, meetings, and persons in prayer.
3. Be open to new ways in which God by his Spirit may be speaking to the Church.
4. Recognize that even though spiritual gifts may be abused, this does not mean that they should be prohibited.
5. Remember that like other new movements in church history, Neo-Pentecostalism may have a valid contribution to make to the ecumenical Church.[16]

The Roman Catholic bishops of the United States also appointed a committee (this time, an episcopal commission) to study Charismatic Renewal in its Catholic form. Like the United Presbyterian document, this report, presented in November 1969, does not equate Pentecostalism merely with speaking in tongues. It shows an awareness of problems raised by the movement and calls for the exercise of critical judgment, while it too encourages further study. The report is essentially positive, affirming that "theologically the movement has legitimate reasons for existence. It has a strong biblical basis."[17] Stressing the need for adequate ecclesiastical supervision of Charismatic Renewal in the Catholic context, the episcopal commission recommends the following:

> It is the conclusion of the Committee on Doctrine that the movement should at this point not be inhibited but allowed to develop. Certain cautions, however, must be expressed. Proper supervision can be effectively exercised only if the Bishops keep in mind their pastoral responsibility to oversee and guide this movement in the Church. We must be on guard that they avoid the mistakes of classic Pentecostalism. It must be recognized that in our culture there is a tendency to substitute religious experience for religious doctrine. In practice we recommend that Bishops involve prudent priests to be associated with this movement. Such involvement and guidance would be welcomed by the Catholic Pentecostals.[18]

Reasons why the historic denominations have moved from opposition (in some cases) to acceptance (even approval) of Neo-Pentecostalism are rather easily discerned. First, these denominations now understand that the Pentecostal experience is not inherently schismatic (nor psychologically damaging), and quite often tends to *increase* a person's commitment to his church instead. Second, they are convinced that, by and large, Neo-Pentecostals today are rejecting the cultural baggage (and doctrinal adiaphora) of Classical Pentecostalism. Third, the historic denominations would find it increasingly difficult to effectively suppress a movement that embraces as many individuals as are present in Charismatic Renewal. Finally, they have listened to the voices of some of their own theologians and other leaders who have spoken publicly in approval of the Pentecostal experience and of the Pentecostal movement more generally.

SOME GUARDED OPINIONS

Leaders of the historic denominations began to take positive notice of the Pentecostal movement by the early 1950s. It is probable that this new recognition was at least partly the result of David Du Plessis' contacts with the ecumenical movement since 1951.[19] Out of these contacts, Du Plessis became a personal friend of John Mackay, a one-time Presbyterian missionary to Latin America (where Pentecostalism had been experiencing dramatic growth), prominent ecumenical leader, and former president of Princeton Theological Seminary. This friendship developed to the point where Mackay invited Du Plessis to attend the Eighteenth Council of the Presbyterian World Alliance in São Paulo, Brazil, during 1959, and to give the regularly scheduled missions lectures at Princeton Seminary that same year.[20] As president of the Council, John Mackay introduced the Pentecostal leader to the assembly with the following words:

> Whatever else history may have to say about our friend, this fact will surely be recorded. This is the first confessional body that has extended recognition to the Pentecostal Movement as a sound Christian Body. The records will also show that Princeton Seminary was the first institution to recognize this by inviting our friend as missions lecturer.[21]

The Presbyterian ecumenical leader (who has been characterized as a politically radical evangelical) seems to have been impressed by Pentecostalism chiefly because of its phenomenal growth throughout the world, and its intense spirituality. Hence, he states (referring to the Pentecostals):

> Never . . . be afraid of a young fanatic or what appears to be a fanatical movement, if Jesus Christ is the supreme object of devotion. On the other hand I am ter-

ribly afraid of a cold, frigid, professionally-aired Christianity which is interested only in form. The young fanatic, if wisely dealt with, can be toned down and mellowed. However, nothing short of the sepulcher awaits those who identify conventional order and aesthetic devotion with spiritual life.[22]

In 1954 (in *The Household of God*), Lesslie Newbigin, then a bishop of the Church of South India, and later associate general secretary of the World Council of Churches, described Pentecostalism as a third stream in contemporary Christianity—with Protestantism (emphasizing faith) and Catholicism (stressing order).[23] He suggested that Pentecostalism, with its emphasis on experience and the Holy Spirit (doctrinally central to the ecumenical movement), is needed, therefore, to supplement the Protestant-Catholic ecumenical debate. In this connection, Newbigin declares:

> May it not be that the great Churches of the Catholic and Protestant traditions will have to be humble enough to receive it [i.e., illumination] in fellowship with their bretheren in various groups of the Pentecostal type with whom at present they have scarcely any Christian fellowship at all?[24]

Another very positive assessment of the Pentecostal movement was voiced in 1958 by the late Henry P. Van Dusen, a liberal Presbyterian, then president of Union Theological Seminary, and chairman of the Joint Committee of the World Council of Churches and the International Missionary Council. In an article in *Life* magazine (June 9, 1958), Van Dusen (like Newbigin) referred to Pentecostalism as a "Third Force" in modern Christianity (though he also includes other distinctively fundamentalist and evangelical churches). And like Mackay, he was impressed by the Third Force's growth, deep spirituality, and sense of commitment:

> Its groups preach a direct biblical message readily understood. They commonly promise an immediate, life-trans-

forming experience of the living God-in-Christ. . . .
They directly approach people . . . anywhere—and do
not wait for them to come to church. They have great
spiritual ardor. . . . They shepherd their converts in an
intimate, sustaining group-fellowship. . . . They place
strong emphasis on the Holy Spirit . . . as the immediate potent presence of God. . . . Above all, they expect
their followers to practice an active, untiring, seven-day-
a-week Christianity. . . . Until lately, other Protestants
regarded the movement as a temporary and passing phenomenon, not worth much attention. Now there is a
growing, serious recognition of its true dimensions and
probable permanence. The tendency to dismiss its Christian message as inadequate is being replaced by a chas-
tened readiness to investigate the secrets of its mighty
sweep, especially to learn if it may have important,
neglected elements in full and true Christian witness.[25]

By the end of the 1950s, it was clear that the ecumenical movement and some of its most prominent leaders had begun to take
the Pentecostal movement seriously as a legitimate Christian expression. This new positive attitude toward what is now Classical
Pentecostalism has been extended toward Charismatic Renewal in
the course of its development during the 1960s and 1970s to the
point where Krister Stendahl, dean of the Harvard Divinity
School, said in his 1972 address to the Society for Pentecostal
Studies:

The "flashlight church" does not have enough to offer.
The high voltage religious experience is a breakthrough
phenomenon because it is needed. If churches are not
open to an infusion of high voltage, they are in real trou-
ble. . . .
    God is upping the voltage in many places. He knows
that it could be dangerous but he knows that it is
needed, and that is the new Pentecostalism.[26]

Slower to respond were leaders of the distinctively evangelical
community (who, theologically, were closer to the Pentecostals
than were mainline ecumenical liberals). Among the most impor-

tant evangelical voices to speak positively (though not uncritically) of Classical Pentecostalism and, later, Charismatic Renewal, has been *Eternity* magazine, published in Philadelphia. In 1958, *Eternity*'s founding editor, Donald Grey Barnhouse, announced in a major article in the journal that its editors (largely evangelical Presbyterians) had found themselves in "95 per cent agreement" (doctrinally) with the leaders of the Assemblies of God.[27] Later, in 1963, Russell Hitt, Barnhouse's successor, wrote a somewhat critical but still open article on Neo-Pentecostalism.[28] Then, in 1973, an unsigned editorial in *Eternity* put forward a very positive position on the *charismata*:

> More and more evangelical scholars today feel that the traditional, supposed biblical arguments for the cessation of the gifts after completion of the New Testament, cannot be sustained by the Holy Scriptures.
>
> The new stress is on the church as the body of Christ with its various members endowed by the Spirit with differing gifts. The gifts are "apportioned to each of us as the Spirit chooses" (I Cor. 12:11, Goodspeed). And who would rule out tongues as one of these gifts? Certainly Paul didn't.[29]

After a visit in California with Jean Stone in early 1962, Phillip Hughes, a Church of England clergyman and editor of the evangelical quarterly *The Churchman* (and a contributing editor to *Christianity Today*), had high praise for the emerging Charismatic Renewal. In an editorial in *The Churchman* later that year, Hughes made the following comments about Neo-Pentecostalism:

> It is transforming lives. It is revitalizing congregations. It is not confined to one church or to one district. Nor is it induced from without, but has the appearance of being a spontaneous movement of the Holy Spirit. Your Editor met with individuals and groups whose lives had been affected by it. He attended their prayer meetings and worshipped with them, and visited the homes of some. He heard them praying in an unknown tongue. It was all restrained and calm, and immediately someone else would interpret what had been said. . . . Much more

impressive than the glossolalia were the love, the joy, the devotion, which flowed out from their lips and their lives —and their consciousness of spiritual power [Kildahl's observation as well]. . . .

It is a movement, moreover, within the heart of the Church, not away from the Church. . . .[30]

Even *Christianity Today,* evangelicalism's most influential periodical, in 1969 urged a tolerant attitude by churches toward Christians who speak in tongues.[31]

Besides liberal Protestants and Anglicans and evangelical leaders, numerous prominent Roman Catholic scholars and church officials have expressed their (again, not uncritical) approval of the Pentecostal movement. Kilian McDonnell, president of the Institute for Ecumenical and Cultural Research, Collegeville, Minnesota, has conducted research into the movement and written favorably about it in *Worship,*[32] *Journal of Ecumenical Studies,*[33] *Commonweal,*[34] *Dialog,*[35] *Religion in Life,*[36] and elsewhere. Bishop Emmett Carter of London, Ontario, Canada,[37] and Archbishop Philip Hannan of New Orleans[38] (among other bishops) have also praised Charismatic Renewal; while Léon Joseph Cardinal Suenens, archbishop of Malines-Brussels, himself now a participant, speaking at the 1973 Charismatic Renewal conference at Notre Dame University, gave his very enthusiastic endorsement of the movement, declaring: "In the name of the Church we thank you, for the future of the Church is coming out of this."[39] (Roman Catholics usually stress Neo-Pentecostalism's emphasis of "renewal" of the church, particularly as it may relate to the decrees of Vatican II.)

But *some* prominent fundamentalist and evangelical thinkers remain quite negative about Charismatic Renewal and the Pentecostal experience. Dispensational fundamentalists, as we have said, generally insist that the *charismata* disappeared at the close of the apostolic era.[40] Typical of this position is J. Vernon McGee's argument. McGee, former pastor of the independent Church of the Open Door, in Los Angeles, is one of America's foremost dispensational fundamentalist spokesmen. He says:

We have seen the importance of sign gifts [i.e., "supernatural" *charismata*] at the beginning of the transitional

period [between the dispensations of law and grace]. But
these gifts disappeared. You may say to me, "Are you
sure they disappeared?" I want to say to you categorically, and emphatically, that the sign gifts disappeared
and the Scriptures said they would [citing I Cor. 13].[41]

This position has led to the charge commonly made by dispensational fundamentalists that current "Charismatic manifestations" are, in fact, counterfeits—perhaps even "Satanic" in nature.

Less severe, but still negative, in his criticism of the Pentecostal
experience is John Stott, prominent Church of England Evangelical, and former rector of All Souls Church, Langham Place, London. In his widely circulated study *The Baptism and Fullness of
the Holy Spirit*, Stott carefully does exegesis of relevant New Testament passages pertaining to Spirit baptism, and *separates* this
experience of all Christians (he feels)—identified with conversion
—from the variety of spiritual gifts given by God to his people
(including, in some instances, tongues). He concludes his essay by
saying:

It is spiritual *graces* which should be common to all
Christians, not spiritual *gifts* or spiritual *experiences*.
The gifts of the Spirit are distributed among different
Christians (I Cor. 12); it is the fruit of the Spirit which
should characterize all. . . . I would appeal to you not
to urge upon people a baptism with the Spirit as a second and subsequent experience entirely distinct from
conversion, for this cannot be proved from Scripture.[42]

Finally, Francis Schaeffer, an evangelical culture-critic (in *The
New Super-Spirituality*), also puts forward a negative assessment
of Neo-Pentecostalism on the basis of what he feels is its weak-
ened doctrinal commitment—its emphasis on "external signs" instead of theological "content"—and its spiritual elitism. Schaeffer
thinks that one reason why some theological liberals find Charismatic Renewal attractive is the fact that experience ("feeling")
functions as the central "doctrine" of both Pentecostalism (less so
in Classical Pentecostalism than in Neo-Pentecostalism) and

liberalism (with its roots in Schleiermacher and later in existentialism). He declares:

> One can . . . see a parallel between the new Pentecostals and the liberals. The liberal theologians don't believe in content or religious truth. They are really existentialists using theological, Christian terminology. Consequently, not believing in truth, they can enter into fellowship with any other experience-oriented group using religious language.[43]

REACTIONS FROM CLASSICAL PENTECOSTALISM

Since the initial emergence of Charismatic Renewal, Classical Pentecostals and Neo-Pentecostals have, in fact, enjoyed fellowship together and have had mutual "working relationships." Both participate in the Full Gospel Business Men's Fellowship International and in more localized ministries such as those of the Kathryn Kuhlman Foundation and Melodyland Christian Center. Neo-Pentecostals and Classical Pentecostals teach at Oral Roberts University, participate together in the newly formed Society for Pentecostal Studies, and are members of the five-year "dialogue" between Pentecostals and the Vatican's Secretariat for Promoting Christian Unity. Furthermore, we have seen that Classical Pentecostalism, as it continues to lose its sectarian characteristics, moves closer to Neo-Pentecostalism. Protestant and Catholic Neo-Pentecostals often worship regularly in Classical Pentecostal churches (in addition to their own)—and, sometimes, vice versa. Some Classical Pentecostal congregations, moreover, without forsaking denominational identity (usually congregations of the Assemblies of God or the International Church of the Foursquare Gospel), have gone so far as to remove the denominational title from their local church name, replacing it with a name that would appeal to a wider spectrum of people (e.g., Christian Center [after Melodyland], Christian Life Church, and The Church on the Way,[44]). Such a change in name usually has been preceded by a distinct modification of worship style approximating that of Charismatic Renewal.

Already in 1961, Donald Gee, the British Assemblies of God

leader, welcomed the fellowship of Neo-Pentecostals. Writing in *Pentecost,* he said:

> We are thrilled at what God is doing these days in bringing so many hundreds of our fellow-believers in the older denominations into Pentecostal blessing. This grace is being bestowed conspicuously, though by no means exclusively, among our friends of the Anglican Communion. They are speaking with new tongues as the Spirit gives them utterance, even as we. Let us unitedly worship God for this and other manifestations of His Spirit.[45]

But American Assemblies of God leaders were not so quick to approve Charismatic Renewal. Both David Du Plessis and Ralph Wilkerson lost their ministerial status in and were "disfellowshiped" by the denomination for their ecumenical activities. Yet, by 1963, officials of the Assemblies of God and the Episcopal Church (which at that time, perhaps, embraced more Neo-Pentecostals than any other denomination) were already meeting together to "learn from each other about Christian faith and life." The church executives of both denominations indicated

> a mutual recognition that we were servants of the same Father, the same Son and the same Holy Spirit. We are eagerly waiting to be led by the Spirit and believe that He will lead us as we continue our conversation together.[46]

Finally, in 1972, the executive presbytery of the Assemblies of God (U.S.A.) *endorsed* Charismatic Renewal (in principle, at least), wishing "to identify with what God is doing in the world today."[47]

Nevertheless, there remains much suspicion on the part of Classical Pentecostals toward Neo-Pentecostalism. Ray Hughes, former general overseer of the Church of God (Cleveland, Tennessee), is one of Charismatic Renewal's severest critics from the Classical Pentecostal side (especially with respect to non-evangelicals and Roman Catholics who claim the Pentecostal experience). Hughes questions basic Neo-Pentecostal theology and ethics for (1) emphasizing an experience seemingly without major attention to belief and doctrine; (2) denying (in some cases) that speaking in tongues is a *normative* experience integrally linked to Spirit baptism; (3) affirming that glossolalia (apparently) is enough to unite people of very different theologies (i.e., evangelicals with Protestant and Anglican liberals, and Roman Catholics); (4) allowing such practices as social dancing, drinking, and smoking ("A body controlled by lust and sinful habits certainly could not be inhabited by the Holy Ghost."); and (5) regarding "separate" prayer meetings apart from formal services of worship as sufficient for corporate expression of spiritual gifts.[48]

Although Ray Hughes probably speaks for the majority of Classical Pentecostal critics of Charismatic Renewal, it is clear that such criticism (and that raised by leaders of the historic denominations and by distinctive evangelicals) is waning. Opposition to Neo-Pentecostalism continues to turn into acceptance, if not approval.

CHAPTER EIGHT: *The Reasons for Success*

We have already considered Luther Gerlach and Virginia Hine's proposal of five factors crucial to the growth and spread of a modern religious movement:

1. reticulate *organization*
2. fervent and convincing *recruitment* along pre-existing lines of significant social relationships
3. a *commitment* act or experience
4. a change-oriented and action-motivating ideology that offers (a) a simple master plan presented in symbolic and easily communicated terms, (b) a sense of sharing in the control and rewards of destiny, (c) a feeling of personal worth and power
5. the perception of real or imagined *opposition*.[1]

As Gerlach and Hine have shown, these factors necessary for the growth and spread of a modern religious movement apply well to the Pentecostal movement as a whole.[2] But a number of other reasons can be suggested for the emergence and success of Neo-Pentecostalism in particular.

THE ECUMENICAL MOVEMENT

"Unity in the Spirit" has become a central theological motif within the ecumenical movement. On the Protestant (and Anglican) side of that movement, a new emphasis upon the doctrine of the Holy Spirit was signaled by the appearance of Lesslie Newbigin's book *The Household of God* in 1954. (Newbigin, then a bishop of the Church of South India, later became an associate general secretary of the World Council of Churches.) In *The Household of God*, he maintains that Catholicism, stressing the given structure (order), and Protestantism, emphasizing the given message (faith), have been engaged in an "incomplete dialogue" —lacking the Holy Spirit aspect of theology, which is crucial to Christian unity. To remedy this incompleteness, Newbigin, as we have already seen, suggests conversations with a "third stream" of Christian tradition—the Pentecostal—whose central theological element is

> the conviction that the Christian life is a matter of *the experienced power and presence of the Holy Spirit today* [emphasis mine]; that neither orthodoxy of doctrine nor impeccability of succession can take the place of this; that an excessive emphasis upon those immutable elements in the Gospel upon which orthodox Catholicism and Protestantism have concentrated attention, may, and in fact often does, result in a Church which is a mere shell, having the form of a Church but not the life; that if we would answer the question "Where is the Church?," we must ask, "Where is the Holy Spirit recognizably present with power?"[3]

The former WCC associate general secretary then goes on to declare:

> Unless the living Spirit Himself takes the things of Christ and shows them to us, we cannot know them. Unless *He* unites us to the ascended Christ we cannot be united.[4]

In 1961, in New Delhi, the Third General Assembly of the World Council of Churches reiterated this theological tenet that the Spirit functions as the key to Christian unity by saying:

> We believe that the unity which is God's will and his gift to his Church is being made visible as all in each place who are baptized into Jesus Christ and confess him as Lord and Saviour are *brought by the Holy Spirit* [emphasis mine] into one fully committed fellowship.[5]

And Newbigin's plea for ecumenical-Pentecostal contact was also realized largely, as we have seen, through the personal efforts of David Du Plessis.

It is clear that the theological stress within the ecumenical movement upon the doctrine of the Holy Spirit (since 1953, at least) is one reason for the emergence and success of Charismatic Renewal—emphasizing the Spirit's work—in denominations closely aligned with the ecumenical movement throughout the world. But it is the Roman Catholic Church, through Pope John XXIII and Vatican II, which has been primarily responsible for the development of a modern theology of the Holy Spirit pertaining to ecumenism. That theological emphasis (rooted in Pope John's "New Pentecost") is a prime factor to explain the growth and spread of the Pentecostal movement within Catholicism.

VATICAN II

Stephen Neill declares: "Nothing in the records of the Vatican Council is more remarkable than the constant references, both in speeches and in documents, to the Holy Spirit. . . ."[6] Again, much of Vatican's focus upon the work of the Spirit can be traced to Pope John's prayer for a New Pentecost marked by unity in the Holy Spirit:

> May there be repeated thus in the Christian families the spectacle of the apostles gathered together in Jerusalem after the Ascension of Jesus to heaven, when the newborn Church was completely united in communion of thought and prayer. . . . And may the Divine Spirit deign to answer in a most comforting manner the prayer that rises daily to Him from every corner of the earth: "Renew your wonders in our time, as though for a new Pentecost. . . ."[7]

That the Spirit is, in fact, the center of Christian unity is affirmed in the Vatican Council's decree "On Ecumenism":

> It is the Holy Spirit, dwelling in those who believe, pervading and ruling over the entire Church, who brings about that marvelous communion of the faithful and

joins them together so intimately in Christ that He is the *principle* of the Church's unity [emphasis mine].[8]

With respect to spiritual gifts in particular—so important in Pentecostal theology—Vatican II accepted and encouraged the continued operation of *charismata* in the life of the church. The document entitled "The Church" declares:

It is not only through the sacraments and Church ministries that the same Holy Spirit sanctifies and leads the people of God and enriches it with virtues. Allotting his gifts to everyone according as he will (I Cor. 12:11), he distributes special graces among the faithful of every rank. By these gifts he makes them fit and ready to undertake the various tasks or offices advantageous for the renewal and upbuilding of the Church, according to the words of the Apostle: "The manifestation of the Spirit is given to everyone for profit" (I Cor. 12:7). These charismatic gifts, whether they be the most outstanding or the more simple and widely diffused, are to be received with thanksgiving and consolation, for they are exceedingly suitable and useful for the needs of the Church.[9]

If the ecumenical movement itself together with its growing stress on the Holy Spirit as the principle of Christian unity is one factor to explain the emergence and success of Charismatic Renewal, Pope John's New Pentecost, with its implications for Vatican II and the Roman Catholic Church thereafter, represents another factor—especially with respect to Catholic participation in the Pentecostal movement since 1967 (two years after the close of the Vatican Council). For, by emphasizing the unifying work of the Spirit (even more than ecumenical Protestantism had done until then), Vatican II officially sanctioned the operation of *charismata* in the contemporary Catholic Church (though it certainly did not endorse the Pentecostal experience per se).[10] Furthermore, the Vatican Council *encouraged* Roman Catholics to build positive relationships with their Protestant—albeit separated"—brethren by visiting their services of worship and other meetings. It was these new relationships that brought Catholics and Pentecostals together in a significant way and that obviously, first introduced Catholics to the Pentecostal experience as a *legitimate* experience of Christian spirituality.[11]

WIDER ACCEPTANCE OF THEOLOGICAL DISSENT

The decade of the 1960s was marked by an increasing toleration of (even radical) theological dissent within the historic denominations. If the iconoclastic views of the late Episcopal Bishop James Pike of California and those of Bishop J. A. T. Robinson (formerly of Woolwich) could be tolerated (and sometimes applauded) within the Anglican Communion, then it was perhaps not difficult for this church to accommodate Pentecostal priests like Dennis Bennett, Michael Harper, and Graham Pulkingham. The same is generally true of other historic denominations as well. Furthermore, wider acceptance of theological dissent within the institutional church (epitomized, perhaps, by the "death of God" movement in the late 1960s) has actually helped bring about the growth and spread of Charismatic Renewal in those denominations. Thus, in 1968, Oral Roberts was welcomed into the ministry of the United Methodist Church. Roberts felt that if the United Methodist Church could embrace theological radicals, it could also accept Pentecostals (even one as "notorious" as himself). His words praising the inclusive character of modern Methodism apply more or less, to most of the other historic denominations today[12]:

> I began to feel that God was leading me to transfer to the Methodist Church. To my mind, the Methodist Church was more than a denomination. It represented all the diverse elements of historic Christianity. In its membership and ministry were deeply committed evangelicals. Yet it had radical liberals, too. More importantly, it had maintained a free pulpit; Methodist ministers could preach their convictions.[13]

GENERAL SPREAD OF SECULARISM

During the course of the second half of the twentieth century, the secularization of Western culture has become a fact. Among other scholars, Bryan Wilson suggests simply that religion has lost its influence on society and this is evidenced by the atrophy of religious *practice* (as in Scandinavia); by the transformation of religious *institutions* into organizations that incorporate all the rational bureaucratic authority suppositions of other, nonreligious organizations of the wider (advanced, technological) society (as in the United States); and, most of all, by a fundamental change in religious thinking. Wilson declares:

> Men act less and less in response to religious motivation: they assess the world in empirical and rational terms, and find themselves involved in rational organizations and rationally determined roles which allow small scope for such predilections as they might privately entertain. Even if, as some sociologists have argued, non-logical behaviour continues in unabated measure in human society, then at least the terms of non-rationality have changed. It is no longer the dogmas of the Christian Church which dictate behaviour, but quite other irrational and arbitrary assumptions about life, society and the laws which govern the physical universe.[14]

With the advance of secularization, church-going, even in the United States in recent years, is declining in proportion to population growth. People no longer feel *compelled* to attend church on Sunday for reasons of "social respectability." Furthermore, it is the "mainline" denominations—whose clergy and structures have been most thoroughly secularized—that are the ones particularly (and most visibly) affected by declining membership and attendance. Sociologist Peter Berger says:

> *If* there is going to be a renascence of religion, its bearers will *not* be the people who have been falling all over each other to be "relevant to modern man." To the extent that modernity and secularization have been closely linked phenomena in Western history, any movement of countersecularization would imply a repudiation of "modern man" as hitherto conceived. . . .[15]

Among other things, secularization of the wider affluent and technological society has brought with it boredom, loss of meaning, and a sense of aimlessness in life, while increased permissiveness (also associated with secularization) has produced a new interest in discipline. In his recent study of American denominations, *Why Conservative Churches Are Growing*, Dean Kelley maintains that "conservative" (i.e., less secularized) churches are growing because they provide the meaning and insist on the discipline (strictness) that an increasing number of people desire in order to regain direction for their lives.

It is apparent, moreover, that with the ever more pervasive rationalization and routinization of life inherent in secularization, the "nonrational," the ecstatic, has again become appealing. In secular society, it is quite understandable that an experiential religious style that also provides meaning and discipline to those for whom religion is still (potentially, at least) a powerful determinant of the conduct of their lives, has become attractive. Charismatic Renewal, which clearly can be interpreted as a movement of countersecularization, is characterized by such a style, and owes its growth and spread, emergence, and success, in part, to the new enthusiasm for religious experience in Western culture today.[16]

YOUNG PEOPLE

In discussing secularization, Bryan Wilson points out that the sense of mystery, the religious meaning of objects, has waned steadily in the West. A demystified world means that everyday thinking has become more instrumental and matter-of-fact, that emotional involvement with nature, the community, and other humans has been reduced, and that, as we have said, the external world has been drained of meaning.[17] Among young people, the "countercultural" movement of the 1960s was an attempt to challenge these trends—to recover the sense of mystery in life, to reject the matter-of-fact character of everyday life, to build community, and to relate emotionally with nature again. Thus the "back to the land" and ecology movements came into being, as did handicrafts and communes, new ("alternative") life-styles, *and* enthusiastic religion (whether Eastern or Western), with a

transcendent emphasis. Pentecostalism, with its inherent spontaneity (particularly as expressed in the Jesus movement), was
sufficiently compatible with countercultural life-styles to gain acceptance among the young (the institutional church was not). It
provided "instant community" (a major emphasis) and contributed to the restoration of the meaning of life and the mystery
behind it (including the possibilities of predictive prophecy, divine healing, and speaking "a heavenly language" [glossolalia]).
For the young, with whom even the eighteenth- and nineteenth-
century revivalists had their greatest successes,[18] Pentecostalism
has been an attempt to escape the routinization of modern life in
secular society, and it has been a major vehicle through which an
answer to the current search for authenticity or reality in living[19]
(something more often *felt* than learned) is carried—symbolized
by the "One Way" slogan of the Jesus movement (John 14:6).[20]
Hence its emergence and success among young people should
come as no surprise. To quote Pat Boone, a former "teen-age
idol," on the matter:

> These young people are searching for reality. The
> church, as they see it today, doesn't have it. They see its
> failures, double standards, lack of concern, and are
> turned off. Even much of what we call "evangelical
> Christianity" has way too little to offer them. Because
> doctrine, no matter how pure or correct it may be, *is not
> enough*.[21]

IN THE MIDDLE CLASS

Reasons for the continued growth and spread of Charismatic
Renewal in the middle class have already been put forth. Not
unlike those reasons pertinent to the young, they include the appeal to the alleviation of "affluent boredom." Pentecostalism represents something meaningful to do and experience *now*. In the
Pentecostal experience, the life to come can already be "tasted"
(i.e., "new wine") in the here and now. Also, Neo-Pentecostalism
is one manifestation of the increased middle-class acceptance of
emotional expression as part of everyday life. *Men* are now "allowed" to cry in public; speaking in tongues can be "therapeutic";

and nonverbal forms of communication (e.g., distinctive prayer postures, embracing, and the laying-on-of-hands) are acceptable, even encouraged. At the same time, however, the non-middle-class cultural "excesses" of Classical Pentecostalism are rejected. Charismatic Renewal is particularly attractive to the middle class because of its legitimate, rational, educated clergy and lay leadership, and because of its well-conceived, well-ordered evangelism without the revivalistic extremes of Classical Pentecostalism. Kathryn Kuhlman has the support of at least *some* prominent medical doctors, and she is officially received by the Pope.[22] Oral Roberts, the university president, is welcomed into the ministry of the United Methodist Church. And Neo-Pentecostal leaders such as Rodman Williams, Edward O'Connor, Donald Gelpi, and Josephine Ford continue to function as respected members of the academic-theological community. Social or psychic deprivation within Charismatic Renewal, as we have seen, is not easily documented.[23]

STATISTICS

Any discussion of reasons for the emergence and success of Neo-Pentecostalism remains incomplete without at least some attempt to deal with actual constituency statistics. Reliable statistics for Classical Pentecostalism are hard enough to find; but for Charismatic Renewal, the problem is even more severe. First, unlike a church or denomination, there is no formal membership for the movement as a whole. Informal prayer groups come, go, and coalesce. Without a separate organizational structure, numbers and turnover in the movement are hard to estimate. (Neo-Pentecostal literature is purchased both by participants and nonparticipants; thus, publication and distribution figures are not definitive.) Second, enthusiastic religious groups are prone to exaggerate statistics. And third, continuing rapid growth insures that the various "estimates" from whatever source are quickly dated. Some of these "educated guesses"—once we are aware of the limitations— nevertheless are interesting. Citing a 1967 source, Walter Hollenweger has suggested that over 1,000 Presbyterian ministers, 700 Episcopal priests (10 per cent of the total), and 10,000 Roman Catholics in the United States have received the Pentecostal expe-

rience.[24] In 1971, Melodyland Messenger estimated that 300 Neo-
Pentecostal Lutheran pastors, 500 Presbyterian ministers and 800
Baptist ministers in America were Charismatic Renewal participants[25]; while David Du Plessis speculated in 1974 that 10 per
cent of all ministers of denominations affiliated with the National
Council of Churches (about 10,000) have received the baptism of
the Holy Spirit.[26] Among all of the historic denominations in
Great Britain, 300 clergy had experienced Spirit baptism by 1970,
according to Michael Harper.[27] Of the various denominations, the
Roman Catholic Church displays what appear to be the most dramatic statistics: Edward O'Connor has suggested (conservatively)
10,000 American Catholic Pentecostals (1971)[28]; Edward Fiske of
the New York *Times* has estimated 15,000 to 50,000 (1970)[29];
and John Haughey of the Jesuit magazine *America* has brought
the total number of Catholic Pentecostals in America to over
300,000 (1973).[30]

Whatever constituency statistics are available, however, we are
tempted to assume that Neo-Pentecostalism as a movement has
grown steadily since 1960—and, at times, perhaps, dramatically;
although in any one of the historic denominations, it remains no
more than a vocal (but increasingly influential) minority.

Sources of financial support for program and paid personnel
within Charismatic Renewal include, of course, the regular
salaries given to Neo-Pentecostal clergy by their churches, as well
as money collected and distributed by Charismatic Renewal organizations. But far more important, as Luther Gerlach and Virginia Hine have stated:

> Pentecostals give personally to fellow Pentecostals believ-
> ing the recipient has been called by God to do a specific
> work. The giver believes in the work as much as the
> recipient—but thinks the recipient can do it better.[31]

Finally, we ought to say something about constituency transience within Neo-Pentecostalism. Again, any statistics at all are
very hard to locate. Although it is apparent that once-avid participants do occasionally leave the movement, there seems to be a
tendency to do so "quietly." Dissident members of sectarian religious groups often quit (i.e., "defect"), then immediately begin

vocally to "denounce" the group, its teachings, and leadership. But Charismatic Renewal, generally devoid of the ethical rigorism, questionable leadership (e.g., mesmeric "prophets," and charlatans) and esoteric doctrines that are present in many religious sects, does not readily foster transience based upon these sectarian characteristics. A good deal of theological and ethical diversity is tolerated. Thus, those who do leave the movement probably do so, more often than not, for sheer loss of interest.[32]

CHARISMATIC RENEWAL AND TRENDS IN THE WIDER SOCIETY

The emergence, development, and success of Neo-Pentecostalism as a religious movement should not be considered in isolation from the trends in society as a whole that have certainly contributed to the movement's growth.

RELIGIOUS EXPERIENCE AND "INSTANTISM" IN MODERN CULTURE

We have already touched upon the attraction of young people and the middle class more generally to Charismatic Renewal, because it offers something to do and experience now. The new enthusiasm for religious experience is one of the more surprising developments of the past decade in the larger society. Often, moreover, this enthusiasm has occurred in people who have abandoned churches and formal religion. Some are consciously seeking a personal encounter with God; but for others, the search for experience is less consciously religious—involving the use of drugs, certain kinds of music and dancing, even occult practices. In addition, very little *patience* is apparent in this quest; results are expected immediately. The enthusiasm for experience, and impatience for that experience ("instantism") are integrally related in modern culture.

In Classical Pentecostalism, religious experience has indeed been a central feature and attraction. But the Pentecostal experience here has tended to be *cumulative* rather than *intrinsic* (instantaneous). In many Pentecostal denominations, religious experience is still conceived to involve, at its core, *three* stages of development, not necessarily in short succession. Conversion ("a personal experience with Jesus") is the first. Second, there is sanctification as a distinct and identifiable experience (a *gradual* process in some Pentecostal denominations, however). Third, Spirit baptism with the initial evidence of speaking in tongues is sought—followed, in due course, by one or more of the spiritual gifts. The whole experiential process may take many hours of personal and corporate prayer, with "pleading" and "tarrying at the altar" over a period of months or even years. Then, given the strong Arminian character of Classical Pentecostalism, even a Spirit-filled believer may "fall from grace" ("backslide") and have to "do the first works over" again—begin the experiential process anew. Furthermore, it is always quicker and far easier to backslide than to be converted, sanctified, and baptized in the Spirit.

In Charismatic Renewal, however, personal religious experience is largely intrinsic (e.g., the "NOW" experience of Oral Roberts). Sanctification (holiness), as we have said, has been spiritualized and socialized. Conversion—personal commitment to Jesus as an act of the will—is insisted upon; but immediately thereafter, Spirit baptism becomes a real possibility. Sometimes, moreover, conversion and the baptism of the Holy Spirit occur virtually at the same time, so that the experiences of Spirit baptism and conversion can hardly be distinguished from each other.

In Classical Pentecostalism, much time is often spent by a candidate for Spirit baptism *waiting* for the initial evidence and/or gift of tongues. It is something that "just happens"—suddenly, sometimes after years of "seeking." But in Charismatic Renewal, one can expect a much quicker response. Fluency in glossolalia, Neo-Pentecostals admit, comes only with much practice (i.e., it is, obviously, a form of "learned behavior"); but the first "sounds" can be articulated almost at once. Thus, Dennis and Rita Bennett say:

> When you received Jesus as Savior, you believed in your heart and confessed Him with your lips [conversion]. Now confess with your lips, but in the new language that the Lord is ready to give you. Open your mouth and show that you believe the Lord has baptized you in the Spirit by *beginning to speak*. Don't speak English, or any other language you know. . . .
>
> We are teaching . . . that these first efforts at obeying the Spirit are only the beginning. It doesn't matter if

the first sounds are just "priming the pump," for the real
flow will assuredly come. . . .

You may begin to speak, but only get out a few halt-
ing sounds. . . . Offer them to God. . . . As you do,
they will develop and grow into a fully developed language.[33]

It is not uncommon in Charismatic Renewal for a nonbeliever to
be converted to Christ and baptized in the Spirit (with the "beginning of speaking in tongues"[34]) in the course of one experience
of the laying-on-of-hands. Hence, Neo-Pentecostalism, more than
Classical Pentecostalism, accommodates the current enthusiasm
for a "full" religious experience *now*.

INCREASED LEISURE TIME

It is clear that the greatly increased affluence and abundant
spare time characteristic of large segments of modern society—
including those in the historic churches, and even some of the
Pentecostal denominations today—have continued to the emergence and success of Charismatic Renewal. Millionaires and other
well-to-do people in the movement, most of whom are connected
with the Full Gospel Business Men's Fellowship International
(major supporters of Oral Roberts University, for instance[35]),
constitute one important factor in its growth and spread. Included among them are Demos Shakarian, one-time millionaire
dairyman, and founder-president of the FGBMFI[36]; Pat Boone,
the entertainer and businessman[37]; George Otis, an electronics
manufacturer[38] and an early patron of the Blessed Trinity Society.[39] Otis describes the life just before his involvement in Charismatic Renewal (he was encouraged by Shakarian):

That Saturday morning in Bel Air [California], with
more than half of my life gone, something like a video
replay surged before me. An audit of my life flashed by;
listed among the Young Millionaires . . . a member of
Young Presidents' Organization (acquiring the presi-
dency of a million-dollar plus organization before the age
of 40) . . . head of a well-known electronics firm with a

Cadillac in the garage and an airplane at Santa Monica. I was a jet-setter for sure—and this world called me "a big success."[40]

Then he goes on to describe the degree to which his business duties (e.g., travel) have enabled him, after his conversion, to evangelize, to witness to his faith and Pentecostal experience throughout the world:

Desire to proclaim Christ's magnificence has propelled me since that [FGBMFI] chapter meeting some half-million miles. I've traveled from the Arctic Circle to Tasmania and from Tahiti to India, to share with all who will listen—from the children of the night to polished mansion halls; in Rotary clubs, hotels and auditoriums; on aircraft carriers and in dung huts, television stations, government offices, Pentagon corridors, movie studios, monasteries, universities and churches.[41]

The affluence of many participants in Charismatic Renewal (together with the sacrificial giving of ordinary lay people as well) has allowed prominent clergy (preacher-lecturers) in the movement like David Du Plessis, Dennis Bennett, Michael Harper, Ralph Wilkerson, and a host of others to become world travelers in evangelism. The fact that corporate executives can leave their work for weeks at a time whenever they wish has resulted in the feasibility of FGBMFI international airlifts,[42] and international Neo-Pentecostal conventions, held thus far in England; in Notre Dame, Indiana (and other parts of the United States); Rome; and in Jerusalem[43]—even a world tour, sponsored by Melodyland Christian Center in 1972–73[44]—all attended by wealthy supporting lay people, prominent clergy and other leaders, and middle-class participants "on vacation." Active participation in Charismatic Renewal requires the contribution of time and money to *two* religious affiliations—the movement, *and* one's own church (a departure from the long-standing Christian idea that there can be just one central religious loyalty). This kind of costly personal involvement, obviously, could not be so widespread without the increased availability of leisure time and the higher income levels characteristic of large segments of contemporary Western society. And it is manifestly apparent that Charismatic Renewal participants have found the movement to offer an especially viable use for their money and spare time.

It is almost a truism to speak of the pervasiveness of anti-institutional sentiment in contemporary Western culture. There seems to be little interest in building new bureaucratic structures or superstructures to replace old ones. In the religious sector, this feeling is perhaps best illustrated by the virtual collapse of major efforts at organic church union that emerged in the 1960s—most notably, the failures of the Anglican-Methodist merger talks in England and the Consultation on Church Union (COCU), involving ten denominations, in the United States—and the weakening of the World Council of Churches and its regional counterparts, especially the National Council of Churches (U.S.A.). The prevalence of such anti-institutional sentiment makes Charismatic Renewal attractive as a movement of *spiritual* unity in diversity that seeks to revitalize ("renew") *existing* church structures rather than to tear them down to build new ones. In this connection, it is also important to underscore the contemporary viability of the persistence of a *movement* without coherent internal structure, hierarchy, or real membership—given the existence in modern society of a looser affiliation, carried by the mass media (e.g., books, magazines, newspapers, radio, television, cassette tapes, and large gatherings), without the need to bring people together for formal as distinct from expressive (e.g., fellowship and evangelistic) purposes.

"REDISCOVERY" OF THE SUPERNATURAL

Like the contemporary quest for religious experience, the fact of increased affluence and leisure time, and the attempt to destructure society, a "rediscovery" of the supernatural by the middle class in contemporary Western society has also contributed to the emergence and success of Charismatic Renewal. It is easy to understand why, in an age of the resurgence of (1) predictive prophecy, "fore-telling" rather than "forth-telling" (e.g., Jeane Dixon and Edgar Cayce), (2) psychic research (e.g., the late Bishop James Pike), (3) astrology, and (4) interest in the occult, Pentecostal phenomena such as divine healing, glossolalia, prophecy, and exorcism[45] should also be increasingly acceptable and attractive to those who, in past times, would have immediately dismissed such activities as appropriate only for the uninstructed.

CHARISMATIC RENEWAL AND OTHER MOVEMENTS

Black Power

Charismatic Renewal bears resemblance to various other relatively unstructured contemporary religious, quasi-religious, and secular movements. We have already mentioned Luther Gerlach and Virginia Hine's *People, Power, Change: Movements of Social Transformation*. This study is primarily a comparison of (Classical and Neo-) Pentecostalism with black power as movements of social transformation. The authors, interestingly enough, have discovered striking similarities between both movements in their decentralized structure, face-to-face recruitment, personal commitment, kind of ideology, and feeling of real or perceived opposition. Furthermore, Gerlach and Hine insist that there are ways in which Pentecostalism may be considered revolutionary (like black power), and black power religious (like Pentecostalism). On this particular issue, their reasoning is as follows:

> Our survey of Pentecostalism in the United States shows that participants tend to be politically conservative. Furthermore, the Pentecostal ethic militates against social change through social action. Although they envision radical political, economic, and social change here on earth, they expect this to be instituted through supernatural means. The social change associated with Pentecostalism, especially in non-Western societies moving toward industrialization, is largely an inadvertent consequence of personal change, but is nonetheless real. It should be noted that many of the newer converts who have remained in their non-Pentecostal churches, especially clergy and very active lay members, combine the radical personal change involved in the Pentecostal expe-

rience with a radical approach to social action on non-religious issues. Pentecostalism, we suggest, is conceptually revolutionary. It encourages an experience through which an individual believes himself to be radically changed; many converts behave accordingly in social situations.

Black Power, on the other hand, is clearly a movement which seeks to accomplish social change with entirely human means. But it is religious in the sense that it requires the commitment of the individual to something greater than self . . . transcending even the body of believers. . . .[46]

If Pentecostalism as a whole can be likened to black power as a movement, Neo-Pentecostalism, specifically, can also be placed side by side with other contemporary movements that emerged in the 1960s and early 1970s.

The Human Potential Movement

Kilian McDonnell, in 1968, was probably the first scholar to suggest the similarity between Charismatic Renewal and what is now known as the Human Potential movement. There is in each of these movements (one religious, one secular), he points out, a "contemporary quest for transcendence and a new synthesis."[47] Very broadly, in the group dynamics of the Human Potential movement and in the prayer meetings of Neo-Pentecostalism are demonstrated similar experiments in "community building," interpersonal honesty, and nonverbal forms of communication (e.g., hand-holding and embracing), though the ideological bases for such actions are far different.[48]

The Jesus Movement

Another movement analogous to Charismatic Renewal, if not, among young people, at least, interwined with it, was the Jesus movement, which had been visible from about 1967 until 1972.[49] Both can be considered decentralized movements with many diverse segments. The Jesus movement, composed primarily of countercultural young people, was generally open in its various groups to the Pentecostal experience with its inherent spontaneity and spiritual gifts. It was different from Neo-Pentecostalism, however, in that the Jesus People originally functioned mainly *outside* the already established churches, which they viewed as "hypocritical." But in its "maturing" process (institutionalization, perhaps), the Jesus movement began to take on more of the explicit characteristics of Charismatic Renewal. From his own research, Ronald Enroth, an evangelical sociologist and authority on the Jesus movement, has made the following observations:

> It appears that the "Jesus bandwagon" days of superficial fervor are giving way to more committed discipleship. One sign of this can be seen in the growing interest in serious Bible study. . . .
>
> Many of the Jesus people seem to have faded into the crowd—the Christian crowd. . . . [For] the young people are now attending established churches where their influence has been felt mainly in terms of more informal worship and *a new emphasis on the Holy Spirit* [emphasis mine]. . . .
>
> Another trend among young Christians who have been a part of the Jesus people movement is a return to the college campus and an increased concern to become more involved in the larger society.[50]

At the same time, the countercultural communes, collectives, and communities of the early days of the Jesus movement (such as the Christian World Liberation Front in Berkeley, California—now Berkeley Christian Coalition[51]) that are still in existence have become more formally structured—very similar in character to the growing number of Catholic Pentecostal communities.

The New Evangelicalism

Yet another "movement" akin to Charismatic Renewal is what has been termed the New Evangelicalism—an attempt (represented largely by an emerging generation of college and university students, recent theological seminary graduates, intellectuals, former "street people," activists, pastors, evangelists, and ordinary lay people) to repudiate the biblicism, anti-intellectualism, separatism, social unconcern, political conservatism, and culture rejection inherent in modern fundamentalism without forsaking the basic tenets of historic Christian orthodoxy. This developing movement, rooted in the thought of C. S. Lewis and Dietrich Bonhoeffer (his earlier writings, especially), the Radical Reformation and Wesleyan Holiness traditions, the social unrest and counterculture of the 1960s as well as the Jesus movement itself, is in many ways to fundamentalism what Neo-Pentecostalism is to Classical Pentecostalism (see Chapter Six). Like Charismatic Renewal, the New Evangelicalism is a decentralized movement with many diverse segments. It is intellectually motivated, ecumenical in spirit (critical of but not hostile to the historic denominations), and socio-politically activist, yet grounded in transcendent biblical orthodoxy.[52]

Thus we see that Charismatic Renewal shares the decentralized structural features and basic goals of other religious and secular movements that also emerged in the 1960s and early 1970s. Neo-Pentecostalism *can* be interpreted as having the revolutionary potential of black power, the relational dynamics of the Human Potential movement, the spontaneity and "spiritual community" of the Jesus movement, and the "progressive orthodoxy"[53] of the New Evangelicalism.

POSTSCRIPT: *"Beyond Fadism"*

It is apparent that we are living in an era of mesmeric prophets and religious fads that are products of the 1960s and early 1970s. Among these can be numbered Krishna Consciousness, Transcendental Meditation (Maharishi Mahesh Yogi), the Divine Light Mission (Guru Maharaj Ji), Satanism (Anton La Vey), and, in the Christian tradition, the Unification Church (Rev. Sun Myung Moon), and the many groups and cults of the Jesus movement, including the Children of God (David "Moses" Berg). Related to the emergence and success of all such movements are, again, the contemporary quest for religious experience, the trend toward interiorization, and a rediscovery of the supernatural. Their present popularity is, to some degree at least, the product of the times and the concerns of the wider culture (and counterculture). Some of these movements can easily be understood as mere religious "fads" or "crazes." Those centered on the charisma of a particular "prophet" may well rise and fall with his fortunes. The anti-institutional church Jesus movement was more closely aligned with the counterculture and its distinctive style and attire—especially the phenomenon of the "hippies"—than with any one leader. Hence, with the decline of a readily visible counterculture (including street people and "long-hairs"), the Jesus People also have lost visibility over the course of the same few years. As Ronald Enroth has suggested, many of the Jesus People have already gone back to the churches they once branded as hypocritical and "irrelevant."

The situation with Charismatic Renewal, however, is somewhat different. Although this movement's present popularity may indeed be related to contemporary trends in the wider society, we must also acknowledge the fact that Neo-Pentecostalism has apparently grown without abatement since its emergence in 1960; that Classical Pentecostalism has been an important religious force since its inception in 1901; and that Pentecostal phenomena were apparently widespread in the primitive church and in various periods of church history thereafter. To think of Charismatic Renewal as merely a fad, therefore, would probably be a mistake. Furthermore, it is quite reasonable to suppose that, given the strong New Testament justification for the operation of *charismata*, the present "renewal" of those same spiritual gifts in the life of the historic churches may signal their return on an ever-increasing scale to the church as a whole. Charismatic Renewal might well represent a movement "beyond fadism."

A PERSONAL ASSESSMENT:
CAN CHARISMATIC RENEWAL REALLY RENEW THE CHURCH?

Emmanuel Sullivan, a Franciscan friar, proposes at least three ways in which the Pentecostal movement in the historic churches may be regarded as a force for renewal. First, he suggests that there is a real *feeling* that the church, in its teaching and ritual, is not meeting the needs of the human spirit. "A theology of renewal is not renewal." Faith must be *expressed*, he says, emphasizing the fact that perhaps

> too much has been claimed in the past by cerebral theologians who have allowed a chasm to develop between the intellect articulating the faith and the emotions expressing it.[1]

Pentecostals, of course, stress, above all else, the expression of their faith.

Second, Sullivan views the Pentecostal movement as a "prayer movement," leading Christians to appropriate works of love and service. He points out that where it is allowed to grow, Pentecostalism creates "a zealous clergy and a genuinely involved laity." Furthermore, this prayer movement, in his opinion, leads to a sense of community that is much more than a mere expression of "togetherness," in that it is truly a manifestation of the church as the body of Christ.

Third, Sullivan argues that the church is of its very nature "Charismatic." New Testament teaching, to him, stresses that "God is pouring out in his Spirit the richest variety of gifts to bring us to the close of the age when God will be all in all (I Cor. 15:28)." Christians must, therefore, *expect* new and different things to happen while living in a Spirit that is "creative, loving, disturbing, and absolutely free."[2]

For Emmanuel Sullivan, spiritual renewal in the church emphasizes the presence of the Holy Spirit and his gifts. Spiritual ecumenism, he goes on to say, stresses spiritual renewal in the church as an inner law of ecumenical growth and development. Sullivan feels that the Pentecostal witness "unites spiritual renewal and spiritual ecumenism by its emphasis on the role of the Holy Spirit, the diversity of sharing his gifts, the call to conversion."[3]

Whatever we may think of the distinctives of Pentecostal faith and practice, it is necessary for us to admit that the Pentecostal experience in its Charismatic Renewal form has brought together clergy and laity of most Protestant, Anglican, Eastern Orthodox, and Catholic denominations in a heartfelt spiritual unity that the institutional ecumenical movement has been unable to match in the course of all its deliberations and pronouncements. Furthermore, it is readily apparent that Charismatic Renewal does indeed produce among its participants "a zealous clergy and a genuinely involved laity." Thus, if renewal of the church is inherently linked both to the realization of Christian unity and to the re-emergence of enlivened congregations, then Charismatic Renewal ought to be regarded as a legitimate contemporary force for renewal of the church.

APPENDIX: *Scholarly Investigations*

To the average person, glossolalia, as perhaps the most observable Pentecostal phenomenon, is the distinguishing feature of the whole movement. Therefore, it should come as no surprise that much has been written about speaking in tongues per se—both within its organizational context and as an independent phenomenon. Early scholarship on the subject includes two classics: Émile Lombard, *De la Glossolalie chez les Premiers Chrétiens et des Phénomènes Similaires: Étude d'Exégèse et de Psychologie* (1910) —viewing the phenomenon as a kind of "automatic speech"; and Eddison Mosimann, *Das Zungenreden geschichtlich und psychologisch untersucht* (1911)—which likens glossolalia to a hypnotic state. But until quite recently, the most often quoted work in the field was probably George Cutten's *Speaking with Tongues: Historically and Psychologically Considered* (1927). Cutten feels that, as a psychological condition, glossolalia may be ascribed to hysteria (extreme susceptibility to suggestion with exaggerated sensations), ecstasy, or even catalepsy (suspended animation with rigidity of the body). More recent scholarship, however, has tended to move away from the conviction of earlier works that speaking in tongues is a neurotic or psychotic symptom or a hypnotic phenomenon resulting from religious excitement— emphasizing that such assumptions have simply not been supported by conclusive empirical studies.

Lincoln Vivier, in "Glossolalia" (unpublished M.D. thesis, 1960), studied South African Pentecostals as deprived and disadvantaged people. He suggests that speaking in tongues is "dissociative"—cutting the associational bonds between words and ideas—and lists a number of criteria he feels could lead to the glossolalia phenomenon:

1. A complete projection of one's needs to something beyond oneself;
2. The absence of any formalised, traditional concepts;
3. The lack of any egoistical manipulation of the environment;
4. Sufficient emotional intensity; and
5. A "dynamic system" that could cause a dissociative state.[1]

Reflecting Jungian concepts of the collective unconscious, Vivier concludes that speaking in tongues is due to the "impact of a Religious dynamism in all its Power," not to a "basic inherent weakness in the individual."[2]

Another study influenced by Jung is Morton Kelsey's *Tongue Speaking* (1964). Kelsey believes that glossolalia is neither an ecstatic, hysterical experience, nor an innocuous liberation of strong religious emotions. He disagrees with the assertion that speaking in tongues is related to schizophrenic behavior—in that a person suffers no damage to his ego and remains able to differentiate clearly between reality and illusion both before and after the experience. Likewise, hysteria as a cause must be discounted, Kelsey says, on the grounds that hysteria is an illness harming the mind and sometimes the body; whereas glossolalia appears to result in an increased ability to cope with reality. Thus, he feels that speaking in tongues must be regarded as an important psychological and religious phenomenon—a meaningful way to contact the "inner world of the spirit"—best understood (again, like Vivier) in relation to the Jungian idea of the collective unconscious.

William Wood's very scholarly work *Culture and Personality Aspects of the Pentecostal Holiness Religion* (1965) is not concerned with glossolalia per se. Nonetheless, it is a significant, though inconclusive, attempt to determine the psychological nature of Pentecostals by administering the Rorschach test to individuals belonging to two small-town congregations of the Pentecostal Holiness Church. Wood puts forward numerous reasons why he considers Pentecostalism particularly attractive to un-identified, deprived, or disorganized persons.[3]

A notable exception to recent positive treatments of speaking in tongues is that of Wayne Oates, "A Socio-Psychological Study of Glossolalia," in Frank Stagg, Glenn Hinson, and Wayne Oates, *Tongue Speaking in Biblical, Historical, and Psychological Perspective* (1967). Oates believes that intellectualization, institutionalization, and sophistication result in the repression of deep religious emotions by a great many people. Distortions of speech characteristic of early childhood are submerged as a child matures, he feels, but these distortions reappear in glossolalia when an individual tries to verbalize long-repressed religious convictions for the first time; he reverts to an early stage of communicative development. Oates concludes that speakers in tongues tend to have weak egos, confused identities, high levels of anxiety, and generally unstable personalities. To him, Neo-Pentecostals, especially, as members of the affluent middle class, are emotionally rather than economically deprived; they break through their loneliness by speaking in tongues—as others do by using alcohol or drugs.

One of the most creative scholars of contemporary glossolalia in the context of the Pentecostal movement is Virginia Hine. Her important article "Pentecostal Glossolalia: Towards a Functional Interpretation," *Journal for the Scientific Study of Religion* (Fall 1969), pp. 211–26, rejects unequivocally theories explaining speaking in tongues as indicative of psychological pathology, suggestibility, or hypnosis, or as a result of social disorganization and deprivation. She believes, rather (on the basis of recent data), that concepts of glossolalia as learned behavior and as part of the process of personality reorganization are far more useful. For speaking in tongues is one component in the process of commitment to a movement (Pentecostalism) with important implications for both personal and social change.

On the other hand, Felicitas Goodman is less affirmative. In her book, *Speaking in Tongues* (1972), she reports the results of her own anthropological, cross-cultural research on glossolalia, and concludes that the common features in glossolalic (aberrant) behavior within groups of vastly different cultural and linguistic backgrounds can be ascribed to an altered state of consciousness. And for Goodman, there is *nothing* exclusive about Christian or any other kind of speaking in tongues.

William Samarin's highly significant work *Tongues of Men and Angels: The Religious Language of Pentecostalism* (1972) is compatible with Virginia Hine's findings. Samarin views glossolalia as a linguistic phenomenon that can occur independently of any particular psychological or emotional state—characterized by strings of usually simple syllables that are not matched systematically with any semantic system. In the middle-class Pentecostal experience, he feels, the acquisition of speaking in tongues both signals and symbolizes transition—as in the case of evangelical conversion. Glossolalia is symbolic, pleasurable, expressive, and therapeutic. People talk in tongues, says Samarin, because it is part of a movement offering them the fulfillment of aspirations their previous religious experience created in them. Glossolalia is a linguistic symbol of the sacred.

We should also mention Anthony Hoekema's critical theological work, *What About Tongue-Speaking?* (1966), and Watson Mills (ed.), *Speaking in Tongues: Let's Talk About It* (1973), a collection of ten essays by authorities on the subject.

Finally, John Kildahl's study of speaking in tongues within Charismatic Renewal specifically, *The Psychology of Speaking in Tongues* (1972), is very significant. Kildahl, in his ten-year investigation, found that glossolalia often results in a continuing submission to the authority of the "leader" who introduced the phenomenon to the speaker, and a satisfying sense of acceptance following that submission. He reports that in over 85 per cent of the cases examined, a personal crisis of some kind preceded the initial experience of speaking in tongues—evidence absent from Virginia Hine's research. But Kildahl does agree with her that glossolalia is, in fact, learned behavior that makes an individual feel better. And his comments in this regard are very important for a contemporary understanding of the phenomenon:

> One of the characteristics invariably noted by new tongue-speakers was a greater sense of power. This took the form of a stronger sense of identity and self-confidence in interpersonal relations. New tongue-speakers reported

a greater sense of purpose and meaning in their lives and a deepening of its spiritual quality. Whereas religious matters often had been important to them before, after speaking in tongues they became increasingly involved with their religious convictions. They felt bolder in their business dealings, in their marriage relationships, and in teaching Sunday School. . . .

The practitioners of glossolalia whom we surveyed were joyful and warm in one another's company. Their sense of community crossed ethnic, socioeconomic, and educational lines. Their common overwhelming experience surmounted their barriers.

We noted a tremendous openness, concern, and care for one another . . . and the highest ethical mandates were a part of their camaraderie. . . . They reported being less annoyed by frustrations, showing patience in their families and a deeper love for mankind in general.[4]

Kildahl's conclusions, then, are quite the opposite of those expressed by Wayne Oates.

Although the present work is not greatly concerned about the nature of the glossolalia phenomenon, I find the generally positive assessments of Hine, Samarin, and Kildahl most compatible with the results of my research. Especially important, I believe, has been the attempt of these scholars to study speaking in tongues, and its consequences, within the context of the related organization or movement, rather than as a totally independent occurrence.[5]

THE HISTORY, SOCIOLOGY, ANTHROPOLOGY, AND THEOLOGY OF PENTECOSTALISM

In the category of historical studies, first mention should be made of Donald Gee's work. Until his death in 1966, Gee was a leader in world Pentecostalism—eight times chairman of the General Conference of the Assemblies of God in Great Britain and a dominant figure at the Pentecostal World Conferences. From 1947 to 1966, he edited for the Pentecostal World Conferences

Pentecost, a quarterly review of news concerning Pentecostalism throughout the world, and a valuable historical source for the movement. Gee's *magnum opus* is *Wind and Flame* (1967) (formerly *The Pentecostal Movement* [1941, 1949]), a historical account of the development of Pentecostalism—not scholarly, yet fair, and based upon firsthand experience of the movement.

Nils Bloch-Hoell's *The Pentecostal Movement* (1964) treats the historical development of Classical Pentecostalism, and its character as a religious movement. Although already a classic, the book is belittling. A more objective historical study of Classical Pentecostalism and early Charismatic Renewal is offered by John Nichol, himself a former Pentecostal, in *The Pentecostals* (1966). Another basically historical account—again somewhat belittling —is Prudencio Damboriena's *Tongues as of Fire: Pentecostalism in Contemporary Christianity* (1969), which is particularly valuable for its (now-dated) statistics on the Pentecostal movement throughout the world, its treatment of the Holiness movement as a predecessor of Pentecostalism, and its discussion of the Pentecostal movement and ecumenism.

Unquestionably, the single most significant contribution to Pentecostal studies is Walter Hollenweger's ten-volume "Handbuch der Pfingstbewegung" (unpublished doctoral thesis, 1965–67). This veritable encyclopedia of almost all Pentecostal denominations and groups throughout the world includes a chapter on early Charismatic Renewal. Although chiefly historical, Hollenweger's study does not neglect sociological, psychological, and political implications of the movement. Perhaps the only major weakness of the work, and its thoroughly revised one-volume abridgment, *The Pentecostals* (1972), is Hollenweger's "anti-fundamentalist" theological biases, which sometimes distort the presentation and may even have seriously affected his selection of source materials.

Finally, we should mention three recent historical works. The first is Vinson Synan's *The Holiness-Pentecostal Movement in the United States* (1972), which offers a good discussion of black Pentecostalism and attempts to place the major Holiness and Pentecostal bodies in America in their proper historical setting. Synan believes that almost all Holiness people are heirs of the Wesleyan movement, but he tends to read Pentecostal history only from the perspective of his own denomination, the Pentecostal Holiness Church, and oversimplifies historical causation. The second study is Steve Durasoff's *Bright Wind of the Spirit: Pentecostalism Today* (1972). Durasoff's very readable account provides new information on Oral Roberts and Oral Roberts University (where the former teaches), the Full Gospel Business Men's Fellowship International, and Kathryn Kuhlman; yet his work is basically an uncritical apologetic for the Pentecostal movement as a whole. The third work is Peter Wagner's *Look Out! The Pentecostals Are Coming* (1973), a very helpful account of the development of Classical Pentecostalism and Neo-Pentecostalism in Latin America.

The present study borrows freely from these scholarly and popular histories of Pentecostalism, but deals more thoroughly with contemporary developments in Charismatic Renewal specifically —as a distinct phenomenon within the larger Pentecostal movement in the United States and Great Britain.

Moving on to sociological and anthropological investigations of Pentecostalism, we should mention first the pioneering work by Liston Pope, *Millhands and Preachers: A Study of Gastonia* (1942), assessing the role of the churches (including the Church of God [Cleveland, Tennessee]) in the strike of textile workers in Gastonia, North Carolina, during the 1930s. One of the most important recent sociological contributions to Pentecostal studies has been made by Bryan Wilson—best known in this field, perhaps, for his classic article "An Analysis of Sect Development" (1959) in Bryan Wilson (ed.), *Patterns of Sectarianism* (1967); his study of the Pentecostal ministry, "The Pentecostalist Minister: Role Conflicts and Contradictions of Status" (1959), also in *Patterns of Sectarianism*; and his investigation of the Elim Church (Great Britain) in *Sects and Society* (1961).

Also highly significant for the study of the sociological and anthropological character of Pentecostalism is the work of Luther Gerlach and Virginia Hine, whose very important article, "Five Factors Crucial to the Growth and Spread of a Modern Religious Movement," *Journal for the Scientific Study of Religion* (Spring 1968), pp. 23–40, has been expanded into a book comparing the movement dynamics of Pentecostalism and black power with respect to organization, recruitment, commitment, ideology, and the perception of opposition—*People, Power, Change: Movements of Social Transformation* (1970). One of their co-workers in the aforementioned study was Kilian McDonnell, who has himself written a number of notable articles on the Pentecostal movement. These include "The Ideology of Pentecostal Conversion," *Journal of Ecumenical Studies* (Winter 1968), pp. 105–26, an attempt to understand the growth of Classical Pentecostalism from its own theology and spirituality; and "Catholic Pentecostalism: Problems in Evaluation," *Dialog* (Winter 1970), pp. 35–54, in which he discusses a number of difficulties inherent in the scholarly investigation of Pentecostalism in general, and Catholic Pentecostalism in particular.

Another significant sociological study is Christian Lalive d'Epinay's *Haven of the Masses: A Study of the Pentecostal Movement in Chile* (1969), marred only by the author's particular theological biases. Finally, we should mention Gary Schwartz's *Sect Ideologies and Social Status* (1970), and the very recent work of Joseph Fichter, including "Liberal and Conservative Catholic Pentecostals," *Social Compass*, XXI (1974), 303–10; and *The Catholic Cult of the Paraclete* (1975). Schwartz interprets Pentecostal belief systems as a response to social circumstances, but does not adequately relate his theory to the data collected. Fichter surveys conservative and liberal trends among Catholic Charismatics.

The present work takes into account the conclusions of McDonnell, Gerlach, and Hine regarding Pentecostal ideology and movement dynamics, and applies them, in specific instances, to Charismatic Renewal in the United States and Great Britain.

A variety of recent theological and exegetical examinations of Pentecostalism have appeared—each of which tends to reflect the characteristic (pro or con) stance of the author. Some of these works are the product of a high degree of scholarly competence.

First to be noted is Howard Ervin's *These Are Not Drunken, As Ye Suppose* (1968). The author (who teaches at Oral Roberts University) has produced here an exegetical and theological study of the Holy Spirit, particularly in Acts and I Corinthians—sound in its scholarship. Like other Pentecostal religious thinkers, Ervin feels that the Book of Acts bears witness to normative Christian experience. In the same general vein is John Rea (ed.), *Laymen's*

Commentary on the Holy Spirit (1972), an exegetical and expositional examination of New Testament passages on the person and work of the Holy Spirit by seven Classical Pentecostal and Neo-Pentecostal scholars and ministers. Less positive about New Testament legitimation of Pentecostal Spirit baptism is Dale Bruner's thorough theological and exegetical investigation *A Theology of the Holy Spirit: The Pentecostal Experience and the New Testament Witness* (1970), which rejects the notion that glossolalia must be the initial evidence of the baptism of the Holy Spirit. Another largely, but not totally, unsympathetic and very scholarly exegetical study is James Dunn's *Baptism in the Holy Spirit* (1970). The author here criticizes Pentecostalism for separating Spirit baptism from conversion-initiation (represented in water baptism), then chides it for separating faith from water baptism.

Probably the most important Roman Catholic appraisal of the Pentecostal movement from a theological perspective is Edward O'Connor's *The Pentecostal Movement in the Catholic Church* (1971). A Catholic Pentecostal himself, O'Connor discusses the character of Catholic Pentecostalism, its development since 1967, and how it differs from both Classical Pentecostalism and other clearly Protestant expressions of Charismatic Renewal. Another Catholic Pentecostal, Donald Gelpi, has attempted to theologically "systematize" the Pentecostal experience from a Catholic standpoint in his book, *Pentecostalism: A Theological Viewpoint* (1971). To these works should be added Josephine Ford's biblical and theological study of Spirit baptism, *Baptism of the Spirit* (1971); Simon Tugwell's *Did You Receive the Spirit?* (1972), an erudite biblical and theological examination of Pentecostal spirituality as it relates to the Roman Catholic and Eastern Orthodox traditions; and Léon Joseph Cardinal Suenens' recent book, *A New Pentecost?* (1974). All three authors are Catholic Pentecostals.

Rodman Williams, a Neo-Pentecostal theologian, has written two important studies. The first, *The Era of the Spirit* (1971), relates the Pentecostal experience in a very positive way to views of the Holy Spirit held by Karl Barth, Emil Brunner, Paul Tillich, and Rudolf Bultmann; while the second, *The Pentecostal Reality* (1972), is a collection of articles dealing with the significance of the Pentecostal experience in contemporary Christianity—again, citing numerous seemingly supportive Protestant and Catholic theologians.

Finally, we ought to mention the book by James Jones, *Filled with New Wine: The Charismatic Renewal of the Church* (1974), which deals with Pentecostal spirituality from the perspective of the author's own involvement in Charismatic Renewal as an Episcopal (Anglo-Catholic) priest.

THIS WORK IN RELATION TO PREVIOUS STUDIES

Unlike a church or denomination, a religious *movement* presents to the scholar distinct research hazards, one of which is the fact that its structural and ideological boundaries are not easily defined. Furthermore, in the case of Neo-Pentecostalism, the movement is contemporary and still in the process of development, necessitating the establishment of some kind of *provisional* theological and organizational consensus within the course of its continuing evolution.

The primary sources of Charismatic Renewal themselves place a hardship on the researcher, because they often cannot be found in even the best university libraries, and are generally very difficult to locate elsewhere. A good number of these sources take the form of books, pamphlets, and brochures issued by little-known publishers and privately. Many are personal "testimonies" and longer "spiritual autobiographies" of prominent figures in the movement. They function not only as theological sources, but also as primary sources of the movement's history. These testimonies and autobiographies often answer important historical questions—the who, what, when, where, and how—of Neo-Pentecostalism. Since many such works are published with evangelistic intent, they are frequently similar in basic content.

"Charismatic magazines and newspapers" constitute another highly significant source for the history of the movement—especially in their presentation of news items concerning Charismatic Renewal throughout the world. Editorial opinions here are also noteworthy, since the periodical editor in a relatively unstructured movement often emerges to a position of leadership—depending, of course, on the degree of acceptance of his newspaper or magazine. (In screening manuscripts for publication, and by his own comments, he has a special role in setting the ideological tone and direction of the movement in question.) What is unfortunate, however, is the fact that back issues of various important Pentecostal serials are not easy to obtain anywhere. Some magazines and newspapers have already ceased publication, while the editors of most others do not usually keep back numbers in reserve for purchase.

In addition to the foregoing types of primary sources, a small (but increasing) number of more scholarly works by Neo-Pentecostals themselves has appeared (most, quite recently). Among these studies, especially important are the rather sophisticated attempts at a theological self-understanding by a few Roman Catholic, Anglican, and Protestant authors.

I have restricted myself to the use of published and other written sources. But I have also found useful—specifically to determine consensus—my own observation of Charismatic Renewal in the United States and Great Britain. It is partially for this reason that my work is limited, by and large, to the movement in these two countries.

The scope of the present study embraces a historical, sociological, and ecclesiastical appraisal of Neo-Pentecostalism. I am chiefly concerned with its origins, development, and significance as a contemporary movement within the recent history of Christianity and the history of culture more generally. The strictly theological character of Charismatic Renewal, however—except for its concrete effect on the movement as a whole—does not play a major role in this presentation, though I have endeavored to emphasize pertinent theological and exegetical views of its most articulate and representative spokespersons, believing that, in the words of Jeffrey Hadden:

> It is a fundamental sociological principle that the leadership of a voluntary association can only be so far out of line with the expectations of its constituency before that leadership is questioned.[6]

What is particularly original about the present study is its treatment of Neo-Pentecostal *distinctives*—leadership, faith and practice, causes for the movement's emergence and success, its relationship to trends in the wider society—and its examination of Classical Pentecostalism and Charismatic Renewal contrasted with each other.

Notes

Chapter One

1. Thomas F. O'Dea, *The Sociology of Religion* (Englewood Cliffs, N.J.: Prentice-Hall, 1966), p. 81.
2. Quoted ibid., p. 17.
3. See Andrew M. Greeley, *Unsecular Man* (New York: Dell, 1972).
4. O'Dea, p. 13.
5. Ibid., p. 24.
6. Ibid., p. 26.
7. Ibid., p. 116.
8. Edward D. O'Connor, *The Pentecostal Movement in the Catholic Church* (Notre Dame, Ind.: Ave Maria Press, 1971), pp. 33–34.
9. Michael Harper, "On to Maturity," *Renewal* (Dec. 1972–Jan. 1973), p. 34.
10. Harper, *None Can Guess* (Plainfield, N.J.: Logos International, 1971), p. 154.
11. Ibid., pp. 149, 153.
12. David J. Du Plessis, "A Statement by Pentecostal Leaders," *Missions Under the Cross*, ed. Normal Goodall (London: Edinburgh House, 1953), pp. 249–50.
13. See, for instance, Jamie Buckingham, "Breakthrough in Unity," *Logos Journal* (Sept.–Oct. 1972), pp. 37–39. E. J. Carnell defines historic orthodoxy as "that branch of Christendom which limits the ground of religious authority to the Bible" in *The Case for Biblical Christianity*, ed. Ronald H. Nash (Grand Rapids, Mich.: Eerdmans, 1969), p. 168.
14. O'Connor, *The Pentecostal Movement in the Catholic Church*, p. 159.
15. Harper, *None Can Guess*, pp. 154–55.
16. See Richard Quebedeaux, "Evangelicals: Ecumenical Allies," *Christianity and Crisis* (Dec. 27, 1971), pp. 286–88; and *The Young Evangelicals* (New York: Harper & Row, 1974).
17. McCandlish Phillips, "And There Appeared to Them Tongues of Fire," *The Saturday Evening Post* (May 16, 1964), p. 40.
18. Quoted in Walter J. Hollenweger, "Handbuch der Pfingstbewegung" (Zurich: unpublished doctoral thesis, Faculty of Theology, University of Zurich, 1965–67), pp. 824–25 (02a. 02.206).
19. See D. G. Lillie, "Renewal in Historic Churches," *Renewal* (Oct.–Nov. 1966), pp. 7–9.

20. See Harper, "First Edify, Then Evangelize," *Trinity* (Whitsuntide 1965), p. 25.

21. See Robert L. Dean, "Strange Tongues: A Psychologist Studies Glossolalia," *Trinity* (Trinitytide 1964), pp. 37–39; and, for instance, Pat Boone, *A New Song* (Carol Stream, Ill.: Creation House, 1970); Thomas R. Nickel, *The Shakarian Story*, 2nd ed. (Los Angeles: Full Gospel Business Men's Fellowship International, 1964); and George Otis, *High Adventure* (Van Nuys, Calif.: Time-Light Publishing, 1971).

22. United Presbyterian Church, U.S.A., *The Work of the Holy Spirit* (Philadelphia: UPCUSA, 1970), p. 30.

23. Ibid., p. 36.

24. Ibid., p. 37.

25. O'Connor, *The Laying On of Hands* (Pecos, N.M.: Dove Publications, 1969), pp. 5–7.

26. Ibid., pp. 3–4.

27. United Presbyterian Church, U.S.A., p. 37.

28. Ibid., p. 38.

29. Ibid., p. 39.

30. John T. Nichol, *The Pentecostals* (Plainfield, N.J.: Logos International, 1966), p. 9.

31. United Presbyterian Church, U.S.A., p. 5. This is, of course, subject to disagreement, and perhaps also to cultural conditions.

32. See Kilian McDonnell, "Catholic Pentecostalism: Problems in Evaluation," *Dialog* (Winter 1970), pp. 35–54.

33. Sociologically, there is a point to be made here. "New" religious movements and new styles of religiosity, particularly if they involve emotional display, almost always appear to be avenues of spiritual mobility—faster ways to reach desired but hitherto hard to attain goals. Classical Pentecostalism itself was that—getting further and with more certainty than was possible in the formalized churches. There is often a "spiritual inflation" with a consequent debasement of the existing spiritual coinage and a demand for its faster circulation and availability. Status inflation is an interesting social phenomenon; and it is possible to see Pentecostalism as two waves of a demand for a wider redistribution of spiritual statuses than the formal organization of the churches otherwise would admit.

34. See, for instance, R. Leonard Carroll, "Glossolalia: Apostles to the Reformation," *The Glossolalia Phenomenon*, ed. Wade H. Horton (Cleveland, Tenn.: Pathway Press, 1966), pp. 67–94; and Vessie D. Hargrave, "Glossolalia: Reformation to the Twentieth Century," *The Glossolalia Phenomenon*, pp. 95–139.

35. Nichol, p. 24.

36. See John P. Kildahl, *The Psychology of Speaking in Tongues* (New York: Harper & Row, 1972), pp. 14–18; Morton T. Kelsey, *Tongue Speaking* (Garden City, N.Y.: Doubleday & Company, 1964), pp. 32–68; George H. Williams and Edith Waldvogel, "A History of Speaking in Tongues and Related Gifts," *The Charismatic Movement*, ed. Michael P. Hamilton (Grand Rapids, Mich.: Eerdmans, 1974), pp. 61–113 (these scholars find more glos-

solalia in Christian history than most others do); Émile Lombard, *De la Glossolalie chez les Premiers Chrétiens et des Phénomènes Similaires: Étude d'Exégèse et de Psychologie* (Lausanne: Imprimeries Réunies, 1910); and Eddison Mosimann, *Das Zungenreden geschichtlich und psychologisch untersucht* (Tübingen: J. C. B. Mohr, 1911).

37. William J. Samarin, *Tongues of Men and Angels: The Religious Language of Pentecostalism* (New York: Macmillan, 1972), p. 13.

Chapter Two

1. Nils Bloch-Hoell, *The Pentecostal Movement* (Oslo: Universitetsforlaget, 1964), pp. 5–17. In making these assertions, Bloch-Hoell relies heavily on the works of a number of prominent American religious historians such as Willard L. Sperry, *Religion in America* (New York: Macmillan, 1946); Kenneth Scott Latourette, *A History of the Expansion of Christianity*, IV (New York: Harper & Brothers, 1941); William W. Sweet, *The American Churches* (London: Epworth Press, 1947); and *The History of Religion in the United States* (New York: Macmillan, 1924). For specific citation of sources, see the relevant Notes in *The Pentecostal Movement* (Chapter I).

2. Donald Gee, *Wind and Flame* (formerly *The Pentecostal Movement*) (Nottingham, England: Assemblies of God Publishing House, 1967), p. 4.

3. Nichol, p. 28.

4. Ibid., pp. 25–35; and Bloch-Hoell, pp. 18–54. For a contemporary account of the Azusa Street revival by a participant, see Frank Bartelman, *Another Wave Rolls In!* (formerly *What Really Happened at Azusa Street?*), ed. John Walker and John G. Myers (Monroeville, Pa.: Whitaker Books, 1970).

5. See Bloch-Hoell, p. 48.

6. See McDonnell, "The Ideology of Pentecostal Conversion," *Journal of Ecumenical Studies* (Winter 1968), pp. 105–26.

7. Nichol, p. 5; and Donald W. Dayton, "The Evolution of Pentecostalism," *The Covenant Quarterly* (Aug. 1974), pp. 29–32.

8. Prudencio Damboriena, *Tongues as of Fire: Pentecostalism in Contemporary Christianity* (Washington, D.C.: Corpus Books, 1969), pp. 29–30.

9. Nichol, pp. 5–6.

10. Damboriena, p. 24.

11. Nichol, p. 7. See also Damboriena, pp. 20–36.

12. Nichol, pp. 54–69.

13. See Luther P. Gerlach and Virginia H. Hine, "Five Factors Crucial to the Growth and Spread of a Modern Religious Movement," *Journal for the Scientific Study of Religion* (Spring 1968), pp. 23–40; and *People, Power, Change: Movements of Social Transformation* (Indianapolis, Ind.: Bobbs-Merrill, 1970), pp. 183–97.

14. Nichol, pp. 70–80.

15. Ibid., pp. 81–93.

16. See Hollenweger, *The Pentecostals* (Minneapolis, Minn.: Augsburg Publishing House, 1972), pp. 29–46.

17. See ibid., pp. 47–62.

18. See Aimee Semple McPherson, *The Story of My Life*, ed. Raymond L. Cox (Waco, Tex.: Word, 1973).

19. See Hollenweger, *The Pentecostals*, pp. 191–93, 196.

20. See ibid., pp. 197–205; and Bryan R. Wilson, *Sects and Society* (London: Heinemann, 1961).

21. See Hollenweger, *The Pentecostals*, pp. 206–17.

22. See Nichol, pp. 94–122, 180–86; and Frank S. Mead, *Handbook of Denominations in the United States*, 6th ed. (Nashville, Tenn. and New York: Abingdon, 1975).

23. See Hollenweger, *The Pentecostals*, pp. 218–43.

24. On Pentecostalism in the Soviet Union, see ibid., pp. 267–87.

25. See ibid., pp. 120–22, 124–25.

26. Nichol, pp. 40–53. For an excellent recent study of Pentecostalism in Chile, see Christian Lalive d'Epinay, *Haven of the Masses: A Study of the Pentecostal Movement in Chile* (London: Lutterworth Press, 1969).

27. Nichol, pp. 40–53. On Brazil, see Hollenweger, *The Pentecostals*, pp. 75–110.

28. On Italy, see Hollenweger, *The Pentecostals*, pp. 251–66.

29. See Nichol, pp. 158–207.

30. On Latin American Pentecostalism in general, see C. Peter Wagner, *Look Out! The Pentecostals Are Coming* (Carol Stream, Ill.: Creation House, 1973).

31. Nichol, pp. 208–39.

32. For details concerning the establishment of Classical Pentecostalism and its later denominational development in specific countries of the world, the reader is referred especially to Walter Hollenweger's "Handbuch der Pfingstbewegung"; and also Prudencio Damboriena's *Tongues as of Fire: Pentecostalism in Contemporary Christianity*; John Nichol's *The Pentecostals*; and Nils Bloch-Hoell's *The Pentecostal Movement*.

33. See Damboriena and Hollenweger for "exact" statistics relevant to specific countries and denominations in those countries.

34. Gee, *Wind and Flame*, p. 50.

35. Harper, *As at the Beginning* (Plainfield, N.J.: Logos International, 1965), pp. 34–39; and Gee, *Wind and Flame*, pp. 20–50. For an interesting exegetical and theological treatise on the *charismata* by an English Anglican (vicar of Ham, Surrey, and sometime chaplain of Clare College, Cambridge) sympathetic to the basic Pentecostal stance, see J. R. Pridie, *The Spiritual Gifts* (London: Robert Scott, 1921).

36. Gee, *Wind and Flame*, p. 88.

37. Ibid.

38. Ibid., p. 89.

39. Ibid., pp. 87–91. He feels that the lack of Pentecostal denominations in the early period actually hindered the movement's growth in Great Britain and the influence of British Pentecostalism throughout the world.

Chapter Three

1. McDonnell, "The Ecumenical Significance of the Pentecostal Movement," *Worship* (Dec. 1966), p. 628. See also, for instance, Dennis Bennett, *Nine O'Clock in the Morning* (Plainfield, N.J.: Logos International, 1970), pp. 33–35, 78; James Brown, "Every Christian Must Become a Pentecostal," *Full Gospel Men's Voice* (Sept. 1959), pp. 7–8; Du Plessis, "Pentecostal Revival Inside the Historic Churches," *Pentecost*, No. 50 (1959), pp. 1–2; "The World-Wide Pentecostal Movement," *Pentecost*, No. 53 (Sept.–Nov. 1960), back cover; Harper, *As at the Beginning*, pp. 56–66; Kelsey, pp. 102–4; O'Connor, *The Pentecostal Movement in the Catholic Church*, pp. 24–25; and Phillips, pp. 32–33.

2. See Lesslie Newbigin, *The Household of God* (New York: Friendship Press, 1954); and Henry P. Van Dusen, "Force's Lessons for Others," *Life* (June 9, 1958), pp. 122, 124.

3. See Hollenweger, "Handbuch der Pfingstbewegung," pp. 823–28 (02a. 02.206); and Harper, *As at the Beginning*, pp. 60–65.

4. See "Rector and a Rumpus," *Newsweek* (July 4, 1960), p. 77; and "Speaking in Tongues," *Time* (Aug. 15, 1960), pp. 53, 55.

5. Harper, *As at the Beginning*, pp. 56–66. See also Dennis Bennett, *Nine O'Clock in the Morning*; and Frank Farrell, "Outburst of Tongues: The New Penetration," in *Christianity Today* (formerly A *Christianity Today Reader*), ed. Frank E. Gaebelein (Old Tappan, N.J.: Spire Books, 1968), pp. 194–205.

6. See Dennis Bennett, *Nine O'Clock in the Morning*, pp. 66–122.

7. See, for instance, *Trinity* (Trinitytide 1961); and *Trinity* (Eastertide 1963), pp. 30–33.

8. *Trinity* (Eastertide 1963), p. 32.

9. Ibid., p. 33.

10. Kelsey, pp. 110–12.

11. See Herald Bredesen, "Leaves from a Campus Diary," *Trinity* (Transfiguration 1963), pp. 6–9; and his spiritual autobiography, *Yes, Lord* (Plainfield, N.J.: Logos International, 1972).

12. See *Trinity* (Whitsuntide 1964), pp. 50–51; and, especially, Howard M. Ervin, *These Are Not Drunken, As Ye Suppose* (Plainfield, N.J.: Logos International, 1968).

13. See Larry Christenson, "Speaking in Tongues," *Trinity* (Transfiguration 1963), pp. 13–16; and, especially, *Speaking in Tongues and Its Significance for the Church* (Minneapolis, Minn.: Bethany Fellowship, 1968).

14. See *Trinity* (Eastertide 1963), pp. 4–16; and, especially, Robert C. Frost, *Aglow with the Spirit*, rev. ed. (Plainfield, N.J.: Logos International, 1972).

15. See "Church of the Redeemer: Miracle in the Inner City," *Acts*, I, No. 5 (1968), 21–30; and, especially, W. Graham Pulkingham, *Gathered for*

Power: Charisma, Communalism, Christian Witness (New York: Morehouse-Barlow, 1972).

16. See *Trinity* (Transfiguration 1963), pp. 32–33; and Donovan Bess, "'Speaking in Tongues': The High Church Heresy," *The Nation* (Sept. 28, 1963), pp. 173–77.

17. See, for instance, *Trinity* (Eastertide 1963), pp. 48–49; *Trinity* (Transfiguration 1963), pp. 28–39; and *Trinity* (Christmastide 1965–66), pp. 28–33.

18. See *Trinity* (Christmastide 1962–63), pp. 2–17; and "Blue Tongues," *Time* (Mar. 29, 1963), p. 52.

19. Phillips, pp. 31–40. For testimonies of early Neo-Pentecostals, see, for instance, Jerry Jensen (ed.), *Baptists* (1963), *Episcopalians* (1964), *Lutherans* (1966), *Methodists* (1963), and *Presbyterians and the Baptism of the Holy Spirit* (Los Angeles: FGBMFI, 1963).

20. See for instance, D. G. Lillie, *Tongues Under Fire* (London: Fountain Trust, 1966).

21. Reprinted in *Trinity* (Christmastide 1962–63), pp. 20–22.

22. Harper, *As at the Beginning*, pp. 80–85. See also Harper's spiritual autobiography, *None Can Guess*; "The 'New' Pentecost in England," *Pentecost* (Mar.–May 1964), pp. 4–5; "News from Michael Harper: Visit of David Du Plessis," *Pentecost* (Dec. 1964–Feb. 1965), back cover, p. 3; *Trinity* (Whitsuntide 1964), pp. 26–31; and *Trinity* (Trinitytide 1964), pp. 54–55.

23. *Renewal* (Jan. 1966), pp. 16–19. See also Bennett, *Nine O'Clock in the Morning*, pp. 129–45.

24. See "Stirrings in Northern Ireland," *Renewal* (Dec. 1968–Jan. 1969), pp. 20–21; John L. Wynne, *This New Pentecostalism* (Belfast, Northern Ireland: John L. Wynne, 1967); and *Logos Journal* (Sept.–Oct. 1972), pp. 6–15.

25. "A New Breath of Life," *Renewal* (Jan. 1966), pp. 4–10; and FGBMFI, *Airlift to London* (Los Angeles: FGBMFI, n.d.).

26. See *Renewal* (Dec. 1967–Jan. 1968), pp. 16, 18; Bennett, *Nine O'Clock in the Morning*, pp. 156–63; and Harper, *None Can Guess*, pp. 108–18.

27. See *Renewal* (Dec. 1967–Jan. 1968), pp. 18–19; and *Renewal* (Apr.–May 1970), p. 35.

28. See "South Africa's Move of the Spirit," *Renewal* (Oct.–Nov. 1968), pp. 5–6; and Harper, *None Can Guess*, pp. 108–18.

29. "Bill Burnett—A Break with Tradition," Johannesburg *Star* (May 4, 1974), pp. 10–11.

30. James D. G. Dunn, "Spirit Baptism and Pentecostalism," *Scottish Journal of Theology* (Nov. 1970), pp. 397–407. See also *Renewal* (Aug.–Sept. 1970), pp. 9, 11–12; Arnold Bittlinger, *Gifts and Graces* (1967) and *Gifts and Ministries* (Grand Rapids, Mich.: Eerdmans, 1973); and Hollenweger, *The Pentecostals*, pp. 244–50.

31. See *Renewal* (Aug.–Sept. 1970), pp. 8–9; and "Church Renewal in Norway," *Renewal* (Aug.–Sept. 1972), pp. 6–7.

32. McDonnell, "Catholic Pentecostalism: Problems in Evaluation," *Dialog* (Winter 1970), p. 35.

33. Kevin and Dorothy Ranaghan, *Catholic Pentecostals* (Paramus, N.J.: Paulist Press, 1969), p. 8.

34. Ibid., p. 10.

35. It is somewhat ironic that Wilkerson still maintains very anti-ecumenical attitudes, and holds a rigorous stance on personal ethics. See David Wilkerson, *The Vision* (New York: Pyramid Books, 1974).

36. Kevin and Dorothy Ranaghan, *Catholic Pentecostals*, pp. 6–23.

37. O'Connor, *The Pentecostal Movement in the Catholic Church*, pp. 15–16.

38. Kevin and Dorothy Ranaghan, *Catholic Pentecostals*, pp. 40–41. For the full story of the Ranaghans' experience, see the entire book; Kevin Ranaghan, "The Essential Element in the Church," *Charisma Digest*, No. 2 (1969), pp. 14–18, 22–24; "A Roman Catholic Discovers New Life in His Church," *Christian Life* (May 1968), pp. 30–31, 57–60; and "The Power that Fell at Pentecost," *Testimony* (Second Quarter 1969), pp. 1–3.

39. See O'Connor, "The Pentecostal Movement Has Brought Joy to My Ministry," *Testimony* (Third Quarter 1969), pp. 14–16.

40. See J. Massyngberde Ford, *The Pentecostal Experience* (Paramus, N.J.: Paulist Press, 1970).

41. Kevin and Dorothy Ranaghan, *Catholic Pentecostals*, pp. 38–57.

42. See Bertil W. Ghezzi, "Three Charismatic Communities," *As the Spirit Leads Us*, ed. Kevin and Dorothy Ranaghan (Paramus, N.J.: Paulist Press, 1971), pp. 164–86; and *New Covenant* (Feb. 1975).

43. O'Connor, *The Pentecostal Movement in the Catholic Church*, pp. 15–19. See also Jim Cavnar, "Catholics: Pentecostal Movement," *Acts*, I, No. 5 (1968), pp. 14–19; James Connelly, "The Charismatic Movement," *As the Spirit Leads Us*, ed. Kevin and Dorothy Ranaghan, pp. 211–32; Edward B. Fiske, "Pentecostals Gain Among Catholics," *New York Times* (Nov. 3, 1970), pp. 37, 56; James W. L. Hills, "The New Charismatics, 1973," (Mar. 1973), pp. 24–25, 33; O'Connor, *The Pentecostal Movement in the Catholic Church*, pp. 13–107; R. Douglas Wead, *Catholic Charismatics: Are They for Real?* (formerly *Father McCarthy Smokes a Pipe and Speaks in Tongues*) (Carol Stream, Ill.: Creation House, 1973); and *Full Gospel Business Men's Voice* (Sept. 1971), pp. 3–17.

44. O'Connor, *The Pentecostal Movement in the Catholic Church*, pp. 99–101; and Rick Casey, "Charismatics II," *National Catholic Reporter* (Aug. 29, 1975), pp. 1, 4, 10.

45. John C. Haughey, "Holy Spirit: A Ghost No Longer," *America* (June 16, 1973), p. 551. See Léon Joseph Cardinal Suenens, *A New Pentecost?* (New York: Seabury Press, 1974); and Elizabeth Hamilton, *Suenens: A Portrait* (Garden City, N.Y.: Doubleday & Company, 1975).

46. Mary Ann Jahr, "A Turning Point," *New Covenant* (Aug. 1974), p. 4.

47. See *New Covenant* (July 1975).

48. See Wagner, pp. 167–69.

49. Harper, "Catholic Pentecostals," *Renewal* (Feb.–Mar. 1970), p. 4. For Catholic Pentecostal testimonies, see FGBMFI, *Catholics and the Baptism in the Holy Spirit* (n.d.) and *The Acts of the Holy Spirit Among the Catholics Today* (Los Angeles: FGBMFI, 1974); Joseph E. Orsini, *Hear My Confession* (Plainfield, N.J.: Logos International, 1971); Kevin and Dorothy Ranaghan, *Catholic Pentecostals;* Maria von Trapp, *Maria* (Carol Stream, Ill.: Creation House, 1972); and R. Russell Bixler (ed.), *The Spirit Is A-Movin'* (Carol Stream, Ill.: Creation House, 1974).

50. See Ralph Martin, *Hungry for God* (Garden City, N.Y.: Doubleday & Company, 1974), p. 164, for addresses.

51. Hollenweger, *The Pentecostals*, p. 15.

52. See "Early Stages of Agreement in Roman Catholic/Pentecostal Dialogue," *Renewal* (Aug.–Sept. 1972), pp. 2–4.

53. Dennis Bennett, "Lutheran Conference on the Holy Spirit," *Logos Journal* (Nov.–Dec. 1972), p. 46. See the magazine now published by Eastern Orthodox Charismatics: *Logos.*

54. Harper, "On to Maturity," *Renewal* (Dec. 1972–Jan. 1973), p. 34.

Chapter Four

1. Luther P. Gerlach and Virginia H. Hine, *People, Power, Change: Movements of Social Transformation* (Indianapolis, Ind.: Bobbs-Merrill, 1970), pp. 33–37.

2. Ibid., p. 38.

3. Gerlach and Hine apply Weber's definition of charismatic leadership to Pentecostalism.

4. Gerlach and Hine, *People, Power, Change*, pp. 41–45.

5. Ibid., p. 52.

6. Ibid., pp. 55–60.

7. Ibid., pp. 65–70.

8. Kildahl, pp. 50–51.

9. William Willoughby, "How to Pubblish a Best Sellur," *Logos Journal* (Nov.–Dec. 1972), pp. 48–49 (repr. from Washington, D.C. *Evening Star and Daily News*).

10. "Statement of Ownership," *Logos Journal* (Nov.–Dec. 1973), p. 252.

11. "Miracle Woman," *Time* (Sept. 14, 1970), p. 62.

12. James Morris, *The Preachers* (New York: St. Martin's Press, 1973), p. 252.

13. Ibid., pp. 237, 240.

14. Ibid., p. 239.

15. Ibid., p. 252.

16. *I Believe in Miracles* (Old Tappan, N.J.: Spire Books, 1962); *God Can Do It Again* (Old Tappan, N.J.: Spire Books, 1969); and *Nothing Is Impossible with God* (Englewood Cliffs, N.J.: Prentice-Hall, 1974).

17. Steve Durasoff, *Bright Wind of the Spirit: Pentecostalism Today* (Englewood Cliffs, N.J.: Prentice-Hall, 1972), p. 185.

18. Quoted in Morris, p. 239.

19. Ibid., p. 242.

20. Ibid., p. 247.

21. Ibid., p. 241.

22. Durasoff, pp. 184–85.

23. Morris, p. 252.

24. "Miracle Woman," *Time* (Sept. 14, 1970), p. 62.

25. "Kathryn Kuhlman: 25 Years in Pittsburgh," *Logos Journal* (Nov.–Dec. 1972), pp. 33–36.

26. Morris, p. 243.

27. Quoted in "Kathryn Kuhlman: 25 Years In Pittsburgh," *Logos Journal* (Nov.–Dec. 1972), p. 35. The Kathryn Kuhlman Foundation receives an annual income of about $2 million, largely from collections at services. It has been alleged, moreover, that Kuhlman is, in fact, a woman of considerable personal wealth. Dino Kartsonakis, her former pianist, estimates the value of "antiques and museum pieces" in Kuhlman's Pittsburgh home and Newport Beach, California, apartment at about $1.4 million, and her jewelry at $1 million. See R. Chandler, "Ex-Aides Sue Kathryn Kuhlman," Los Angeles *Times* (July 3, 1975), Part II, pp. 1–2.

28. *Logos Journal* (Jan.–Feb. 1973), p. 32. For a parapsychological interpretation of Kuhlman, see Allen Spraggett, *Kathryn Kuhlman: The Woman Who Believes in Miracles* (New York: New American Library, 1971). A less positive assessment of her ministry is offered by William A. Nolen, *Healing* (New York: Random House, 1974), pp. 41–102.

29. Durasoff, pp. 113, 126.

30. See Oral Roberts, *The Call: An Autobiography* (Old Tappan, N.J.: Spire Books, 1971), pp. 93–112.

31. Durasoff, p. 119.

32. Ibid., pp. 114–26; and Roberts, pp. 93–96.

33. Roberts, p. 175.

34. Ibid., p. 158.

35. Hollenweger, *The Pentecostals*, p. 365.

36. Durasoff, pp. 135–37.

37. Ibid., p. 133.

38. Roberts, p. 134.

39. Ibid., p. 137.

40. Ibid., p. 131.

41. Dunn, "Spirit Baptism and Pentecostalism," *Scottish Journal of Theology* (Nov. 1970), p. 403. See "Oral Roberts Joins the Methodists," *Renewal* (Aug.–Sept. 1968), pp. 4–5; and Jeanne Hinton, "Oral Roberts and the Heart of British Methodism," *Renewal* (Apr.–May 1970), pp. 7, 9–10.

42. Roberts, p. 177.

43. Ibid., pp. 185–96.

44. For a less positive treatment of Roberts and his career, see Morris, pp. 57–126.

45. Harper, *None Can Guess*, p. 6.

46. Ibid., pp. 44, 58.

47. Du Plessis, *The Spirit Bade Me Go*, rev. ed. (Plainfield, N.J.: Logos International, 1970), p. 10.

48. Ibid., p. 122.

49. Hollenweger, *The Pentecostals*, p. 7.

50. Du Plessis, *The Spirit Bade Me Go*, p. 11.

51. Ibid., p. 122.

52. Ibid., pp. 12, 122.

53. Ibid., p. 122.

54. Ibid., p. 13.

55. Ibid.

56. Ibid., pp. 15, 122.

57. Ibid., p. 16.

58. Ibid., p. 122.

59. Hollenweger, *The Pentecostals*, p. 7.

60. "Early Stages of Agreement in Roman Catholic/Pentecostal Dialogue," *Renewal* (Aug.–Sept. 1972), p. 2.

61. Du Plessis, *The Spirit Bade Me Go*, p. 122.

62. Hollenweger, *The Pentecostals*, p. 7.

63. Du Plessis, *The Spirit Bade Me Go*, p. 20.

64. Ibid., p. 27. See also Hollenweger, "Handbuch der Pfingstbewegung" (08.137.002).

65. See James A. Taylor, "A Search for Giants," *A.D.* (Sept. 1974), pp. 20–23.

66. Harper, *None Can Guess*, pp. 12–14.

67. Ibid., p. 14.

68. Ibid., pp. 17–19.

69. Ibid., pp. 20–28.

70. Ibid., p. 33.

71. Ibid., pp. 38–41.

72. Ibid., p. 43.

73. Ibid., pp. 44–47.

74. Ibid., pp. 54–57.

75. Ibid., p. 54.

76. Ibid., pp. 58, 60.

77. Ibid., p. 60.

78. See John R. W. Stott, *The Baptism and Fullness of the Holy Spirit* (Downers Grove, Ill.: InterVarsity Press, 1964).

79. Harper, *None Can Guess*, p. 63.

80. Ibid., pp. 90–93.

81. Ibid., pp. 108–18.

82. "Early Stages of Agreement in Roman Catholic/Pentecostal Dialogue," *Renewal* (Aug.–Sept. 1972), p. 4.

83. "Fountain Trust Gets New General Secretary," *Logos Journal* (Sept.–Oct. 1972), p. 60.

84. *New Covenant* (Aug. 1975), p. 23.

85. Durasoff, p. 145. See Nickel.

86. See Kelsey, pp. 65–68.

87. Durasoff, p. 146.

88. Ibid., p. 147.

89. Hollenweger, *The Pentecostals*, p. 6.

90. See William C. Armstrong, "Demos Shakarian: A Man and His Message," *Logos Journal* (Sept.–Oct. 1971), pp. 13–14.

91. Durasoff, pp. 148–49.

92. Ibid., p. 150.

93. Quoted ibid.

94. See Kevin and Dorothy Ranaghan, *As the Spirit Leads Us*, pp. 118–25.

95. Quoted in Durasoff, p. 150.

96. Ibid., p. 151.

97. "Pentecostal Unit Gains Followers," *Full Gospel Business Men's Voice* (Oct. 1972), pp. 2–3, 26 (repr. from New York *Times*, July 16, 1972).

98. Durasoff, p. 155.

99. Ibid., pp. 151–55.

100. Ibid., p. 156.

101. Ibid.

102. Hollenweger, *The Pentecostals*, p. 5.

103. See Jean Stone, "A High Church Episcopalian Becomes Pentecostal, *Full Gospel Men's Voice* (Oct. 1960), pp. 9–10 (repr. from *The Living Church*).

104. See *Trinity* (Christmastide 1961–62), p. 49.

105. John L. Sherrill, *They Speak with Other Tongues* (New York: Pyramid Books, 1964), p. 122.

106. *Trinity* (Transfiguration 1963), p. 50.

107. See, for instance, *Trinity* (Transfiguration 1963), pp. 28–39.

108. Harper, *As at the Beginning*, p. 72.

109. Conversation with Walter Hollenweger (Jan. 1970).

110. See Jean Stone Willans, *The Acts of the Green Apples* (Altadena, Calif.: Society of Stephen, 1973), a somewhat misleading spiritual autobiography.

111. Harper, *None Can Guess*, pp. 60–64.

112. Ibid., p. 64.

113. Michael Harper letter (Sept. 11, 1975).

114. Letter to the author from Michael Harper (Feb. 1, 1974).

115. R. Chandler, "Charismatic Clinics: Instilling Maturity," *Christianity Today* (Sept. 28, 1973), pp. 44–45; "Christian Center: Charismatic Clinic," *Acts*, I, No. 5 (1968), pp. 19–20; *Melodyland Messenger* (Aug. 1969; Aug. 1970); special charismatic clinic edition (1970; Mar. 1971; June 1971; and Jan. 1973).

Chapter Five

1. McDonnell, "The Ideology of Pentecostal Conversion," *Journal of Ecumenical Studies* (Winter 1968), pp. 114–15.

2. See *Melodyland Messenger* (Sept. 1969), p. 6.

3. Harper, *None Can Guess*, pp. 149, 153.

4. See, for instance, Ralph Martin, "Life in Community," pp. 145–63, and Bertil W. Ghezzi, "Three Charismatic Communities," *As the Spirit Leads Us*, ed. Kevin and Dorothy Ranaghan, pp. 164–86.

5. George Martin, "Charismatic Renewal and the Church of Tomorrow," *As the Spirit Leads Us*, ed. Kevin and Dorothy Ranaghan, p. 242.

6. See *Trinity* (Christmastide 1963), pp. 2–17.

7. See, for instance, *Trinity* (Eastertide 1963), pp. 4–25; and *Trinity* (Transfiguration 1963), pp. 6–9, 20–21.

8. See Ghezzi, "Three Charismatic Communities," *As the Spirit Leads Us*, ed. Kevin and Dorothy Ranaghan, pp. 164–86.

9. See, for instance, Jerry Jensen, "Charismata in the Twentieth Century," *Full Gospel Business Men's Voice* (June 1965), pp. 3–21.

10. Conversation with Jerry Jensen, former editor of *Full Gospel Business Men's Voice* (Autumn 1970).

11. See, for instance, Pat King, "The Jesus People Are Coming," *Logos Journal* (Sept–Oct. 1971), pp. 6–7; J. Rodman Williams, "Charismatic Journey" (Nov.–Dec. 1971), pp. 13–15; and "Adventure into Faith," *Full Gospel Business Men's Voice* (Oct. 1972), pp. 39–42.

12. Ronald M. Enroth, "Where Have All the Jesus People Gone?," *Eternity* (Oct. 1973), pp. 14–15, 17, 28, 30.

13. See her spiritual autobiography, *Sealed Orders* (Plainfield, N.J.: Logos International, 1972).

14. See Jeanne Hinton, "Breakfast with the Darnalls," *Renewal* (Dec. 1969–Jan. 1970), pp. 9, 11–12.

15. Marshall's latest book tells of her Pentecostal experience: *Something More* (New York: McGraw-Hill, 1974).

16. This fact is well known but not widely publicized by the church.

17. Ford, *The Pentecostal Experience*, p. 37. Ford's criticism of male domination in Catholic Pentecostalism apparently caused her to break with the Notre Dame community. See her article, "Biblical Material Relevant to the Ordination of Women," *Journal of Ecumenical Studies* (Fall 1973), pp. 669–99. On the role of women in Catholic Pentecostalism, see Joseph H. Fichter, "How It Looks to a Social Scientist," *New Catholic World* (Nov.–Dec. 1974), pp. 244–48.

18. Harper, "Christian Unity—the Growing Fact," *Renewal* (Dec. 1970–Jan. 1971), pp. 4–5.

19. J. Rodman Williams, *The Era of the Spirit* (Plainfield, N.J.: Logos International, 1971), p. 16.

20. Marshall, p. 270.

21. For a contrary evangelical view, see Palmer Robertson, "Neo-Pentecostalism and the Freedom of the Christian," *The Presbyterian Guardian* (Jan. 1975), pp. 18–19.

22. For one important example of "deprivation theory" in this context, see Charles Y. Glock and Rodney Stark, *Religion and Society in Tension* (Chicago: Rand McNally, 1965), pp. 242–59.

23. Gerlach and Hine, "Five Factors Crucial to the Growth and Spread of

a Modern Religious Movement," *Journal for the Scientific Study of Religion* (Spring 1968), pp. 30–31.

24. Kildahl, p. 78.

25. See, for instance, Leon and Virginia Kortenkamp, "Power to Witness," *As the Spirit Leads Us*, ed. Kevin and Dorothy Ranaghan, pp. 103–13.

26. Kildahl, p. 84.

27. Don Basham, *A Handbook on Holy Spirit Baptism* (Monroeville, Pa.: Whitaker Books, 1969), p. 85.

28. Ibid., p. 114.

29. See Blessed Trinity Society, *Return to the Charismata* (Van Nuys, Calif.: Blessed Trinity Society, 1962), p. 8.

30. Harper, "On to Maturity," *Renewal* (Dec. 1972–Jan. 1973), p. 34.

31. Ibid.

32. Harper, *None Can Guess*, pp. 158–59.

33. Williams, *The Era of the Spirit*, p. 58.

34. See Frost, *Aglow with the Spirit*.

35. Basham, p. 115.

36. Larry Christenson, *Speaking in Tongues and Its Significance for the Church* (Minneapolis, Minn.: Bethany Fellowship, 1968), p. 107.

37. Ibid., pp. 105–6.

38. Harper, *Walk in the Spirit* (Plainfield, N.J.: Logos International, 1968), pp. 88–89.

39. O'Connor, *The Pentecostal Movement in the Catholic Church*, p. 112.

40. Ibid., pp. 112–17. Also see Jim Cavnar, *Prayer Meetings* (Pecos, N.M.: Dove Publications, 1969).

41. See John Randall, *In God's Providence: The Birth of a Catholic Charismatic Parish* (Plainfield, N.J.: Logos International, 1973).

42. Ghezzi, "Three Charismatic Communities," *As the Spirit Leads Us*, ed. Kevin and Dorothy Ranaghan, pp. 179–86. See, for instance, Steven B. Clark, *Building Christian Communities* (Notre Dame, Ind.: Ave Maria Press, 1971); and *New Covenant* (Feb. 1975).

43. See James Byrne, *Threshold of God's Promise*, rev. ed. (Notre Dame, Ind.: Ave Maria Press, 1971).

44. See, for instance, "Charismatic Presbyterian Ministers Meet for National Conference," *Logos Journal* (Mar.–Apr. 1972), p. 43; and Edward E. Plowman, "Mission to Orthodoxy: The 'Full' Gospel," *Christianity Today* (Apr. 26, 1974), pp. 44–45.

45. Dennis Bennett, "Lutheran Conference on the Holy Spirit," *Logos Journal* (Nov.–Dec. 1972), pp. 44–46; and Norris Wogen (ed.), *Jesus, Where Are You Taking Us?: Lutheran Conference on the Holy Spirit* (Carol Stream, Ill.: Creation House, 1973). On Charismatic Renewal within Lutheranism, also see Erling Jorstad, *Bold in the Spirit: Lutheran Charismatic Renewal in America Today* (Minneapolis, Minn.: Augsburg Publishing House, 1974); and John Stevens Kerr, *The Fire Flames Anew: A Look at the New Pentecostalism* (Philadelphia: Fortress Press, 1974).

46. *Melodyland Messenger* (Aug. 1969), p. 7.

47. *Melodyland Messenger* (Aug. 1969 and special charismatic clinic edition 1970); and Melodyland Christian Center, *Official Report for 1971* (Anaheim, Calif.: MCC, 1972).

48. Harper, "Christian Unity—the Growing Fact," *Renewal* (Dec. 1970–Jan. 1971), pp. 4–5.

49. Leonard Evans, "A Personal Itinerary in the Charismata," *View*, No. 2 (1964), p. 14.

50. Quoted in Buckingham, "Breakthrough in Unity," *Logos Journal* (Sept.–Oct. 1972), p. 38.

51. Harper, *None Can Guess*, pp. 154–55.

52. Clark, "Charismatic Renewal in the Church," *As the Spirit Leads Us*, ed. Kevin and Dorothy Ranaghan, pp. 24–25.

53. Gelpi, *Pentecostalism: A Theological Viewpoint*, p. 35.

54. Ibid., p. 99.

55. Quoted in Buckingham, "Breakthrough in Unity," *Logos Journal* (Sept.–Oct. 1972), p. 39.

56. Carnell, p. 168.

57. Kevin Ranaghan, "Catholics and Pentecostals Meet in the Spirit," *As the Spirit Leads Us*, ed. Kevin and Dorothy Ranaghan, pp. 138–39.

58. Hollenweger, "Charismatic Movements Today" (Birmingham, England: prepublication essay, 1974), p. 4.

59. Ibid., p. 5.

60. See Robert Doolittle, "Denominational Renewal," *Unitarian Universalist World* (May 1, 1975), p. 3.

61. Ervin, *These Are Not Drunken, As Ye Suppose* (Plainfield, N.J.: Logos International, 1968, pp. 225–26.

62. Basham, p. 10.

63. Hollenweger, "Charismatic Movements Today," p. 12.

64. Ibid.

65. Basham, p. 26.

66. Dennis and Rita Bennett, *The Holy Spirit and You* (Plainfield, N.J.: Logos International, 1971), pp. 71–72.

67. Ibid., pp. 84–88.

68. See, especially, George B. Cutten, *Speaking in Tongues: Historically and Psychologically Considered* (New Haven, Conn.: Yale University Press, 1927).

69. Samarin, pp. 199, 231, 235.

70. Hollenweger, "Charismatic Movements Today," p. 12.

71. Christenson, *Speaking in Tongues and Its Significance for the Church*, pp. 25–27.

72. Basham, *A Handbook on Holy Spirit Baptism*, p. 26.

73. Christenson, *Speaking in Tongues and Its Significance for the Church*, p. 129.

74. O'Connor, *The Pentecostal Movement in the Catholic Church*, p. 134.

75. Dennis and Rita Bennett, p. 83.

76. Bittlinger, *Gifts and Graces*, pp. 26–27.

77. See Frederick Dale Bruner, *A Theology of the Holy Spirit: The Pentecostal Experience and the New Testament Witness* (Grand Rapids, Mich.: Eerdmans, 1970); and Dunn, *Baptism in the Holy Spirit* (Naperville, Ill.: Allenson, 1970).

78. Hollenweger, "Charismatic Movements Today," pp. 10–11.

79. O'Connor, *The Pentecostal Movement in the Catholic Church*, pp. 132–35.

80. Kevin and Dorothy Ranaghan, *Catholic Pentecostals*, p. 142.

81. Williams, *The Era of the Spirit*, p. 41 n. On the relationship of Spirit baptism to sacramental life, see McDonnell and Bittlinger, *The Baptism in the Holy Spirit as an Ecumenical Problem* (Notre Dame, Ind.: Charismatic Renewal Services, 1972).

82. Williams, *The Era of the Spirit*, p. 45 n.

83. Frost, *Overflowing Life* (Plainfield, N.J.: Logos International, 1971), p. 115.

84. Kevin Ranaghan, "Catholics and Pentecostals Meet in the Spirit," *As the Spirit Leads Us*, ed. Kevin and Dorothy Ranaghan, p. 129.

85. Kevin and Dorothy Ranaghan, *Catholic Pentecostals*, pp. 142–43.

86. Hollenweger, *The Pentecostals*, p. 8.

87. Pat Boone, *A New Song* (Carol Stream, Ill.: Creation House), p. 46.

88. Ibid., pp. 5–6.

89. See Boone's spiritual autobiography, *A New Song*.

90. Kevin and Dorothy Ranaghan, *Catholic Pentecostals*, pp. 188–89.

91. McDonnell, "Catholic Pentecostalism: Problems in Evaluation," *Dialog* (Winter 1970), p. 51.

92. See Quebedeaux, *The Young Evangelicals*.

93. McDonnell, "Catholic Pentecostalism: Problems in Evaluation," *Dialog* (Winter 1970), p. 51.

94. Harper, *Walk in the Spirit*, pp. 59–60.

95. O'Connor, *The Pentecostal Movement in the Catholic Church*, p. 106.

96. Kevin and Dorothy Ranaghan, *Catholic Pentecostals*, pp. 211–12.

97. See *Melodyland Messenger* (June 1970), pp. 4–5; and *Melodyland in Motion* (Oct. 1973), p. 128.

98. Pulkingham, *Gathered for Power: Charisma, Communalism, Christian Witness*, p. 128.

99. Ibid., p. 135. Also see this book as a whole in addition to the same author's *They Left Their Nets: A Vision for Community Ministry* (New York: Morehouse-Barlow, 1973); Harper, *A New Way of Living* (Plainfield, N.J.: Logos International, 1973); and Hollenweger, *New Wine in Old Wineskins* (Gloucester, England: Fellowship Press, 1973), pp. 27–28. A very moderate work on social concern in Charismatic Renewal has recently been written by Larry Christenson, *A Charismatic Approach to Social Action* (Minneapolis, Minn.: Bethany Fellowship, 1974). On social concern within Catholic Pentecostalism, specifically, see *New Covenant* (June 1974) and especially Joseph H. Fichter, "Liberal and Conservative Catholic Pentecostals," *Social Compass*, XXI (1974), pp. 303–10; and *The Catholic Cult of the Paraclete* (New York: Sheed and Ward, 1975).

100. McDonnell, "Catholic Pentecostalism: Problems in Evaluation," *Dialog* (Winter 1970), pp. 41–42.

101. Quoted ibid., p. 41.

102. Du Plessis, *The Spirit Bade Me Go*, p. 93.

103. Christenson, *Speaking in Tongues and Its Significance for the Church*, pp. 107–8.

104. Harper, *Walk in the Spirit*, pp. 74–75, 77–78.

Chapter Six

1. Bryan R. Wilson, "Sect Development," *Patterns of Sectarianism*, ed. Bryan R. Wilson (London: Heinemann, 1967), pp. 23–24.

2. Ibid., p. 27.

3. Nichol, pp. 236–37.

4. Wilson, *Patterns of Sectarianism*, p. 25.

5. Quoted in Dean, "Strange Tongues: A Psychologist Studies Glossolalia," *Trinity* (Trinitytide 1964), p. 39.

6. The major work on dispensational fundamentalism is Clarence B. Bass, *Backgrounds to Dispensationalism* (Grand Rapids, Mich.: Eerdmans, 1960).

7. See, for instance, the relevant articles in Mead.

8. Quoted in Hollenweger, "Handbuch der Pfingstbewegung," p. 825 (02a.02.206).

9. For a discussion of the specific differences between fundamentalism and evangelicalism, see Quebedeaux, *The Young Evangelicals*, pp. 1–45.

10. Harper, "On to Maturity," *Renewal* (Dec. 1972–Jan. 1973), p. 34.

11. See James S. Tinney, "Black Origins of the Pentecostal Movement," *Christianity Today* (Oct. 8, 1971), pp. 4–6.

12. See Bloch-Hoell, pp. 161–64.

13. Quoted ibid., p. 161.

14. Quoted ibid., pp. 161–62.

15. Hollenweger, *The Pentecostals*, pp. 53–59.

16. Wade H. Horton, "Introduction," *The Glossolalia Phenomenon*, ed. Wade H. Horton, p. 17.

17. Quoted in Dean, "Strange Tongues: A Psychologist Studies Glossolalia," *Trinity* (Trinitytide 1964), p. 39.

18. See Hollenweger, *The Pentecostals*, pp. 429–51.

19. Nichol, pp. 209–11.

20. See ibid., pp. 211–15.

21. See Hollenweger, *The Pentecostals*, pp. 438–51. Also see Roberto Barbosa, "Bread and Gospel: Affirming a Total Faith—An Interview with Brazilian Pentecostalist Manoel de Mello," *The Christian Century* (Dec. 25, 1974), pp. 1,223–26.

22. Quoted in Hollenweger, "Handbuch der Pfingstbewegung," p. 825 (02a.02.206); and Harper, *As at the Beginning*, p. 63.

23. See, for instance, Hollenweger, *The Pentecostals*, pp. 38–40.

24. For instance, Lee College (Church of God) Cleveland, Tenn.; Emmanuel College (Pentecostal Holiness Church), Franklin Springs, Ga.; Cen-

tral Bible College (Assemblies of God), Springfield, Mo.; and Southern California College (Assemblies of God), Costa Mesa, Calif.

25. James M. Beaty, "Society for Pentecostal Studies to Meet," *Church of God Evangel* (Nov. 12, 1973), p. 11.

26. *Society for Pentecostal Studies: Pneuma '74* (Costa Mesa, Calif.: Southern California College, 1974).

27. See, for instance, *Trinity* (Christmastide 1962–63), pp. 2–17; Bredesen, "Leaves from a Campus Diary," *Trinity* (Transfiguration 1963), pp. 6–9; Jensen, "Charismata in the Twentieth Century," *Full Gospel Business Men's Voice* (June 1965), pp. 3–21; and "Former Professor Head of Melodyland Schools," *Melodyland Messenger* (Nov. 1972), p. 1.

28. See, for instance, Roberts, pp. 197–216; and "ORU: New Charismatic University," *Acts* (July–Aug. 1967), pp. 17–18.

29. See *Melodyland School of Theology: Catalog 1974–76* (Anaheim, Calif.: MCC, 1974).

30. See Quebedeaux, *The Young Evangelicals*, pp. 1–45.

31. Williams, *The Era of the Spirit*, p. 58.

32. Harper, "On to Maturity," *Renewal* (Dec. 1972–Jan. 1973), p. 34.

33. See Harper, "Are You a Gnostic?," *Renewal* (Oct.–Nov. 1972), pp. 28–29.

34. See Hollenweger, *The Pentecostals*, pp. 399–410; and Quebedeaux, *The Young Evangelicals*, pp. 129–34.

35. McDonnell, "Catholic Pentecostalism: Problems in Evaluation," *Dialog* (Winter 1970), p. 41.

36. See Mead, Damboriena, Lalive d'Epinay, and Wagner.

37. Hollenweger, *The Pentecostals*, pp. 474–76.

38. See ibid., pp. 489–92.

39. Stanley C. Plog, "UCLA Conducts Research on Glossolalia," *Trinity* (Whitsuntide 1964), pp. 38–39.

40. See Dean, "Strange Tongues: A Psychologist Studies Glossolalia," *Trinity* (Trinitytide 1964), pp. 37–39.

41. This chapter is largely an expansion of the author's article "The Old Pentecostalism and the New Pentecostalism," *Theology, News and Notes* (March 1974), pp. 6–8, 23. A number of differences between Classical Pentecostalism and Charismatic Renewal have also been suggested by Erling Jorstad (ed.), *The Holy Spirit in Today's Church: A Handbook of the New Pentecostalism* (Nashville and New York: Abingdon, 1973), pp. 22–23.

Chapter Seven

1. Greg S. Forster, "The Third Arm 2," *TSF Bulletin* (Autumn 1972), pp. 19–20.

2. Harper, *As at the Beginning*, p. 56.

3. See McDonnell, "Catholic Pentecostalism: Problems in Evaluation," *Dialog* (Winter 1970), p. 52 n.

4. "Taming the Tongues," *Time* (July 10, 1964), pp. 64, 66.

5. Bess, p. 173.

6. On the background of Pike's pastoral letter, see *Trinity* (Transfiguration 1963), pp. 28–37. The center of Pentecostal phenomena in Pike's diocese was (at the time) Holy Innocents Parish, Corte Madera, California. Its rector, Todd Ewald, an Anglo-Catholic, is still a leader in Charismatic Renewal today. He is discussed in the sources cited in notes 5 and 6.

7. Quoted in McDonnell, "Catholic Pentecostalism: Problems in Evaluation," *Dialog* (Winter 1970), p. 52.

8. Ibid.

9. Du Plessis, *The Spirit Bade Me Go*, p. 27.

10. See *Trinity* (Whitsuntide 1964), pp. 26–31; and *Trinity* (Trinitytide 1964), pp. 28–29, 32–33.

11. *The Person and Work of the Holy Spirit* (Oklahoma City: Presbyterian Charismatic Communion, 1971).

12. *The Charismatic Movement in the Lutheran Church in America: A Pastoral Perspective* (New York: LCA, 1974).

13. United Presbyterian Church, U.S.A., *The Work of the Holy Spirit* (Philadelphia: UPCUSA, 1970).

14. See McDonnell, "Catholic Pentecostalism: Problems in Evaluation," *Dialog* (Winter 1970), p. 53.

15. United Presbyterian Church, U.S.A., pp. 22–28.

16. Ibid., p. 23.

17. Quoted in McDonnell, "Catholic Pentecostalism: Problems in Evaluation," *Dialog* (Winter 1970), p. 54.

18. Ibid.

19. See Du Plessis, *The Spirit Bade Me Go*.

20. Repr. ibid., pp. 35–60.

21. Quoted ibid., p. 19.

22. Quoted in Gee, *All with One Accord* (Springfield, Mo.: Gospel Publishing House, 1961), pp. 9–10.

23. See Newbigin, pp. 94–122.

24. Newbigin, p. 122.

25. Van Dusen, pp. 122, 124.

26. Quoted in "High Voltage Religion," *Melodyland Messenger* (Jan. 1973), p. 2.

27. Donald Grey Barnhouse, "Finding Fellowship with Pentecostals," *Eternity* (Apr. 1958), pp. 8–10.

28. Russell T. Hitt, "The New Pentecostalism," *Eternity* (Apr. 1970), pp. 12–13 (repr.). See also the Blessed Trinity Society's response to this article: Jean Stone and Herald Bredesen, *The Charismatic Renewal in the Historic Churches* (Van Nuys, Calif.: Blessed Trinity Society, 1963).

29. "Tongues: Updating Some Old Issues" (editorial), *Eternity* (Mar. 1973), p. 8.

30. Philip E. Hughes, "From England, an Editorial," *Trinity* (Christmastide 1962–63), pp. 20–22 (repr. from *The Churchman* [Sept. 1962]).

31. "The Gift of Tongues" (editorial), *Christianity Today* (Apr. 11, 1969), pp. 27–28.

32. McDonnell, "The Ecumenical Significance of the Pentecostal Movement," *Worship* (Dec. 1966), pp. 608–29, and "New Dimensions in Research on Pentecostalism," *Worship* (Apr. 1971), pp. 214–19.

33. McDonnell, "The Ideology of Pentecostal Conversion," *Journal of Ecumenical Studies* (Winter 1968), pp. 105–26.

34. McDonnell, "Holy Spirit and Pentecostalism," *Commonweal* (Nov. 8, 1968), pp. 198–204.

35. McDonnell, "Catholic Pentecostalism: Problems in Evaluation," *Dialog* (Winter 1970), pp. 35–54.

36. McDonnell, "The Catholic Charismatic Renewal: Reassessment and Critique," *Religion in Life* (Summer 1975), pp. 138–54.

37. G. Emmett Carter, "The Pentecostal Renewal in the Catholic Church," *Testimony* (First Quarter 1972), p. 1.

38. Philip M. Hannan, "We Thank God for the Charismatic Renewal!," *Testimony* (First Quarter 1972), pp. 2–3.

39. Quoted in Haughey, p. 551.

40. This is somewhat ironic, because most Classical Pentecostals are, in fact, dispensational fundamentalists.

41. Quoted in Ervin, *And Forbid Not to Speak with Tongues*, rev. ed. (Plainfield, N.J.: Logos International, 1971), p. 26.

42. Stott, p. 59.

43. Francis A. Schaeffer, *The New Super-Spirituality* (Downers Grove, Ill.: InterVarsity Press, 1972), p. 16. Two attempts by evangelicals to "make peace" with Pentecostals are Michael Griffiths, *Three Men Filled with the Spirit* (London: Overseas Missionary Fellowship, 1969); and Peter E. Gillquist, *Let's Quit Fighting About the Holy Spirit* (Grand Rapids, Mich.: Zondervan, 1974).

44. See Jack W. Hayford, "The Church on the Way," *Logos Journal* (Mar.–Apr. 1972), pp. 20–22, 39.

45. Gee, "To Our New Pentecostal Friends," *Pentecost* (Dec. 1961–Feb. 1962), back cover.

46. Quoted in "Episcopal and Pentecostal Leaders Confer," *Pentecost* (Mar.–May 1963), p. 8.

47. See "American Assemblies of God Welcome Charismatic Movement," *Renewal* (Dec. 1972–Jan. 1973), p. 8.

48. Ray H. Hughes, "A Traditional Pentecostal Looks at the New Pentecostalism," *Christianity Today* (June 7, 1974), pp. 6–10. See also Bennie S. Triplett, *A Contemporary Study of the Holy Spirit* (Cleveland, Tenn.: Pathway Press, 1970), pp. 111–37.

Chapter Eight

1. Gerlach and Hine, "Five Factors Crucial to the Growth and Spread of a Modern Religious Movement," *Journal for the Scientific Study of Religion* (Spring 1968), pp. 23–24.

2. See Gerlach and Hine, *People, Power, Change: Movements of Social Transformation*.

3. Newbigin, p. 95.

4. Ibid., p. 101. For comments by Pentecostals on Newbigin's work, see Gee, *All with One Accord*, pp. 14–18; and Forster, "The Third Arm 1," *TSF Bulletin* (Summer 1972), p. 6.

5. Quoted in Harold E. Fey (ed.), *A History of the Ecumenical Movement: 1948–1968* (Philadelphia: Wesminster Press, 1970), p. 43.

6. Stephen Neill, *The Church and Christian Union* (London: Oxford University Press, 1968), p. 318. One can, perhaps, argue that Vatican II's stress on the Holy Spirit was the result of the failure of all other legitimations for doctrine, social policy, etc. When legitimations (papal infallibility, for instance) fail or become suspect, then the Holy Spirit might be a very useful (extremely general and unspecific) legitimation for any cause or policy.

7. Quoted in Kevin and Dorothy Ranaghan, *Catholic Pentecostals*, p. vi.

8. Quoted in Robert McAfee Brown, *The Ecumenical Revolution* (Garden City, N.Y.: Doubleday & Company, 1967), p. 10.

9. Quoted in Byrne, p. 72.

10. A case has been made for a woman, Elena Guerra, as the "real" forerunner of Catholic Pentecostalism (rather than Pope John XXIII). See Val Gaudet, "Fore-runner of the Charismatic Renewal!," *Testimony* (Third Quarter 1974), pp. 5–9.

11. For a report on an early post-Vatican II Pentecostal-Catholic encounter, see Daniel J. O'Hanlon, "The Pentecostals and Pope John's 'New Pentecost,'" *View*, No. 2 (1964), pp. 44–47.

12. See Jeffrey K. Hadden, *The Gathering Storm in the Churches* (Garden City, New York: Doubleday & Company, 1969).

13. Roberts, p. 131.

14. Wilson, *Religion in Secular Society* (Baltimore: Penguin Books, 1966), p. 10.

15. Peter L. Berger, "A Call for Authority in the Christian Community," *The Christian Century* (Oct. 27, 1971), p. 1,262.

16. For an attempt to deal with "secularism" in the context of Charismatic Renewal, see O'Connor, *Pentecost in the Modern World* (Notre Dame, Ind.: Ave Maria Press, 1972), pp. 14–17.

17. Wilson, *Religion in Secular Society*, p. 78.

18. Ibid., p. 33.

19. Hence, the title of Rodman Williams' book, *The Pentecostal Reality*.

20. See, for instance, the testimonies of young people who were early participants in Catholic Pentecostalism in Kevin and Dorothy Ranaghan, *Catholic Pentecostals*, pp. 58–106.

21. Boone, p. 184.

22. See *Logos Journal* (Jan.–Feb. 1973), p. 32.

23. Pentecostalism was a legitimated way to dismantle inhibition and to enjoy emotional release, which for a long time was limited in modern society. In some ways, it may be anticultural (or countercultural?), but it may also function as a safety valve, and may thus in the long run prevent emotions from running into socially nihilistic channels. If might be interesting to speculate why in the 1900–60 period the lower socio-economic levels of society

needed this kind of release; and why in the 1960s and 1970s the middle class needs it. The need could, perhaps, be linked to the declining relative position of the middle class in a period of economic redistribution and the reduction of status differences (i.e., a limited experience of relative deprivation).

24. Hollenweger, *The Pentecostals*, p. 15.

25. *Melodyland Messenger* (Feb. 1971), p. 4.

26. "'Mainline' Charismatics," *The Christian Century* (Oct. 30, 1974), pp. 1,006–7.

27. Harper, "Baptism in the Spirit," *Transmit* (Sept. 1970), p. 2.

28. O'Connor, *The Pentecostal Movement in the Catholic Church*, pp. 16–18.

29. Fiske, p. 37.

30. Haughey, p. 551.

31. Gerlach and Hine, *People, Power, Change: Movements of Social Transformations*, p. 52.

32. But see Casey.

33. Dennis and Rita Bennett, pp. 69–72.

34. Ibid., p. 72.

35. Hollenweger, *The Pentecostals*, p. 365.

36. See Nickel.

37. See Boone.

38. See George Otis, *High Adventure* (Van Nuys, Calif.: Time-Light Publishing, 1971).

39. *Trinity* (Transfiguration 1963), p. 50.

40. Otis, "High Adventure," *Full Gospel Business Men's Voice* (Mar. 1972), p. 6.

41. Ibid., p. 29.

42. See, for instance, FGBMFI, *Airlift to London*; and Raymond W. Becker, "A Report of the 1972 Scandinavian-European Airlift," *Full Gospel Business Men's Voice* (Oct. 1972), pp. 5–14, 19–22, 30–33, 35–38, 42–45.

43. See "World Conference on the Holy Spirit," *Logos Journal* (Sept.–Oct. 1973), p. 46.

44. See *Melodyland World Tour* (Anaheim, Calif.: MCC, 1972).

45. On exorcism in Charismatic Renewal, see Harper, *Spiritual Warfare* (Plainfield, N.J.: Logos International, 1970), a very moderate treatment.

46. Gerlach and Hine, *People, Power, Change*, p. xix.

47. McDonnell, "Holy Spirit and Pentecostalism," *Commonweal* (Nov. 8, 1968), p. 204.

48. For somewhat contrary views on this comparison, however, see Ford, *The Pentecostal Experience*, p. 56; and O'Connor, *Pentecost in the Modern World*, pp. 41–48.

49. See Robert S. Ellwood, *One Way: The Jesus Movement and Its Meaning* (Englewood Cliffs, N.J.: Prentice-Hall, 1973).

50. Enroth, pp. 14–15, 17.

51. See Quebedeaux, *The Young Evangelicals*, pp. 94–97.

52. For further information on the New Evangelicalism and its relationship to Charismatic Renewal, see Quebedeaux, *The Young Evangelicals*.

53. For the nature of "progressive orthodoxy," see ibid., especially pp. 37–41.

Postscript

1. Emmanuel Sullivan, "Can the Pentecostal Movement Renew the Churches?," *Study Encounter*, VIII (4) (1972), p. 12.
2. Ibid., p. 13.
3. Ibid., p. 10.

Appendix

1. Lincoln M. Van E. Vivier, "Glossolalia" (Johannesburg, South Africa: unpublished M.D. thesis, University of the Witwatersrand, 1960), p. 434.
2. Ibid., p. vi.
3. See William W. Wood, *Culture and Personality Aspects of the Pentecostal Holiness Religion* (The Hague and Paris: Mouton, 1965), pp. 65–66.
4. Kildahl, pp. 83–84.
5. See Watson E. Mills, "Literature on Glossolalia," *Journal of the American Scientific Affiliation* (Dec. 1974), pp. 169–73.
6. Hadden, pp. 258–59.

Bibliography

Primary Sources (works by Pentecostals)

Acts. Los Angeles, 1967–70. Serial.

Bartelman, Frank. *Another Wave Rolls In!* (formerly *What Really Happened at Azusa Street?*), ed. John Walker and John G. Myers. Monroeville, Pa.: Whitaker Books, 1970.

Basham, Don. *A Handbook of Holy Spirit Baptism*. Monroeville, Pa.: Whitaker Books, 1969.

Beaty, James M. "Society for Pentecostal Studies to Meet," *Church of God Evangel* (Cleveland, Tenn.), Nov. 12, 1973, p. 11.

Bennett, Dennis. *Nine O'Clock in the Morning*. Plainfield, N.J.: Logos International, 1970.

Bennett, Dennis and Rita. *The Holy Spirit and You*. Plainfield, N.J.: Logos International, 1971.

Bittlinger, Arnold. *Gifts and Graces*. Grand Rapids, Mich.: Eerdmans, 1967.

———. *Gifts and Ministries*. Grand Rapids, Mich.: Eerdmans, 1973.

Bixler, R. Russell (ed.). *The Spirit Is A-Movin'*. Carol Stream, Ill.: Creation House, 1974.

Blessed Trinity Society. *Return to the Charismata*. Van Nuys, Calif.: Blessed Trinity Society, 1962.

Boone, Pat. *A New Song*. Carol Stream, Ill.: Creation House, 1970.

Bredesen, Herald. *Yes, Lord*. Plainfield, N.J.: Logos International, 1972.

Byrne, James. *Threshold of God's Promise* (rev. ed.). Notre Dame, Ind.: Ave Maria Press, 1971.

Carothers, Merlin R. *Power in Praise*. Plainfield, N.J.: Logos International, 1972.

———. *Prison to Praise*. Plainfield, N.J.: Logos International, 1970.

———. *Walking and Leaping*. Plainfield, N.J.: Logos International, 1974.

Cavnar, Jim. *Prayer Meetings*. Pecos, N.M.: Dove Publications, 1969.

Chandler, R. "Charismatic Clinics: Instilling Maturity," *Christianity Today* (Sept. 28, 1973), pp. 44–45.

————. "Ex-Aides Sue Kathryn Kuhlman," Los Angeles *Times* (July 3, 1975), Part II, pp. 1–2.

Charisma Digest (previously *View*). Los Angeles: Full Gospel Business Men's Fellowship International, 1966–69. Serial.

Christenson, Larry. *A Charismatic Approach to Social Action*. Minneapolis, Minn.: Bethany Fellowship, 1974.

————. *Speaking in Tongues: A Gift for the Body of Christ*. London: Fountain Trust, 1963.

————. *Speaking in Tongues and Its Significance for the Church*. Minneapolis, Minn.: Bethany Fellowship, 1968.

Clark, Steven B. *Building Christian Communities*. Notre Dame, Ind.: Ave Maria Press, 1972.

Doolittle, Robert. "Denominational Renewal," *Unitarian Universalist World* (May 1, 1975), p. 3.

Du Plessis, David J. *The Spirit Bade Me Go* (rev. ed.). Plainfield, N.J.: Logos International, 1970.

————. "A Statement by Pentecostal Leaders," *Missions Under the Cross*, ed. Norman Goodall. London: Edinburgh House, 1953, pp. 249–50.

Durasoff, Steve. *Bright Wind of the Spirit: Pentecostalism Today*. Englewood Cliffs, N.J.: Prentice-Hall, 1972.

Ervin, Howard M. *And Forbid Not to Speak with Tongues* (rev. ed.). Plainfield, N.J.: Logos International, 1971.

————. *These Are Not Drunken, As Ye Suppose*. Plainfield, N.J.: Logos International, 1968.

Ford, J. Massyngberde. *Baptism of the Spirit*. Techny, Ill.: Divine Word Publications, 1971.

————. "Biblical Material Relevant to the Ordination of Women," *Journal of Ecumenical Studies* (Fall 1973), pp. 669–99.

————. *The Pentecostal Experience*. Paramus, N.J.: Paulist Press, 1970.

Forster, Greg S. "The Third Arm 1," *TSF Bulletin* (London) (Summer 1972), pp. 5–9.

————. "The Third Arm 2," *TSF Bulletin* (Autumn 1972), pp. 16–21.

Fountain Trust, *The Fountain Trust: What It Is and What It Does*. London: Fountain Trust, n.d.

Frost, Robert C. *Aglow with the Spirit* (rev. ed.). Plainfield, N.J.: Logos International, 1971.

————. *Overflowing Life*. Plainfield, N.J.: Logos International, 1971.

Full Gospel Business Men's Fellowship International. *The Acts of the Holy Spirit Among the Catholics Today*. Los Angeles: FGBMFI, 1974.

————. *Airlift to London*. Los Angeles: FGBMFI, n.d.

————. *Catholics and the Baptism in the Holy Spirit.* Los Angeles: FGBMFI, n.d.

Full Gospel Business Men's Voice (formerly *Full Gospel Men's Voice*). Los Angeles: FGBMFI, 1953–. Serial.

Gee, Donald. *All with One Accord.* Springfield, Mo.: Gospel Publishing House, 1961.

————. *Wind and Flame* (formerly *The Pentecostal Movement*). Nottingham, England: Assemblies of God Publishing House, 1967.

Gelpi, Donald L. *Pentecostalism: A Theological Viewpoint.* Paramus, N.J.: Paulist Press, 1971.

Gift. Nigel. Transvaal, South Africa, 1968–. Serial.

Harper, Michael. *As at the Beginning.* Plainfield, N.J.: Logos International, 1965.

————. "Baptism in the Spirit," *Transmit* (Kelham, Newark, Nottinghamshire, England), Sept. 1970, pp. 2–3.

————. *A New Way of Living.* Plainfield, N.J.: Logos International, 1973.

————. *None Can Guess.* Plainfield, N.J.: Logos International, 1971.

————. *Spiritual Warfare.* Plainfield, N.J.: Logos International, 1970.

————. *Walk in the Spirit.* Plainfield, N.J.: Logos International, 1968.

Horton, Wade H. (ed.). *The Glossolalia Phenomenon.* Cleveland, Tenn.: Pathway Press, 1966.

Hughes, Ray H. "A Traditional Pentecostal Looks at the New Pentecostalism," *Christianity Today*, June 7, 1974, pp. 6–10.

Jensen, Jerry (ed.). *Baptists* (1963), *Episcopalians* (1964), *Lutherans* (1966), *Methodists* (1963), and *Presbyterians and the Baptism of the Holy Spirit.* Los Angeles: FGBMFI, 1963.

Jones, James W. *Filled with New Wine: The Charismatic Renewal of the Church.* New York: Harper & Row, 1974.

Kelsey, Morton T. *Tongue Speaking.* Garden City, N.Y.: Doubleday & Company, 1964.

Kuhlman, Kathryn. *God Can Do It Again.* Old Tappan, N.J.: Spire Books, 1969.

————. *I Believe in Miracles.* Old Tappan, N.J.: Spire Books, 1962.

————. *Nothing Is Impossible with God.* Englewood Cliffs, N.J.: Prentice-Hall, 1974.

Lillie, D. G. *Tongues Under Fire.* London: Fountain Trust, 1966.

Logos. Christchurch, New Zealand, 1966–. Serial.

Logos. Ft. Wayne, Ind., 1968–. Serial.

Logos Journal. Plainfield, N.J., 1971–. Serial.

Marshall, Catherine. *Something More*. New York: McGraw-Hill, 1974.

Martin, Ralph. *Hungry for God*. Garden City, N.Y.: Doubleday & Company, 1974.

McPherson, Aimee Semple. *The Story of My Life*, ed. Raymond L. Cox. Waco, Tex.: Word, 1973.

Melodyland Christian Center. *Melodyland School of Theology: Catalog 1974–76*. Anaheim, Calif.: MCC, 1974.

———. *Melodyland World Tour*. Anaheim, Calif.: MCC, 1972.

———. *Official Report for 1971*. Anaheim, Calif.: MCC, 1972.

Melodyland in Motion (formerly *Melodyland Messenger*). Anaheim, Calif., 1969–. Serial.

New Covenant. Ann Arbor, Mich., 1971–. Serial.

New Wine. Ft. Lauderdale, Fla., 1968–. Serial.

Nickel, Thomas R. *The Shakarian Story* (2nd ed.). Los Angeles: FGBMFI, 1964.

O'Connor, Edward D. *The Laying On of Hands*. Pecos, N.M.: Dove Publications, 1969.

———. *Pentecost in the Modern World*. Notre Dame, Ind.: Ave Maria Press, 1972.

———. *The Pentecostal Movement in the Catholic Church*. Notre Dame, Ind.: Ave Maria Press, 1971.

Otis, George. *High Adventure*. Van Nuys, Calif.: Time-Light Publishing, 1971.

Pentecost. London, 1947–66. Serial.

Pridie, J. R. *The Spiritual Gifts*. London: Robert Scott, 1921.

Pulkingham, W. Graham. *Gathered for Power: Charisma, Communalism, Christian Witness*. New York: Morehouse-Barlow, 1973.

———. *They Left Their Nets: A Vision for Community Ministry*. New York: Morehouse-Barlow, 1973.

Ranaghan, Kevin. "A Roman Catholic Discovers New Life in His Church," *Christian Life* (Wheaton, Ill.), May 1968, pp. 30–31, 57–60.

Ranaghan, Kevin and Dorothy (eds.). *Catholic Pentecostals*. Paramus, N.J.: Paulist Press, 1969.

——— (eds.). *As the Spirit Leads Us*. Paramus, N.J.: Paulist Press, 1971.

Randall, John. *In God's Providence: The Birth of a Catholic Charismatic Parish*. Plainfield, N.J.: Logos International, 1973.

Rea, John (ed.). *Layman's Commentary on the Holy Spirit*. Plainfield, N.J.: Logos International, 1972.

Renewal. London, 1966–. Serial.

Roberts, Oral. *The Call: An Autobiography.* Old Tappan, N.J.: Spire Books, 1971.

Sanford, Agnes. *Sealed Orders.* Plainfield, N.J.: Logos International, 1972.

Sherrill, John L. *They Speak with Other Tongues.* New York: Pyramid Books, 1964.

Society for Pentecostal Studies: Pneuma '74. Costa Mesa, Calif.: Southern California College, 1974.

Stone, Jean, and Bredesen, Herald. *The Charismatic Renewal in the Historic Churches.* Van Nuys, Calif.: Blessed Trinity Society, 1963.

Suenens, Léon Joseph Cardinal. *A New Pentecost?* New York: Seabury Press, 1974.

Synan, Vinson. *The Holiness-Pentecostal Movement in the United States.* Grand Rapids, Mich.: Eerdmans, 1972.

Testimony. Hanford, Calif., 1962–. Serial.

Trinity. Van Nuys, Calif., 1961–66. Serial.

Triplett, Bennie S. *A Contemporary Study of the Holy Spirit.* Cleveland, Tenn.: Pathway Press, 1970.

Tugwell, Simon. *Did You Receive the Spirit?* Paramus, N.J.: Paulist Press, 1972.

Vivier, Lincoln M. Van E. "Glossolalia." Johannesburg, South Africa: unpublished M.D. thesis, University of the Witwatersrand, 1960.

Von Trapp, Maria. *Maria.* Carol Stream, Ill.: Creation House, 1972.

Wead, R. Douglas. *Catholic Charismatics: Are They for Real?* (formerly *Father McCarthy Smokes a Pipe and Speaks in Tongues*). Carol Stream, Ill.: Creation House, 1973.

Wilkerson, David. *The Cross and the Switchblade.* Old Tappan, N.J.: Spire Books, 1964.

———. *The Vision.* New York: Pyramid Books, 1974.

Willans, Jean Stone. *The Acts of the Green Apples.* Altadena, Calif.: Society of Stephen, 1973.

Williams, J. Rodman. *The Era of the Spirit.* Plainfield, N.J.: Logos International, 1971.

———. *The Pentecostal Reality.* Plainfield, N.J.: Logos International, 1972.

Wogen, Norris (ed.). *Jesus, Where Are You Taking Us?: Lutheran Conference on the Holy Spirit.* Carol Stream, Ill.: Creation House, 1973.

Wynne, John L. *This New Pentecostalism.* Belfast, Northern Ireland: John L. Wynne, 1967.

Secondary Sources (works by non-Pentecostals)

Barbosa, Roberto. "Bread and Gospel: Affirming a Total Faith—An Inter-

238   *Bibliography*

view with Brazilian Pentecostalist Manoel de Mello," *The Christian Century* (Dec. 25, 1974), pp. 1,223–26.

Barnhouse, Donald Grey. "Finding Fellowship with Pentecostals," *Eternity* (Philadelphia), Apr. 1958, pp. 8–10.

Bass, Clarence B. *Backgrounds to Dispensationalism*. Grand Rapids, Mich.: Eerdmans, 1960.

Berger, Peter L. "A Call for Authority in the Christian Community," *The Christian Century*, Oct. 27, 1971, pp. 1,257–63.

Bess, Donovan. " 'Speaking in Tongues': The High Church Heresy," *The Nation*, Sept. 28, 1963, pp. 173–77.

"Bill Burnett—A Break with Tradition," Johannesburg *Star*, May 4, 1974, pp. 10–11.

Bloch-Hoell, Nils. *The Pentecostal Movement*. Oslo: Universitetsforlaget, 1964.

"Blue Tongues," *Time*, Mar. 29, 1963, p. 52.

Brown, Robert McAfee. *The Ecumenical Revolution*. Garden City, N.Y.: Doubleday & Company, 1967.

Bruner, Frederick Dale. *A Theology of the Holy Spirit: The Pentecostal Experience and the New Testament Witness*. Grand Rapids, Mich.: Eerdmans, 1970.

Carnell, E. J. *The Case for Biblical Christianity*, ed. Ronald H. Nash. Grand Rapids, Mich.: Eerdmans, 1969.

Casey, Rick. "Charismatics II," *National Catholic Reporter* (Aug. 29, 1975), pp. 1, 4, 10.

Cutten, George B. *Speaking with Tongues: Historically and Psychologically Considered*. New Haven, Conn.: Yale University Press, 1927.

Damboriena, Prudencio. *Tongues as of Fire: Pentecostalism in Contemporary Christianity*. Washington, D.C.: Corpus Books, 1969.

Dayton, Donald W. "The Evolution of Pentecostalism," *The Covenant Quarterly* (Chicago), Aug. 1974, pp. 28–40.

Dunn, James D. G. *Baptism in the Holy Spirit*. Naperville, Ill.: Allenson, 1970.

———. "Spirit Baptism and Pentecostalism," *Scottish Journal of Theology*, Nov. 1970, pp. 397–407.

Ellwood, Robert S. *One Way: The Jesus Movement and Its Meaning*. Englewood Cliffs, N.J.: Prentice-Hall, 1973.

Enroth, Ronald M. "Where Have All the Jesus People Gone?," *Eternity*, Oct. 1973, pp. 14–15, 17, 28, 30.

Farrel, Frank. "Outburst of Tongues: The New Penetration," *Christianity Today* (formerly *A Christianity Today Reader*), ed. Frank E. Gaebelein. Old Tappan, N.J.: Spire Books, 1968, pp. 194–205.

Fey, Harold E. (ed.). *A History of the Ecumenical Movement: 1948–1968.* Philadelphia: Westminster Press, 1970.

Fichter, Joseph H. *The Catholic Cult of the Paraclete.* New York: Sheed and Ward, 1975.

———. "How It Looks to a Social Scientist," *New Catholic World,* Nov.–Dec. 1974, pp. 244–48.

———. "Liberal and Conservative Catholic Pentecostals," *Social Compass,* XXI, 1974, pp. 303–10.

Fiske, Edward B. "Pentecostals Gain Among Catholics," New York *Times,* Nov. 3, 1970, pp. 37, 56.

Gerlach, Luther P., and Hine, Virginia H. "Five Factors Crucial to the Growth and Spread of a Modern Religious Movement," *Journal for the Scientific Study of Religion,* Spring 1968, pp. 23–40.

———. *People, Power, Change: Movements of Social Transformation.* Indianapolis, Ind.: Bobbs-Merrill, 1970.

"The Gift of Tongues" (editorial), *Christianity Today,* Apr. 11, 1969, pp. 27–28.

Gillquist, Peter E. *Let's Quit Fighting About the Holy Spirit.* Grand Rapids, Mich.: Zondervan, 1974.

Glock, Charles Y., and Stark, Rodney. *Religion and Society in Tension.* Chicago: Rand McNally, 1965.

Goodman, Felicitas D. *Speaking in Tongues: A Cross-Cultural Study.* Chicago: University of Chicago Press, 1972.

Greeley, Andrew M. *Unsecular Man,* New York: Dell, 1972.

Griffiths, Michael. *Three Men Filled with the Spirit.* London: Overseas Missionary Fellowship, 1969.

Hadden, Jeffrey K. *The Gathering Storm in the Churches.* Garden City, N.Y.: Doubleday & Company, 1969.

Hamilton, Elizabeth. *Suenens: A Portrait.* Garden City, N.Y.: Doubleday & Company, 1975.

Hamilton, Michael (ed.). *The Charismatic Movement.* Grand Rapids, Mich.: Eerdmans, 1974.

Haughey, John C. "Holy Spirit a Ghost No Longer," *America,* June 16, 1973, p. 551.

Hills, James W. L. "The New Charismatics, 1973," *Eternity,* Mar. 1973, pp. 24–25, 33.

Hine, Virginia H. "Pentecostal Glossolalia: Towards a Functional Interpretation," *Journal for the Scientific Study of Religion,* Fall 1969, pp. 211–26.

Hitt, Russell T. "The New Pentecostalism," *Eternity,* Apr. 1970, pp. 12–13 (repr.).

Hoekema, Anthony A. *What About Tongue Speaking?* Grand Rapids, Mich.: Eerdmans, 1966.

Hollenweger, Walter J. "Charismatic Movements Today." Birmingham, England: prepublication essay, 1974.

———. "Handbuch der Pfingstbewegung," 10 vols. Zurich: unpublished doctoral thesis, Faculty of Theology, University of Zurich, 1965–67.

———. *New Wine in Old Wineskins.* Gloucester, England: Fellowship Press, 1973.

———. *The Pentecostals.* Minneapolis, Minn.: Augsburg Publishing House, 1972.

Jorstad, Erling. *Bold in the Spirit: Lutheran Charismatic Renewal in America Today.* Minneapolis, Minn.: Augsburg Publishing House, 1974.

——— (ed.). *The Holy Spirit in Today's Church: A Handbook of the New Pentecostalism.* Nashville and New York: Abingdon, 1973.

Kelley, Dean M. *Why Conservative Churches Are Growing.* New York: Harper & Row, 1972.

Kerr, John Stevens. *The Fire Flames Anew: A Look at the New Pentecostalism.* Philadelphia: Fortress Press, 1974.

Kildahl, John P. *The Psychology of Speaking in Tongues.* New York: Harper & Row, 1972.

Lalive d'Epinay, Christian. *Haven of the Masses: A Study of the Pentecostal Movement in Chile.* London: Lutterworth Press, 1969.

Lombard, Émile. *De la Glossolalie chez les Premiers Chrétiens et des Phénomènes Similaires: Étude d'Exégèse et de Psychologie.* Lausanne: Imprimeries Réunies, 1910.

Lutheran Church in America. *The Charismatic Movement in the Lutheran Church in America: A Pastoral Perspective.* New York: LCA, 1974.

" 'Mainline' Charismatics," *The Christian Century,* Oct. 30, 1974, pp. 1,006–7.

McDonnell, Kilian. "The Catholic Charismatic Renewal: Reassessment and Critique," *Religion in Life* (Summer 1975), pp. 138–54.

———. "Catholic Pentecostalism: Problems in Evaluation," *Dialog* (Minneapolis, Minn.), Winter 1970, pp. 35–54.

———. "The Ecumenical Significance of the Pentecostal Movement," *Worship* (Collegeville, Minn.), Dec. 1966, pp. 609–29.

———. "Holy Spirit and Pentecostalism," *Commonweal,* Nov. 8, 1968, pp. 198–204.

———. "The Ideology of Pentecostal Conversion," *Journal of Ecumenical Studies,* Winter 1968, pp. 105–26.

———. "New Dimensions in Research on Pentecostalism," *Worship,* Apr. 1971, pp. 214–19.

McDonnell, Kilian, and Bittlinger, Arnold. *The Baptism in the Holy Spirit as an Ecumenical Problem*. Notre Dame, Ind.: Charismatic Renewal Services, 1972.

Mead, Frank S. *Handbook of Denominations in the United States* (6th ed.). Nashville and New York: Abingdon, 1975.

Mills, Watson E. "Literature on Glossolalia," *Journal of the American Scientific Affiliation* (Elgin, Ill.), Dec. 1974, pp. 169–73.

—— (ed.). *Speaking in Tongues: Let's Talk About It*. Waco, Texas: Word, 1973.

"Miracle Woman," *Time*, Sept. 14, 1970, pp. 62, 64.

Morris, James. *The Preachers*. New York: St. Martin's Press, 1973.

Mosimann, Eddison. *Das Zungenreden geschichtlich und psychologisch untersucht*. Tübingen: J. C. B. Mohr, 1911.

Neill, Stephen. *The Church and Christian Union*. London: Oxford University Press, 1968.

Newbigin, Lesslie. *The Household of God*. New York: Friendship Press, 1954.

Nichol, John T. *The Pentecostals*. Plainfield, N.J.: Logos International, 1966.

Nolen, William A. *Healing*. New York: Random House, 1974.

O'Dea, Thomas F. *The Sociology of Religion*. Englewood Cliffs, N.J.: Prentice-Hall, 1966.

Phillips, McCandlish. "And There Appeared to Them Tongues of Fire," *The Saturday Evening Post*, May 16, 1964, pp. 31–40.

Plowman, Edward E. "Mission to Orthodoxy: The 'Full' Gospel," *Christianity Today*, Apr. 26, 1974, pp. 44–45.

Pope, Liston. *Millhands and Preachers: A Study of Gastonia*. New Haven: Yale University Press, 1942.

Presbyterian Church in the United States. *The Person and Work of the Holy Spirit*. Oklahoma City: Presbyterian Charismatic Communion, 1971.

Quebedeaux, Richard. "Evangelicals: Ecumenical Allies," *Christianity and Crisis*, Dec. 27, 1971, pp. 286–88.

——. "The Old Pentecostalism and the New Pentecostalism," *Theology, News and Notes* (Pasadena, Calif.: Fuller Theological Seminary), Mar. 1974, pp. 6–8, 23.

——. *The Young Evangelicals*. New York: Harper & Row, 1974.

"Rector and a Rumpus," *Newsweek*, July 4, 1960, p. 77.

Robertson, Palmer. "Neo-Pentecostalism and the Freedom of the Christian," *The Presbyterian Guardian* (Philadelphia), Jan. 1975, pp. 18–19.

Samarin, William J. *Tongues of Men and Angels: The Religious Language of Pentecostalism*. New York: Macmillan, 1972.

Schaeffer, Francis A. *The New Super-Spirituality*. Downers Grove, Ill.: Inter-Varsity Press, 1972.

Schwartz, Gary. *Sect Ideologies and Social Status*. Chicago: University of Chicago Press, 1970.

"Speaking in Tongues," *Time*, Aug. 15, 1960, pp. 53, 55.

Spragett, Allen. *Kathryn Kuhlman: The Woman Who Believes in Miracles*. New York: New American Library, 1971.

Stagg, Frank E.; Hinson, Glenn; and Oates, Wayne E. *Glossolalia*. Nashville and New York: Abingdon, 1967.

Stott, John R. W. *The Baptism and Fullness of the Holy Spirit*. Downers Grove, Ill.: InterVarsity Press, 1964.

Sullivan, Emmanuel. "Can the Pentecostal Movement Renew the Churches?," *Study Encounter* (Geneva: World Council of Churches), VIII (4), 1972, pp. 1–16.

"Taming the Tongues," *Time*, July 10, 1964, pp. 64, 66.

Taylor, James A. "A Search for Giants," *A.D.*, Sept. 1974, pp. 20–23.

Tinney, James S. "Black Origins of the Pentecostal Movement," *Christianity Today*, Oct. 8, 1971, pp. 4–6.

"Tongues: Updating Some Old Issues" (editorial), *Eternity*, Mar. 1973, p. 8.

United Presbyterian Church, U.S.A. *The Work of the Holy Spirit*. Philadelphia: UPCUSA, 1970.

Van Dusen, Henry P. "Force's Lessons for Others," *Life*, June 9, 1958, pp. 122, 124.

Wagner, C. Peter. *Look Out! The Pentecostals Are Coming*. Carol Stream, Ill.: Creation House, 1973.

Wilson, Bryan R. *Religion in Secular Society*. Baltimore: Penguin Books, 1966.

———. *Sects and Society*. London: Heinemann, 1961.

——— (ed.). *Patterns of Sectarianism*. London: Heinemann, 1967.

Wood, William W. *Culture and Personality Aspects of the Pentecostal Holiness Religion*. The Hague and Paris: Mouton, 1965.

INDEX

C.R. means Charismatic Renewal